Building Big Data Pipelines with Apache Beam

Use a single programming model for both batch and stream data processing

Jan Lukavský

BIRMINGHAM—MUMBAI

Building Big Data Pipelines with Apache Beam

Publishing Product Manager: Reshma Raman
Senior Editor: David Sugarman
Content Development Editor: Nathanya Dias
Technical Editor: Devanshi Ayare
Copy Editor: Safis Editing
Project Coordinator: Aparna Ravikumar Nair
Proofreader: Safis Editing
Indexer: Sejal Dsilva
Production Designer: Ponraj Dhandapani
Marketing Coordinator: Priyanka Mhatre

First published: January 2022

Production reference: 1161221

Published by Packt Publishing Ltd.
Livery Place
35 Livery Street
Birmingham
B3 2PB, UK.

ISBN 978-1-80056-493-0

www.packt.com

Contributors

About the author

Jan Lukavský is a freelance big data architect and engineer who is also a committer of Apache Beam. He is a certified Apache Hadoop professional. He is working on open source big data systems combining batch and streaming data pipelines in a unified model, enabling the rise of real-time, data-driven applications.

I want to thank my family for all their support and patience, especially my wife, Pavla, and my children.

About the reviewer

Marcelo Henrique Neppel currently works as a software engineer at Canonical, interacting with technologies including Kubernetes and Juju. Previously, he worked at a big data company coordinating two teams and developing pipelines for projects using Apache Beam, and also at BPlus Tecnologia, working with databases and integrations.

I would like to thank Packt for giving me the opportunity to contribute to this excellent book. I would like to thank my wife, Janaina, and my family, for always supporting me, and also Gabriel Verani, who introduced me to Apache Beam.

Table of Contents

Preface

Section 1: Apache Beam: Essentials

1

Introduction to Data Processing with Apache Beam

Technical requirements	4	States and triggers	16
Why Apache Beam?	5	Timers	18
Writing your first pipeline	6	Assigning data to windows	18
Running our pipeline against streaming data	10	Defining the life cycle of a state in terms of windows	20
Exploring the key properties of unbounded data	12	Pane accumulation	23
Measuring event time progress inside data streams	15	Unifying batch and streaming data processing	24
		Summary	28

2

Implementing, Testing, and Deploying Basic Pipelines

Technical requirements	30	Task 1 – calculating the K most frequent words in a stream of lines of text	35
Setting up the environment for this book	31		
Installing Apache Kafka	31	Defining the problem	35
Making our code accessible from minikube	33	Discussing the problem decomposition	36
		Implementing the solution	39
Installing Apache Flink	34	Testing our solution	41
Reinstalling the complete environment	35	Deploying our solution	44

Task 2 – calculating the
maximal length of a word in
a stream   45
Defining the problem   45
Discussing the problem decomposition   46
Implementing the solution   46
Testing our solution   48
Deploying our solution   50

Specifying the PCollection
Coder object and the
TypeDescriptor object   53
Understanding default triggers,
on time, and closing behavior   56
Introducing the primitive
PTransform object – Combine   59
Task 3 – calculating the average
length of words in a stream   62
Defining the problem   62
Discussing the problem decomposition   63
Implementing the solution   63
Testing our solution   66
Deploying our solution   67

Task 4 – calculating the average

length of words in a stream
with fixed lookback   69
Defining the problem   69
Discussing the problem decomposition   69
Implementing the solution   69
Testing our solution   69
Deploying our solution   71

Ensuring pipeline upgradability   72
Task 5 – calculating
performance statistics for
a sport activity tracking
application   74
Defining the problem   74
Discussing the problem decomposition   75
Solution implementation   76
Testing our solution   78
Deploying our solution   79

Introducing the primitive
PTransform object –
GroupByKey   80
Introducing the primitive
PTransform object – Partition   81
Summary   82

3

Implementing Pipelines Using Stateful Processing

Technical requirements   86
Task 6 – Using an external
service for data augmentation   86
Defining the problem   87
Discussing the problem decomposition   87
Implementing the solution   88
Testing our solution   91
Deploying our solution   92

Introducing the primitive
PTransform object – stateless
ParDo   92
Task 7 – Batching queries to an
external RPC service   95
Defining the problem   95
Discussing the problem decomposition   95
Implementing the solution   96

Task 8 – Batching queries to
an external RPC service with
defined batch sizes   99
Defining the problem   99
Discussing the problem decomposition 100
Implementing the solution   100

Introducing the primitive
PTransform object –
stateful ParDo   107
Describing the theoretical properties
of the stateful ParDo object   108
Applying the theoretical properties
of the stateful ParDo object to the API
of DoFn   112

Using side outputs   115
Defining droppable data
in Beam   118

Task 9 – Separating droppable
data from the rest of the
data processing   120
Defining the problem   121
Discussing the problem decomposition 121
Implementing the solution   122
Testing our solution   127
Deploying our solution   129

Task 10 – Separating droppable
data from the rest of the data
processing, part 2   130
Defining the problem   130
Discussing the problem decomposition 131
Implementing the solution   133
Testing our solution   137
Deploying our solution   139

Using side inputs   139
Summary   142

Section 2: Apache Beam: Toward Improving Usability

4

Structuring Code for Reusability

Technical requirements   148
Explaining PTransform
expansion   148
Task 11 – enhancing
SportTracker by runner
motivation using side inputs   149
Problem definition   150
Problem decomposition discussion   150
Solution implementation   152
Testing our solution   157
Deploying our solution   160

Introducing composite
transform – CoGroupByKey   161
Task 12 – enhancing
SportTracker by runner
motivation using
CoGroupByKey   162
Problem definition   162
Problem decomposition discussion   163
Solution implementation   163

Introducing the Join library DSL 165

Stream-to-stream joins
explained   168
Task 13 – writing a reusable
PTransform –
StreamingInnerJoin   172
Problem definition   172

Problem decomposition discussion   173
Solution implementation   177
Testing our solution   183
Deploying our solution   185
Table-stream duality   186
Summary   188

5
Using SQL for Pipeline Implementation

Technical requirements   190
Understanding schemas   191
Attaching a schema to a PCollection   191
Transforms for PCollections
with schemas   194
Implementing our first
streaming pipeline using SQL   197
Task 14 – implementing
SQLMaxWordLength   200
Problem definition   200
Problem decomposition discussion   200
Solution implementation   201
Task 15 – implementing

SchemaSportTracker   204
Problem definition   204
Problem decomposition discussion   205
Solution implementation   205
Task 16 – implementing
SQLSportTrackerMotivation   208
Problem definition   208
Problem decomposition discussion   208
Solution implementation   209
Further development of Apache
Beam SQL   212
Summary   213

6
Using Your Preferred Language with Portability

Technical requirements   216
Introducing the portability layer   217
Portable representation of the pipeline   218
Job Service   219
SDK harness   219
Implementing our first
pipelines in the Python SDK   220
Implementing our first Python pipeline   220

Implementing our first streaming
Python pipeline   222
Task 17 – implementing
MaxWordLength in the
Python SDK   223
Problem definition   224
Problem decomposition discussion   224
Solution implementation   224
Testing our solution   226

Deploying our solution 227

Python SDK type hints and coders 230

Task 18 – implementing SportTracker in the Python SDK 231

Problem definition 231
Solution implementation 231
Testing our solution 234
Deploying our solution 235

Task 19 – implementing RPCParDo in the Python SDK 236

Problem definition 236
Solution implementation 236
Testing our solution 240

Deploying our solution 241

Task 20 – implementing SportTrackerMotivation in the Python SDK 242

Problem definition 242
Solution implementation 242
Deploying our solution 246

Using the DataFrame API 247

Interactive programming using InteractiveRunner 248

Introducing and using cross-language pipelines 250

Summary 253

Section 3: Apache Beam: Advanced Concepts

7

Extending Apache Beam's I/O Connectors

Technical requirements 258

Defining splittable DoFn as a unification for bounded and unbounded sources 258

Task 21 – Implementing our own splittable DoFn – a streaming file source 262

The problem definition 262
Discussing the problem decomposition 263
Implementing the solution 264
Testing our solution 275
Deploying our solution 277

Task 22 – A non-I/O application of splittable DoFn – PiSampler 278

The problem definition 278
Discussing the problem decomposition 280
Implementing the solution 281
Testing our solution 283
Deploying our solution 283

The legacy Source API and the Read transform 284

Writing a custom data sink 285

The inherent non-determinism of Apache Beam pipelines 286

Summary 288

8

Understanding How Runners Execute Pipelines

Describing the anatomy of an Apache Beam runner 290

Identifying which transforms should be overridden 293

Explaining the differences between classic and portable runners 295

Classic runners 295
Portable pipeline representations 296
The executable stage concept and the pipeline fusion process 298

Understanding how a runner handles state 301

Ensuring fault tolerance 302

Local state with periodic checkpoints 303
Remote state 304

Exploring the Apache Beam capability matrix 305

Understanding windowing semantics in depth 306

Merging and non-merging windows 307

Debugging pipelines and using Apache Beam metrics for observability 309

Using metrics in the Java SDK 310

Summary 311

Index

Other Books You May Enjoy

Preface

Apache Beam is a unified data processing model for both batching and streaming (real-time) big data workloads. This book explains all the aspects of the technology – starting from a theoretical description of the model through to explaining the basics and then advanced concepts. Reading this book will teach you how to implement, test, and run various real-life examples, but also understand what is hidden underneath a typical Apache Beam runner and how the Apache Beam portability layer works, enabling the decoupling of runners from various programming languages and their respective SDKs.

Who this book is for

This book is for data engineers, data scientists, and data analysts who want to learn how Apache Beam works. Intermediate-level knowledge of the Java programming language is assumed.

What this book covers

Chapter 1, *Introduction to Data Processing with Apache Beam*, provides a description of batch and streaming processing semantics and key insights on how to unify them.

Chapter 2, *Implementing, Testing, and Deploying Basic Pipelines*, provides an examples-driven approach to understanding how to implement and verify some of the most common data processing pipelines.

Chapter 3, *Implementing Pipelines Using Stateful Processing*, explains how to implement more sophisticated data processing requiring the use of user-defined states.

Chapter 4, *Structuring Code for Reusability*, details best practices for structuring code so that it can be reused in multiple data processing pipelines and even for building **Domain-Specific Languages (DSLs)**.

Chapter 5, *Using SQL for Pipeline Implementation*, covers how to make life even easier with a well-known data query language – **Structured Query Language (SQL)**.

Chapter 6, Using Your Preferred Language with Portability, explains how Apache Beam handles the portability of runners among different languages and how to use different SDKs (the Apache Beam Python SDK).

Chapter 7, Extending Apache Beam's I/O Connectors, provides a detailed description of how Apache Beam I/O connectors are written using *splittable DoFn* work and how they can be used for non-I/O applications.

Chapter 8, Understanding How Runners Execute Pipelines, performs a deep dive into the anatomy of an Apache Beam runner.

To get the most out of this book

This book builds on at least a basic knowledge of the Java and Python programming languages. It also requires the ability to run Bash and Docker (`minikube`). All other technologies are included.

Software used in the book	Operating system requirements
Java 11, Python 3	Linux or macOS
Bash	Linux or macOS
Docker	Linux or macOS

Installation instructions are provided in the book.

If you are using the digital version of this book, we advise you to type the code yourself or access the code from the book's GitHub repository (a link is available in the next section). Doing so will help you avoid any potential errors related to the copying and pasting of code.

Download the example code files

You can download the example code files for this book from GitHub at `https://github.com/PacktPublishing/Building-Big-Data-Pipelines-with-Apache-Beam`. If there's an update to the code, it will be updated in the GitHub repository.

We also have other code bundles from our rich catalog of books and videos available at `https://github.com/PacktPublishing/`. Check them out!

Download the color images

We also provide a PDF file that has color images of the screenshots and diagrams used in this book. You can download it here: `https://static.packt-cdn.com/downloads/9781800564930_ColorImages.pdf`.

Conventions used

There are a number of text conventions used throughout this book.

`Code in text`: Indicates code words in the text, database table names, folder names, filenames, file extensions, pathnames, dummy URLs, user input, and Twitter handles. Here is an example: "For this reason, Beam defined a `RestrictionTracker` object."

A block of code is set as follows:

```
ClassLoader loader = FirstPipeline.class.
getClassLoader();
String file = loader.getResource("lorem.txt").getFile();
List<String> lines = Files.readAllLines(
Paths.get(file), StandardCharsets.UTF_8);
```

When we wish to draw your attention to a particular part of a code block, the relevant lines or items are set in bold:

```
@Override
public PCollection<String> expand(PBegin input) {
  return input
    .apply(Impulse.create())
    .apply(MapElements.into(TypeDescriptors.strings())
        .via(e -> directoryPath))
    .apply(new DirectoryWatch())
    .apply(Reshuffle.viaRandomKey())
    .apply(new FileRead());
}
```

Any command-line input or output is written as follows:

```
$ ./mvnw clean install
```

Bold: Indicates a new term, an important word, or words that you see on screen. For instance, words in menus or dialog boxes appear in **bold**. Here is an example: "A typical example of a runner would be **Apache Flink**, **Apache Spark**, or **Google Cloud Dataflow**."

> **Tips or Important notes**
> Appear like this.

Get in touch

Feedback from our readers is always welcome.

General feedback: If you have questions about any aspect of this book, email us at customercare@packtpub.com and mention the book title in the subject of your message.

Errata: Although we have taken every care to ensure the accuracy of our content, mistakes do happen. If you have found a mistake in this book, we would be grateful if you would report this to us. Please visit www.packtpub.com/support/errata and fill in the form.

Piracy: If you come across any illegal copies of our works in any form on the internet, we would be grateful if you would provide us with the location address or website name. Please contact us at copyright@packt.com with a link to the material.

If you are interested in becoming an author: If there is a topic that you have expertise in and you are interested in either writing or contributing to a book, please visit authors.packtpub.com.

Share Your Thoughts

Once you've read *Building Big Data Pipelines with Apache Beam,* we'd love to hear your thoughts! Scan the QR code below to go straight to the Amazon review page for this book and share your feedback.

https://packt.link/r/1-800-56493-7

Your review is important to us and the tech community and will help us make sure we're delivering excellent quality content.

Section 1
Apache Beam: Essentials

This section represents a general introduction to how most streaming data processing systems work, what the general properties of data streams are, and what problems are needed to be solved for computational correctness and for balancing throughput and latency in the context of Apache Beam. This section also covers how pipelines are implemented, tested, and run.

This section comprises the following chapters:

- *Chapter 1, Introduction to Data Processing with Apache Beam*
- *Chapter 2, Implementing, Testing, and Deploying Basic Pipelines*
- *Chapter 3, Implementing Pipelines Using Stateful Processing*

1
Introduction to Data Processing with Apache Beam

Data. Big data. Real-time data. Data streams. Many buzzwords to describe many things, and yet they have many common properties. Mind-blowing applications can be developed from the successful application of (theoretically) simple logic – take data and produce knowledge. However, a simple-sounding task can turn out to be difficult when the amount of data needed to produce knowledge is huge (and still growing). Given the vast volumes of data produced by humanity every day, which tools should we choose to turn our *simple logic* into scalable solutions? That is, solutions that protect our investment in creating the data extraction logic, even in the presence of new requirements arising or changing on a daily basis, and new data processing technologies being created? This book focuses on why **Apache Beam** might be a good solution to these challenges, and it will guide you through the Beam learning process.

In this chapter, we will cover the following topics:

- Why Apache Beam?
- Writing your first pipeline
- Running a pipeline against streaming data
- Exploring the key properties of Unbounded data
- Measuring the event time progress inside data streams
- Assigning data to windows
- Unifying batch and streaming data processing

Technical requirements

In this chapter, we will introduce some elementary pipelines written using Beam's Java **Software Development Kit** (**SDK**).

We will use the code located in the GitHub repository for this book: `https://github.com/PacktPublishing/Building-Big-Data-Pipelines-with-Apache-Beam`.

We will also need the following tools to be installed:

- **Java Development Kit** (**JDK**) **11** (possibly **OpenJDK 11**), with `JAVA_HOME` set appropriately
- **Git**
- **Bash**

> **Important note**
> Although it is possible to run many tools in this book using the **Windows** shell, we will focus on using Bash scripting only. We hope Windows users will be able to run Bash using virtualization or **Windows Subsystem for Linux** (or any similar technology).

First of all, we need to clone the repository:

1. To do this, we create a suitable directory, and then we run the following command:

```
$ git clone https://github.com/PacktPublishing/Building-
Big-Data-Pipelines-with-Apache-Beam.git
```

2. This will result in a directory, `Building-Big-Data-Pipelines-with-Apache-Beam`, being created in the working directory. We then run the following command in this newly created directory:

```
$ ./mvnw clean install
```

Throughout this book, the $ character will denote a Bash shell. Therefore, `$ ./mvnw clean install` would mean to run the `./mvnw` command in the top-level directory of the `git clone` (that is, `Building-Big-Data-Pipelines-with-Apache-Beam`). By using `chapter1$ ../mvnw clean install`, we mean to run the specified command in the subdirectory called `chapter1`.

Why Apache Beam?

There are two basic questions we might ask when considering a new technology to learn and apply in practice:

- What problem am I struggling with that the new technology can help me solve?
- What would the costs associated with the technology be?

Every sound technology has a well-defined *selling point* – that is, something that justifies its existence in the presence of competing technologies. In the case of Beam, this selling point could be reduced to a single word: **portability**. Beam is portable on several layers:

- Beam's pipelines are portable between multiple **runners** (that is, a technology that executes the distributed computation described by a pipeline's author).
- Beam's data processing model is portable between various programming languages.
- Beam's data processing logic is portable between bounded and unbounded data.

Each of these points deserves a few words of explanation. By *runner portability*, we mean the possibility to run existing pipelines written in one of the supported programming languages (for instance, Java, **Python**, **Go**, **Scala**, or even **SQL**) against a data processing engine that can be chosen *at runtime*. A typical example of a runner would be **Apache Flink**, **Apache Spark**, or **Google Cloud Dataflow**. However, Beam is by no means limited to these; new runners are created as new technologies arise, and it's very likely that many more will be developed.

When we say Beam's data processing model is portable between various programming languages, we mean it has the ability to provide support for multiple SDKs, regardless of the language or technology used by the runner. This way, we can code Beam pipelines in the Go language, and then run these against the Apache Flink Runner, written in Java.

Last but not least, the core of Apache Beam's model is designed so that it is portable between bounded and unbounded data. Bounded data is what was historically called *batch processing*, while unbounded data refers to *real-time processing* (that is, an application crunching live data as it arrives in the system and producing a low-latency output).

Putting these pieces together, we can describe Beam as a tool that lets you deal with your big data architecture with the following vision:

Choose your preferred language, write your data processing pipeline, run this pipeline using a runner of your choice, and do all of this for both batch and real-time data at the same time.

Because everything comes at a price, you should expect to pay for flexibility like this – this price would be a somewhat bigger overhead in terms of CPU and/or memory usage. The Beam community works hard to make this overhead as small as possible, but the chances are that it will never be zero.

If all of this sounds compelling to you, then we are ready to start a journey exploring Apache Beam!

Writing your first pipeline

Let's jump right into writing our first pipeline. The first part of this book will focus on Beam's Java SDK. We assume that you are familiar with programming in Java and building a project using **Apache Maven** (or any similar tool). The following code can be found in the com.packtpub.beam.chapter1.FirstPipeline class in the chapter1 module in the GitHub repository. We would like you to go through all of the code, but we will highlight the most important parts here:

1. We need some (demo) input for our pipeline. We will read this input from the resource called lorem.txt. The code is standard Java, as follows:

    ```
    ClassLoader loader = FirstPipeline.class.
    getClassLoader();
    String file = loader.getResource("lorem.txt").getFile();
    List<String> lines = Files.readAllLines(
        Paths.get(file), StandardCharsets.UTF_8);
    ```

2. Next, we need to create a Pipeline object, which is a container for a **Directed Acyclic Graph** (**DAG**) that represents the data transformations needed to produce output from input data:

    ```
    Pipeline pipeline = Pipeline.create();
    ```

> **Important note**
> There are multiple ways to create a pipeline, and this is the simplest. We will see different approaches to pipelines in *Chapter 2, Implementing, Testing, and Deploying Basic Pipelines.*

3. After we create a pipeline, we can start filling it with data. In Beam, data is represented by a PCollection object. Each PCollection object (that is, *parallel collection*) can be imagined as a line (an edge) connecting two vertices (PTransforms, or *parallel transforms*) in the pipeline's DAG.

4. Therefore, the following code creates the first node in the pipeline. The node is a transform that takes raw input from the list and creates a new PCollection:

```
PCollection<String> input = pipeline.apply(Create.
of(lines));
```

Our DAG will then look like the following diagram:

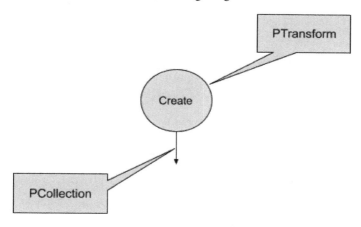

Figure 1.1 – A pipeline containing a single PTransform

5. Each PTransform can have one main output and possibly multiple side output PCollections. Each PCollection has to be consumed by another PTransform or it might be excluded from the execution. As we can see, our main output (PCollection of PTransform, called Create) is not presently consumed by any PTransform. We connect PTransform to a PCollection by *applying* this PTransform on the PCollection. We do that by using the following code:

```
PCollection<String> words = input.apply(Tokenize.of());
```

This creates a new PTransform (Tokenize) and connects it to our input PCollection, as shown in the following figure:

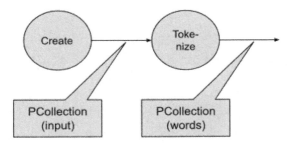

Figure 1.2 – A pipeline with two PTransforms

We'll skip the details of how the Tokenize PTransform is implemented for now (we will return to that in *Chapter 5, Using SQL for Pipeline Implementation*, which describes how to structure code in general). Currently, all we have to remember is that the Tokenize PTransform takes input lines of text and splits each line into words, which produces a new PCollection that contains all of the words from all the lines of the input PCollection.

6. We finish the pipeline by adding two more PTransforms. One will produce the well-known *word count example*, so popular in every big data textbook. And the last one will simply print the output PCollection to standard output:

```
PCollection<KV<String, Long>> result =
    words.apply(Count.perElement());


result.apply(PrintElements.of());
```

Details of both the Count PTransform (which is Beam's built-in PTransform) and PrintElements (which is a user-defined PTransform) will be discussed later. For now, if we focus on the pipeline construction process, we can see that our pipeline looks as follows:

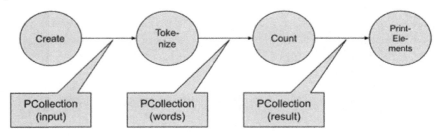

Figure 1.3 – The final word count pipeline

7. After we define this pipeline, we should run it. This is done with the following line:

```
pipeline.run().waitUntilFinish();
```

This causes the pipeline to be passed to a runner (configured in the pipeline; if omitted, it defaults to a runner available on Classpath). The standard default runner is the DirectRunner, which executes the pipeline in the local **Java Virtual Machine (JVM)** only. This runner is mostly only suitable for testing, as we will see in the next chapter.

8. We can run this pipeline by executing the following command in the code examples for the chapter1 module, which will yield the expected output on standard output:

```
chapter1$ ../mvnw exec:java \
    -Dexec.mainClass=com.packtpub.beam.chapter1.
FirstPipeline
```

> **Important note**
> The ordering of output is not defined and is likely to vary over multiple runs. This is to be expected and is due to the fact that the pipeline underneath is executed in multiple threads.

9. A very useful feature is that the application of PTransform to PCollection can be chained, so the preceding code can be simplified to the following:

```
ClassLoader loader = ...
FirstPipeline.class.getClassLoader();
String file =
    loader.getResource("lorem.txt").getFile();
List<String> lines = Files.readAllLines(
    Paths.get(file), StandardCharsets.UTF_8);
Pipeline pipeline = Pipeline.create();
pipeline.apply(Create.of(lines))
    .apply(Tokenize.of())
    .apply(Count.perElement())
    .apply(PrintElements.of());

pipeline.run().waitUntilFinish();
```

When used with care, this style greatly improves the readability of the code.

Now that we have written our first pipeline, let's see how to port it from a bounded data source to a streaming source!

Running our pipeline against streaming data

Let's discuss how we can change this code to enable it to run against a streaming data source. We first have to define what we mean by a data stream. A *data stream* is a continuous flow of data without any prior information about the cardinality of the dataset. The dataset can be either finite or infinite, but we do not know which in advance. Because of this property, the streaming data is often called *unbounded data*, because, as opposed to *bounded data*, no prior bounds regarding the cardinality of the dataset can be made.

The absence of bounds is one property that makes the processing of data streams trickier (the other is that bounded data sets can be viewed as static, while unbounded data is, by definition, changing over time). We'll investigate these properties later in this chapter, and we'll see how we can leverage them to define a Beam unified model for data processing.

For now, let's imagine our pipeline is given a source, which gives one line of text at a time but does not give any signal of how many more elements there are going to be. How do we need to change our data processing logic to extract information from such a source?

1. We'll update our pipeline to use a streaming source. To do this, we need to change the way we created our input `PCollection` of lines coming from a `List` via `Create PTransform` to a streaming input. Beam has a utility for this called **TestStream**, which works as follows.

    Create a `TestStream` (a utility that emulates an unbounded data source). The `TestStream` needs a `Coder` (details of which will be skipped for now and will be discussed in *Chapter 2, Implementing, Testing, and Deploying Basic Pipelines*):

    ```
    TestStream.Builder<String> streamBuilder =
        TestStream.create(StringUtf8Coder.of());
    ```

2. Next, we fill the `TestStream` with data. Note that we need a timestamp for each record so that the `TestStream` can emulate a real stream, which should have timestamps assigned for every input element:

    ```
    Instant now = Instant.now();

    // add all lines with timestamps to the TestStream
    List<TimestampedValue<String>> timestamped =
        IntStream.range(0, lines.size())
    ```

```
          .mapToObj(i -> TimestampedValue.of(
            lines.get(i), now.plus(i)))
          .collect(Collectors.toList());

for (TimestampedValue<String> value : timestamped) {
    streamBuilder = streamBuilder.addElements(value);
}
```

3. Then, we will apply this to the pipeline:

```
// create the unbounded PCollection from TestStream
PCollection<String> input =
    pipeline.apply(streamBuilder.
advanceWatermarkToInfinity());
```

We encourage you to investigate the complete source code of the com.packtpub.
beam.chapter1.MissingWindowPipeline class to make sure everything is
properly understood in the preceding example.

4. Next, we run the class with the following command:

```
chapter1$ ../mvnw exec:java \
    -Dexec.mainClass=\
        com.packtpub.beam.chapter1.MissingWindowPipeline
```

This will result in the following exception:

```
java.lang.IllegalStateException: GroupByKey cannot be
applied to non-bounded PCollection in the GlobalWindow
without a trigger. Use a Window.into or Window.triggering
transform prior to GroupByKey.
```

This is because we need a way to identify the (at least partial) completeness of
the data. That is to say, the data needs (explicit or implicit) markers that define
a condition that (when met) triggers a completion of a computation and outputs
data from a PTransform. The computation can then continue from the values
already computed or be reset to the initial state.

There are multiple ways to define such a condition. One of them is to define
time-constrained intervals called *windows*. A time-constrained window might
be defined as data arriving within a specific time interval – for example, between
1 P.M. and 2 P.M.

5. As the exception suggests, we need to define a window to be applied to the input
    data stream in order to complete the definition of the pipeline. The definition of a
    `Window` is somewhat complex, and we will dive into all its parameters later in this
    book. But for now, we'll define the following `Window`:

```
PCollection<String> windowed =
    words.apply(
        Window.<String>into(new GlobalWindows()
            .discardingFiredPanes()
            .triggering(AfterWatermark.
pastEndOfWindow()));
```

    This code applies `Window.into PTransform` by using `GlobalWindows`, which
    is a specific `Window` that contains whole data (which means that it can be viewed as
    a `Window` containing the whole history and future of the universe).

    The complete code can be viewed in the `com.packtpub.beam.chapter1.`
    `FirstStreamingPipeline` class.

6. As usual, we can run this code using the following command:

```
chapter1$ ../mvnw exec:java \
    -Dexec.mainClass=\
        com.packtpub.beam.chapter1.FirstStreamingPipeline
```

    This results in the same outcome as in the first example and with the same caveat –
    the order of output is not defined and will vary over multiple runs of the same code
    against the same data. The values will be absolutely deterministic, though.

Once we have successfully run our first streaming pipeline, let's dive into what exactly this
streaming data is, and what to expect when we try to process it!

Exploring the key properties of unbounded data

In the previous section, we successfully ran our sample pipeline against simulated
unbounded data. We have seen that only a slight modification had to be made for the
pipeline to produce output in the streaming case. Let's now dive a little deeper into
understanding why this modification was necessary and how to code our pipelines to be
portable from the beginning.

First of all, we need to define a notion of *time*. In our everyday life, time is a common thing we don't think that much about. We know *what time it is* at the moment, and we react to events that happen (more or less) instantly. We can plan for the future, but we cannot change the past.

When it comes to data processing, things change significantly. Let's imagine a smart home application that reads data from various sensors and acts based on the values it receives. Such an application is depicted in the following diagram:

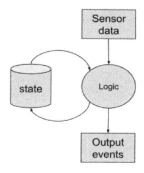

Figure 1.4 – A simple sensor data processing application

The application reads a stream of incoming sensor data, reads the state associated with each device and/or the other settings related to the data being processed, (possibly) updates the state, and (possibly) outputs some resulting events or commands (for example, *turn on a light* if *some condition* is met).

Now, let's imagine we want to make modifications to the application logic. We add some new smart features, and we would like to know how the logic would behave if it had been fed with some *historical events* that we stored for a purpose like this. We cannot simply exchange the logic and push historical data through it because that would result in incorrect modifications of the state – the state might have been changed from the time we recorded our historical data. We see that we cannot mix two times – the time at which we *process* our data and the time at which the data *originated*. We usually call these two times the *processing time* and the *event time*. The first one is the time we see on our clock when an event arrives, while the other is the time at which the event occurred. A beautiful demonstration of these two times is depicted in the following table:

Time	*Star Wars* episodes					
Processing	Episode IV	Episode V	Episode VI	Episode I	Episode II	Episode III
Event	Episode I	Episode II	Episode III	Episode IV	Episode V	Episode VI

Figure 1.5 – Star Wars episodes' processing and event times

For those who are not familiar with the *Star Wars* saga, the *processing time* here represents the order in which the movies were released, while the *event time* represents the order of the episodes in the chronology of the story. By defining the event time and the processing time, we are able to explain another weird aspect of the streaming world – each data stream is inevitably *unordered* in terms of its event time. What do we mean by this? And why should this be inevitable?

The out-of-orderness of a data stream is shown in the following diagram:

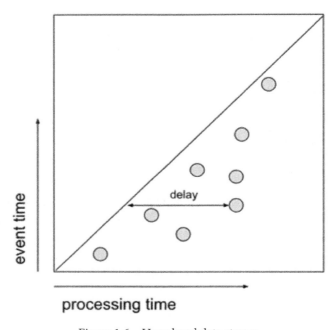

Figure 1.6 – Unordered data stream

The circles represent data points (events), the *x*-axis is *processing time*, and the *y*-axis is *event time*. The upper-left half of the square should be empty under normal circumstances because that area represents events coming from the future – events with a higher event time than the current processing time. The rest of the data points represent events that arrive with a lower or higher delay from the time they occurred (event time). The vast majority of the delay is caused by technical reasons, such as queueing in the network stack, buffering, machine clocks being out of sync, or even outages of some parts of a distributed system. But there are also physical reasons why this happens – a vastly delayed data point is what you see if you look at the sky at night. The light coming from the stars we see with our naked eye is delayed by as much as a thousand years. Because even our physical reality works like this, the out-of-orderness is to be expected and has to be considered 'normal' in any stream processing.

So, we defined what the event and processing times are. We have a clock for measuring processing time. But what about event time? How do we measure that? Let's find out!

Measuring event time progress inside data streams

As we have shown, data streams are naturally unordered in terms of event time. Nevertheless, we need a way of measuring the completeness of our computation. Here is where another essential principle appears – *watermarks*.

A *watermark* is a (heuristic) algorithm that gives us an estimation of how far we have got in the event time domain. A perfect watermark gives the highest possible time (T) that guarantees no further data arrives with an event time $< T$. Let's demonstrate this with the following diagram:

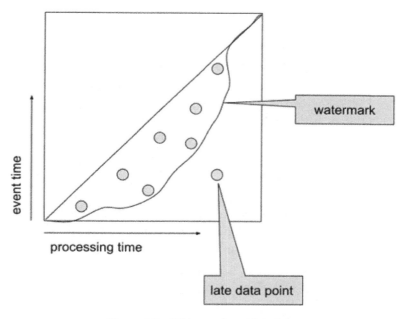

Figure 1.7 – Watermark and late data

We can see from *Figure 1.7* that the watermark is a boundary that moves along with the data points, ideally leaving all of the data on its left side. All data points lying on the right side (with a processing time on the *x*-axis) are called *late data*. Such data typically requires special handling that will be described in *Chapter 2, Implementing, Testing, and Deploying Basic Pipelines*.

There are many ways to implement watermarks. They are typically generated at the source and propagated through the pipeline. We will discuss the details of the implementation of some watermarks in later chapters dedicated to I/O connectors. Typically, users do not have to generate watermarks themselves, although it is very useful to have a very good understanding of the concept.

States and triggers

Each computation on a data stream that takes into account more than a single isolated event needs a *state*. The state holds (accumulates) values derived from the so-far processed stream elements. Let's imagine we want to calculate the current number of elements in a stream. We would do that as follows:

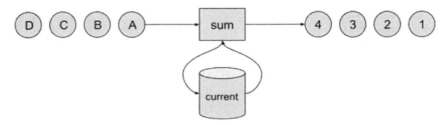

Figure 1.8 – Counting elements in a stream

The computational logic is straightforward – take the incoming element, read the current number of elements from the state, increment that number by one, store the new count into the state, and emit the current value to the output stream.

As simple as this sounds, the overall picture becomes quite complex when we consider that what we are building is an application that is supposed to run for a very long time (theoretically, forever). Such a long-running application will necessarily face disruptions caused by failing hardware, software, or necessary upgrades of the application itself. Therefore, each (sane) stream processing application has to be *fault-tolerant* by design.

Ensuring fault-tolerance puts specific requirements on the state and on the stream itself. Specifically, we must ensure the following:

- We must keep the state in secure, fault-tolerant storage.
- We must retain the ability to restore both the state and the stream to a defined position.

Both of these requirements dictate that every fault-tolerant stream processing engine must provide state management and state access APIs, and it must incorporate the state into its core concepts. The same holds true for Beam, and we'll dive deeper into the state concept in the following chapters.

Our element-count example raises another question: *when should we output the resulting count?* In the preceding example, we output the current count for each input element. This might not be adequate for every application. Other options would be to output the current value in the following ways:

- In fixed periods of processing time (for instance, every 5 seconds)
- When the watermark reaches a certain time (for instance, the output count when our watermark signals that we have processed all data up to 5 P.M.)
- When a specific condition is met in the data

Such emitting conditions are called *triggers*. Each of these possibilities represents one option: a processing time trigger, an event time trigger, and a data-driven trigger. Beam provides full support for processing and event time triggers and supports one data-driven trigger, which is a trigger that outputs after a specific number of elements (for example, after every 10 elements).

If you remember, we have already seen a declaration of a trigger:

```
PCollection<String> windowed =
    words.apply(
        Window.<String>into(new GlobalWindows()
            .discardingFiredPanes()
            .triggering(
                AfterWatermark.pastEndOfWindow()));
```

This is one of many event time triggers, which specifies that we want to *output a result* when our *watermark reaches a time*, and it is defined as an end-of-window. We'll dive deeper into this in later chapters when we discuss the concept of windows.

Timers

Both event time and processing time triggers require an additional stream processing concept. This concept is a *timer*. A timer is a tool that lets an application specify a moment in either the processing time or event time domain, and when that moment is reached, an application-defined callback hook is called. For the same reason as with states, timers also need to be fault-tolerant (that is, they have to be kept in fault-tolerant storage). Beam is purposely designed so that there is actually no way to access a watermark directly, and the only way of observing a watermark is by using event time timers. We will investigate timers in more detail in *Chapter 3, Implementing Pipelines Using Stateful Processing*.

We now know that a streaming data processing engine needs to manage the application's state for us, but what is the life cycle of such a state? Let's find out!

Assigning data to windows

We have already touched on (but have not yet defined) the concept of a *window*. A window is a specific, bounded range of data within a data stream. Beam has several types of pre-defined window functions:

- Tumbling windows
- Sliding windows
- Session windows

Tumbling windows are for assigning data elements into a single window of a pre-defined length, as follows:

Figure 1.9 – Tumbling windows

Tumbling windows can each have exactly the same *fixed length* (for example, 1 hour or 1 day in what are called *fixed windows*), or different lengths (for example, 1 month in what are called *calendar windows*). The common property of tumbling windows is that the event time of each element can be assigned to exactly one window, and that these windows cover a continuous, (possibly) infinite time range, without any gaps.

Sliding windows are windows that assign data elements into multiple windows, shifted by a time period called a *slide*, as shown in the following figure:

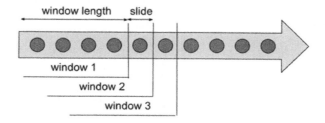

Figure 1.10 – Sliding windows

Sliding windows have the same fixed window length (for example, 1 hour) and the same fixed slide (for example, 10 minutes). A sliding window of 1 hour with a slide of 10 minutes assigns each event time into six distinct windows, each shifted by 10 minutes.

The last type of window is called a *session window*. This type of window is special in several ways. Unlike both previous types, session windows are *key unaligned*. What does that mean? Neither tumbling nor sliding windows depend on the data itself – each data element is assigned to a window (or several windows) based solely on the element's timestamp. The boundary of all the windows in the stream is exactly aligned for all the data. This is not the case for session windows. Session windows split the stream into independent *sub-streams* based on a user-provided key for each element in the stream. We can imagine the key as a color representing each stream element. Session windows group only elements having the same color, therefore, windows in the stream are no longer aligned on the same boundary. We can illustrate this as follows:

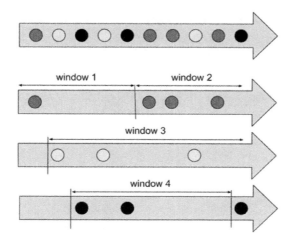

Figure 1.11 – Session windows

We can see from *Figure 1.11* that different keys (types) of elements are grouped in different windows. There, one other parameter that has to be specified: a session *gap duration*. This duration is a timeout (in the event time) that has to elapse between the timestamps of two successive elements with the same key in order to prevent assigning them in the same window. That is to say, as long as elements for a key arrive with a frequency higher than the gap duration, all are placed in the same window. Once there is a delay of at least the gap duration, the window is closed, and another window will be created when a new element arrives. This type of window is frequently used when analyzing user sessions in web clickstreams (which is where the name *session window* came from).

There is one more special window type called a *global window*. This very special type of window assigns all data elements into a single window, regardless of their timestamp. Therefore, the window spans a complete time interval from *–infinity* to *+infinity*. This window is used as a default window before any other window is applied. We'll look into this later in this chapter.

Defining the life cycle of a state in terms of windows

Windows are actually a way of scoping a state in computation. Each state is valid within the context of a window, and each window has its own independent state.

Figure 1.12 illustrates state scoping:

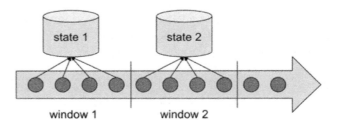

Figure 1.12 – Scoping state within windows

The scoping of states by windows brings up another crucial concept of stream processing: *late data elements*. One such element is shown in *Figure 1.7*.

We can state the problem as follows: *when can we clear and discard the state that belongs to a particular window?* Obviously, it is impractical to keep all states of all windows open forever, because each window carries a non-zero memory footprint, and keeping the window around for an unbounded time would cause the memory to be depleted over time. On the other hand, deleting the state right after the watermark passes the timestamp that marks the end of the window would mean we need a perfect watermark (a watermark that never produces late data). Any possible late data would mean we would produce incorrect outputs – the state would be cleared before all the data elements belonging to the respective window could be processed and therefore would have to be dropped or would produce a completely wrong outcome.

One option would be to define semantics that would require the watermark to advance only when the probability of late data is sufficiently low. We would drop all data that arrived after the watermark and pretend that we didn't see it. If the watermark produces a sufficiently low number of this late data, the error introduced by dropping the late data would be negligible. The crucial problem with this approach is that it necessarily introduces very high latency due to the out-of-orderness of stream processing. We would therefore face a latency versus correctness trade-off, when our goal ideally should be to have both high correctness and low latency.

To resolve this dilemma, stream processing engines introduce an additional concept called *allowed lateness*. This defines a timeout (in the event time) after which the state in a window can be cleared and all remaining data can be cleared. This option gives us the possibility to achieve the following:

- Enable the watermark heuristic to advance sufficiently quickly to not incur unnecessary latency.

- Enable an independent measure of how many states are to be kept around, even after their maximal timestamp has already passed.

We illustrate this concept in *Figure 1.13*, which shows a simple watermark heuristic that just shifts the processing time by a constant duration (which will define minimal latency) and a late data boundary, which shifts the watermark by an additional allowed lateness duration. This might introduce data that will be actually dropped but can now be tuned independently:

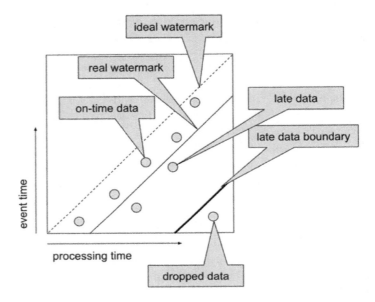

Figure 1.13 – Allowed lateness

> **Important note**
>
> Practical watermark implementations do not typically use a fixed shift between the watermark and processing time, but rather use statistics inferred from consumed data to produce a watermark that is non-linear in terms of the processing time.

The definition of *on-time* and *late data* brings up one last technical term that appears in the context of triggers (see the *States, triggers, and timers* section as a reminder). When a trigger condition is met and the trigger causes output data to be emitted downstream, three possible conditions can occur:

- The watermark has not yet reached the end timestamp of a window.

- The watermark has crossed the window end timestamp, and this is the first activation of a trigger since then.

- The watermark has passed the window end timestamp, and this is not the first activation of a trigger.

According to these three conditions, we can mark the resulting downstream data element as one of the following:

- **Early**: The data is emitted prior to terminating the respective window's end timestamp – this means that we output speculative partial results.

- **On-time**: This marks data that was calculated once the window's end timestamp was reached.

- **Late**: This contains any output with late data incorporated.

Beam calls data emitted as a result of trigger firings a **pane** and puts the information about lateness or earliness of such firing into the `PaneInfo` object.

Pane accumulation

When a trigger fires and causes data to be output from the current window(s) to downstream processing, there are several options that can be used with both the state associated with the window and with the resulting value itself.

After a trigger fires and data is output downstream, we have essentially two options:

- Reset the state to an empty (initial) state (*discard*).

- Keep the state intact (*accumulate*).

This concept might be a little confusing, so we'll demonstrate it with an example. Let's assume that we want to count the number of elements in a stream every minute in the processing time. In general, window functions are based on event time, so to get something that would resemble a processing time window, we can use the following:

```
// Window into single window and specify trigger
PCollection<String> windowed =
    words.apply(
        Window.<String>into(new GlobalWindows()
            .triggering(
                Repeatedly.forever(
                    AfterProcessingTime.pastFirstElementInPane()
                        .plusDelayOf(Duration.standardSeconds(1))))
            .discardingFiredPanes());
```

Please investigate the complete source code in the `com.packtpub.beam.chapter1.ProcessingTimeWindow` class.

We can run this pipeline using the following:

```
chapter1$ ../mvnw exec:java \
  -Dexec.mainClass=com.packtpub.beam.chapter1.
ProcessingTimeWindow
```

Please feel free to experiment with changing `discardingFiredPanes` to `accumulatingFiredPanes` to see how the output differs. In the accumulation mode, the output contains the sum of the elements from the beginning, while in the discarding mode, it contains only increments from the last trigger firing.

Now that we have discussed all the key properties of data streams, let's see how we can use this knowledge to close the gap between batch processing and real-time stream processing!

Unifying batch and streaming data processing

One of the core features that Beam offers is the portability of data processing pipelines between batch and streaming processing. This began around 2004, with the famous white paper, *MapReduce: Simplified Data Processing on Large Clusters*. The idea behind MapReduce is quite simple: divide a complex computation into several parts, each of which consists of two functions – `Map` and `Reduce` – and apply these functions on a large scale using clusters of *commodity hardware*. The simplicity of the two building blocks gives rise to quite simple requirements in terms of fault tolerance, which is essential for any large distributed system.

Details of this system can be easily found online and are out of the scope of this book. We reference it here to demonstrate how and why data processing systems evolved from this moment on. The greatest benefit – massive parallel processing of data on clusters of computers that fail – is what enabled the cost-effectiveness of these large computations and finally led to the development of deep learning applications and other computationally intensive approaches.

The approach has two major drawbacks:

- Complex algorithms typically require a very difficult decomposition into Map and Reduce functions, the chaining of multiple stages, and so on.

- The latency of data processing is very high due to the fact that all data has to be reprocessed from scratch and no continuous updates are possible.

At first, both of these drawbacks were addressed by different systems. Therefore, batch systems with higher-level primitives (such as joins and groupings) came out (for example, **Apache Spark**), while, at the same time, different systems tailored to low-latency processing came out (for example, **Apache Storm**). The evolution of these systems can be illustrated as follows:

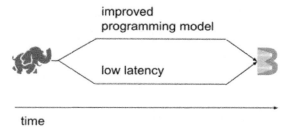

Figure 1.14 – Evolving from Apache Hadoop to Apache Beam

Apache Beam was the first model to unify both of these evolving paths into a single model, and it was targeted at both low-latency and advanced programming models. This was enabled by a simple (but very crucial) insight: *batch semantics can be defined using streaming semantics* (this statement is often rephrased as *batch is a special case of streaming*). Let's see how exactly this was achieved.

Due to the described simplicity of parallelizing a chain of MapReduce operations, practically all batch systems targeted at improving the programming model were defining high-level abstractions, which then, in turn, translated to low-level MapReduce-like operations. Therefore, we can focus on the simple MapReduce paradigm for the batch case, which works as follows:

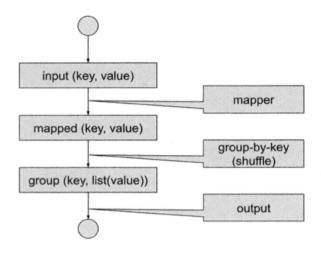

Figure 1.15 – Batch data flow

For clarity, we will briefly describe how the processing works. Each input record is fed into the Map function, producing possibly multiple key-value pairs. Each record with the same key is then grouped together and fed into the Reduce function, which (for the given key and list of values) produces final outputs.

As we have seen in this chapter, in the case of streaming semantics, there are two more things to worry about: an *event time* of a stream element, and a *window function* that assigns these elements into windows (tumbling, sliding, session). Therefore, if we extend the batch processing with the event time of each key-value pair and define a sensible default window, we get the situation depicted in *Figure 1.16*.

Each element is now equipped with a default timestamp (*ts*) and a default window:

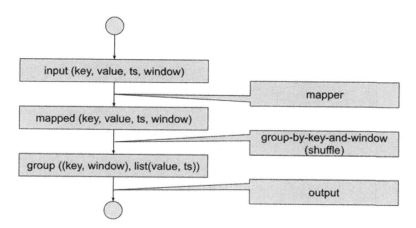

Figure 1.16 – Batch data flow with streaming semantics

We have to define sensible defaults for the timestamp and window. The timestamp can be chosen at a fixed value (typically, either the timestamp of the start of the batch computation, or *–infinity*), and the default window is the global window. The reason why there is no meaningful option other than to put all of the elements into a single window is that we must extend the GroupByKey operation in classical batch mode to GroupByKeyAndWindow to fulfill the streaming constraint that the state is bound to the window. In order to be able to derive the batch semantics from the streaming one, we see that the default window must assign the complete input to a single window (the global window).

Last but not least, we have to deal with how the event time moves in our streaming pipeline-running batch workflow. As we have seen, streaming processing uses watermarks to mark the progress of the event time. Batch semantics have no order in the input dataset (or in how the input data set is processed), therefore, we need to move the watermark from *–infinity* at the beginning and during the job to *+infinity* once the job completes (more exactly, when the job finishes reducing the last key).

> **Important note**
>
> Under special circumstances, it is possible to smoothly advance the event time watermark, even in the case of batch processing. We will learn more about this topic when we explore the stateful processing of time series data.

To sum this up, we can see that we can derive batch semantics from streaming semantics by performing the following:

- Assigning a fixed timestamp to all input key-value pairs.
- Assigning all input key-value pairs to the global window.
- Moving the watermark from *–inf* to *+inf* in one hop once all the data is processed

So, the unified approach of Beam comes from the following logic:

Code your pipeline as a streaming pipeline then run it in both a batch and streaming fashion.

There are some cases where an exception to this rule makes sense, but every time you code a batch-only pipeline in Beam, you should take one step back and think if it is really what you want.

Summary

In this chapter, we went over some of the basic theoretical concepts you will need to understand in order to keep up with the following chapters. These include the difference between *processing time* and *event time*, which is the key knowledge for being able to define the correctness of streaming computation. Processing time is mostly useful for defining the rate of the (partial) result emission via *triggers*, because otherwise you would always have to wait for the end of the *window* to get a result. We have also seen how different *accumulation modes* affect the output of a computation.

We have walked through the life cycle of *states*, as needed for aggregations. We have seen that *watermarks* are a systematic approach for the definition of the position in the event time and, as such, define the relationship between the event time and the processing time. We also walked through how to write your first pipeline using Beam. We'll be using these lessons as a foundation for everything we cover throughout this book.

In *Chapter 2, Implementing, Testing, and Deploying Basic Pipelines*, we'll be developing our understanding of pipelines even further, covering the implementation, testing, and deployment of pipelines to real distributed runners.

2

Implementing, Testing, and Deploying Basic Pipelines

Now that we are familiar with the basic concept of streaming data processing, in this chapter, we will take a deep dive into how to build something practical with **Apache Beam**.

The purpose of this chapter is to give you some hands-on experience of solving practical problems from start to finish. The chapter will be divided into subsections, with each following the same structure:

1. Defining a practical problem

2. Discussing the problem decomposition (and how to solve the problem using Beam's `PTransform`)

3. Implementing a pipeline to solve the defined problem

4. Testing and validating that we have implemented our pipeline correctly

5. Deploying the pipeline, both locally and to a running cluster

During this process (mostly at *Step 2*), we will discuss the various possibilities provided by Beam for addressing the problem, and we will try to highlight any caveats or common issues you might run into.

In this chapter, we will get acquainted with how to implement and test our code and how to work with the GitHub repository for this book. We'll also discuss which tooling to use. The primary aim is to get familiar with Beam and to start *thinking Beam-ish*. We will walk through the following sections:

- Setting up the environment for this book
- Task 1 – Calculating the *K* most frequent words in a stream of lines of text
- Task 2 – Calculating the maximal length of a word in a stream
- Specifying the `PCollection Coder` object and the `TypeDescriptor` object
- Understanding default triggers, on time, and closing behavior
- Introducing the primitive `PTransform` object – `Combine`
- Task 3 – Calculating the average length of words in a stream
- Task 4 – Calculating the average length of words in a stream with fixed lookback
- Ensuring pipeline upgradability
- Task 5 – Calculating performance statistics for a sport activity tracking application
- Introducing the primitive `PTransform` object – `GroupByKey`
- Introducing the primitive `PTransform` object – `Partition`

Technical requirements

In this chapter, we will be installing and setting up the development environment that we will be using throughout the book. In order to carry out the necessary installations, you will need a system capable of running **Bash** and **Docker**. All of the other necessary technologies are self-contained within **minikube**, which we will run on top of the system.

Throughout this chapter, we will use the code from the GitHub repository for this book:

`https://github.com/PacktPublishing/Building-Big-Data-Pipelines-with-Apache-Beam`

Do not forget to clone it or use the cloned version from the previous chapter.

Setting up the environment for this book

In this section, we will set up the environment needed for this chapter and the rest of the book. The technologies we will build upon are Docker and minikube.

Minikube is a local version of **Kubernetes**, which will enable us to easily set up the other technologies we need.

Let's set up everything we need for this chapter now:

1. The steps to install minikube can be found at `https://minikube.sigs.k8s.io/docs/start/`.

2. Next, make sure to install the **kubectl** tool using the official Kubernetes instructions, which can be found at `https://kubernetes.io/docs/tasks/tools/`.

3. After installing minikube, we will start it by executing the following command:

```
$ minikube start
```

> **Important note**
> minikube accepts as an optional parameter a configurable amount of memory and number of CPUs. The `minikube start` command takes the optional `--cpus` and `--memory` arguments, which can be used to tune these settings. We recommend using all of the CPUs available on your local machine and at least 4 GB of RAM.

4. We then validate that we have correctly set up minikube by using the following command:

```
$ kubectl config current-context
minikube
```

The next step is installing **Apache Kafka**, which is an implementation of a distributed commit log, which we will be using as our streaming source for the examples throughout this book.

Installing Apache Kafka

The next step is to get Apache Kafka up and running inside our minikube cluste:

1. We do that with the following command, which is run inside our cloned GitHub repository for this book:

```
$ ./env/install-kafka.sh
```

After this command finishes, we should see two Pods running inside our minikube cluster:

```
$ kubectl get pods
NAME      READY    STATUS     RESTARTS    AGE
kafka-0   1/1      Running    0           25s
zk-0      1/1      Running    0           26s
```

2. After the successful installation of Kafka inside our minikube cluster, we validate that it is up and running by creating a **topic** (if you're not familiar with Kafka, just imagine a *topic* is a named stream inside Kafka). In this case, we will create a topic named `first_topic`:

```
$ ./env/kafka-topics.sh --create \
    --topic first_topic --bootstrap-server kafka:9093
Created topic first_topic.
```

3. Next, we will demonstrate how to read and write data to the topic. By running the following command, we start a **consumer** that will connect to the topic and output data to the console:

```
$ ./env/kafka-consumer.sh --topic first_topic \
        --bootstrap-server kafka:9093
```

This command will start a process that will continuously ask for new data from the topic and as soon as new data arrives, output it to the console. We can break this at any time by pressing *Ctrl + C*.

4. Keeping the consumer running, we can run the following command in a different terminal to produce a single message to the topic:

```
$ echo "First Message!" | ./env/kafka-producer.sh \
        --topic first_topic \
        --bootstrap-server kafka:9093
```

We should see `First Message!` as output text in the consumer terminal.

5. We can run the producer in interactive mode by running the following command:

```
$ ./env/kafka-producer.sh --topic first_topic \
    --bootstrap-server kafka:9093
```

6. Then, we can write lines of text, which will be transformed into messages written to the topic. They will then be displayed in the consumer terminal. Lastly, we'll demonstrate how to send a text file to the topic. Running the following code will produce the text we used in *Chapter 1*, *Introduction to Data Processing with Apache Beam*, for computing word counts:

```
$ cat chapter1/src/main/resources/lorem.txt | \
    ./env/kafka-producer.sh --topic first_topic \
    --bootstrap-server kafka:9093
```

Note that at any time, you can restore Kafka to its initial state by deleting the pod:

```
$ kubectl delete pod kafka-0
```

> **Important note**
>
> On some platforms, the `kafka-0` pod might not start and will end up in `CrashLoopBackOff`. This could be due to the storage provisioner not being able to set a specific kernel parameter. In that case, we would have to set the parameter manually using `$ sudo sysctl net/netfilter/nf_conntrack_max=524288` and then stop and start minikube again.

Next, let's see how to run our code on minikube.

Making our code accessible from minikube

In order to be able to run our code inside the minikube cluster, we need to package it as a Docker image and create a deployment for it. We do that with the following steps:

1. We'll install a deployment that will host all the compiled code from our GitHub repository by running the following:

```
$ ./env/install-packt-beam.sh
```

This command will build a Docker image, push it into the running minikube cluster, and then create a pod that will host our terminal within minikube. We will use this pod to run all of the code examples throughout this book:

```
$ kubectl get pods
```

NAME	READY	STATUS
kafka-0	1/1	Running
packt-beam-5c694d874b-t7mhc	1/1	Running
zk-0	1/1	Running

2. When making any update to the code, we must make sure to update the Docker image and recreate the deployment's pod. We do that by running the following command:

```
$ ./env/build-docker.sh
```

3. If we want to deploy only the code for a specific chapter, we can do that by using an additional parameter with the number of the chapter. The following code will build and deploy code for the second chapter only, which can speed up the build process:

```
$ ./env/build-docker.sh 2
```

Do not forget to run this command after each update to the source code, otherwise, your changes will not be visible to the minikube cluster.

Installing Apache Flink

Apache Flink is a distributed stream processing engine. We will use it to deploy our pipelines to a real-world runner:

1. We will use a *session cluster* (a long-running cluster that is able to accept job submissions), although there are other options for deploying a Flink application. Please consult Flink's online documentation for more information. We will run the session cluster by using the following command:

```
$ ./env/install-flink.sh
```

2. Next, we will verify that our Pods for Flink are running:

```
$ kubectl get pods -l app=flink
```

NAME	READY	STATUS
flink-jobmanager-55bd469755-m6pjz	1/1	Running
flink-taskmanager-6c694df88-794kc	1/1	Running

3. We can look at Flink's web UI by running proxy and then pointing our browser at http://localhost:8001/api/v1/namespaces/default/services/flink-jobmanager:ui/proxy/:

```
$ kubectl proxy
```

Next, let's see how to reinstall the complete environment.

Reinstalling the complete environment

At any time, if we want to (for any reason) return to a clean state, we can delete the minikube cluster and start over from the beginning with the following steps:

1. You can stop and delete minikube by running the following commands:

```
$ minikube stop
$ minikube delete
```

2. Then, you can reinitialize the whole environment using a single command:

```
$ ./env/start-all.sh
```

So, if we have everything ready, we can jump straight to solving our first puzzle!

Task 1 – Calculating the K most frequent words in a stream of lines of text

In the previous chapter, we wrote a very basic pipeline that computed a simple (but surprisingly frequently used) functionality. The pipeline computed the number of occurrences of a word in a text document. We then transformed this to a data stream of lines, which was generated by a TestStream utility.

In the first task of this chapter, we want to extend this simple pipeline to be able to calculate and output only the *K* most frequent words in a stream of lines. So, let's first define the problem.

Defining the problem

Given an input data stream of lines of text, calculate the K most frequent words within a fixed time window of T seconds.

There are many practical applications for solving this problem. For example, if we had a store, we might want to compute daily statistics to find the products with the maximum profit. However, we have chosen the example of counting words in a text stream for its simplicity.

Discussing the problem decomposition

First, we need to split the problem into several pieces:

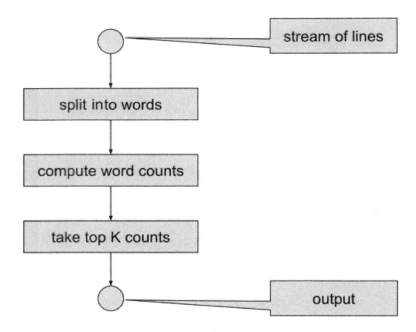

Figure 2.1 – The problem decomposition

We have already seen how to make a pipeline that splits text into words and then computes the number of occurrences of each word. The difference now is that we need a (configurable) way of specifying a fixed time window in which to complete the computation. Then, we need to filter the *K* most frequent words. Luckily, Beam has a PTransform object that can come to the rescue called **Top**.

Another difference is that we need to read data from a real stream – that would be our Apache Kafka topic. Let's put all these pieces together. Note that we have omitted some functions and class definitions that are not directly relevant to Beam but are merely a way of getting input. Please see the complete source code in your cloned GitHub repository in the com.packtpub.beam.chapter2.TopKWords class.

Before digging into the details of the pipeline and the implementation, let's run it and experiment with it a little!

1.   We can run any class in the book with the following command:

```
$ kubectl exec -it <packt-beam> -- \
    run-class.sh com.packtpub.beam.chapter2.TopKWords
```

Note that we must supply an actual name for the pod running the `packt-beam` image instead of the `<packt-beam>` placeholder. We can get the name of the pod using `kubectl get pods`.

Another option would be to replace the pod name with `$(kubectl get pods | grep packt-beam | cut -d' ' -f1)`.

> **Important note**
>
> Throughout this book, we will use the abbreviated form of this command, `$./kubectl exec -it packt-beam`, and we'll let you add the correct pod name yourself.

2. To successfully run the pipeline, we will need input and output topics. We will create these as follows (we can ignore the warnings produced):

```
$ ./env/kafka-topics.sh --create --topic input_topic \
      --bootstrap-server kafka:9093
```

```
WARNING: Due to limitations in metric names, topics with
a period ('.') or underscore ('_') could collide. To
avoid issues it is best to use either, but not both.
Created topic input_topic.
```
```
$ ./env/kafka-topics.sh --create --topic output_topic \
      --bootstrap-server kafka:9093
```

```
WARNING: Due to limitations in metric names, topics with
a period ('.') or underscore ('_') could collide. To
avoid issues it is best to use either, but not both.
Created topic input_topic.
```

3. Now that we have created input and output topics, we can run our pipeline with a required argument supplied (please run the command with the class name only to see the description of the required arguments):

```
$ kubectl exec -it packt-beam -- \
    run-class.sh  com.packtpub.beam.chapter2.TopKWords \
    10 kafka:9093 input_topic output_topic 3
```

This will run the pipeline with a window length of 10 seconds and calculate the top three occurrences of each word in the input topic.

4. To be able to observe the results from our running pipeline, we need to run a
    consumer (in a different terminal):

```
$ ./env/kafka-consumer.sh --bootstrap-server kafka:9093 \
    --topic output_topic \
      --value-deserializer=\
          org.apache.kafka.common.serialization.
LongDeserializer \
        --key-deserializer=\
          org.apache.kafka.common.serialization.
StringDeserializer \
        --property print.key=true
```

The details of this command can be found online in the Kafka documentation for
`kafka-console-consumer`.

5. Once both our pipeline and our consumer are running, we are left with the last step,
    and that's to feed our pipeline some data! We will do that by writing some data to
    our `input_topic`:

```
$ echo "This is first message" | ./env/kafka-producer.sh
\
        --bootstrap-server kafka:9093 --topic input_topic
```

About 10 seconds after we write the message, we should see output similar to the
following:

```
message         1
first     1
This      1
```

6. This is good, but if we want a more streaming experience, we have to create a real
    stream. For that, we will use a very simple utility, `delay_input.sh`, located in
    this book's source code. This tool reads input lines and outputs them after a given
    number of seconds in an unchanged form. To experiment with this, you can try the
    following command:

```
$ cat LICENSE | ./env/delay_input.sh
```

Passing additional parameters changes the rate of output. So, for example, `./env/
delay_input.sh 0.5` outputs two lines per second (that is, every line is delayed
for half a second).

7. We can use the `delay_input.sh` tool for a real streaming experience by running the following command:

```
$ cat LICENSE | ./env/delay_input.sh | \
    ./env/kafka-producer.sh \
    --bootstrap-server kafka:9093 \
    --topic input_topic
```

Please feel free to experiment with this for a while to get a grasp of how the streaming logic behaves. Next, let's get ready for the actual implementation to see how this works in practice!

Implementing the solution

Please see the full implementation of the `om.packtpub.beam.chapter2.TopKWords` class, which is in the `chapter2` directory of the source code located in the cloned GitHub repository. Now, we will walk through this solution:

1. Because our pipeline is supposed to read command-line arguments (for example, the duration of fixed windowing, the number of top elements to output, and so on), we need to parse the arguments from the passed command. We take the required arguments and pass the remaining arguments to `PipelineOptions` because the pipeline can take generic options and runner-dependent options. We'll see how to use these options when we deploy the pipeline to a running cluster:

```
Params = parseArgs(args);
PipelineOptions options = PipelineOptionsFactory.
fromArgs(
    params.getRemainingArgs()).create();
Pipeline = Pipeline.create(options);
```

2. Next, we need to connect our pipeline to our Kafka broker. We do that using the **Apache Maven** Artifact, `org.apache.beam:beam-sdks-java-io-kafka`:

```
PCollection<String> lines = pipeline
    .apply(
        KafkaIO.<String, String>read()
            .withBootstrapServers(params.
getBootstrapServer()))
            .withKeyDeserializer(StringDeserializer.class)
```

```
                  .withValueDeserializer(StringDeserializer.
class)
                  .withTopic(params.getInputTopic()))
         .apply(MapToLines.of());
```

We must specify our input topic, where to connect, for example, any bootstrap servers – in our case, that is the `kafka:9093` host port – and the key and value deserializers (please see the list of available options in the Kafka documentation).

For those interested in the details of `MapToLines PTransform`, please refer to the source code in the GitHub repository. We will skip these details for now. What is important is that it transforms the `KafkaRecord` object coming from the `KafkaIO` object to text lines.

> **Important note**
> Beam is packaged into many modules so when building a pipeline, we have to pick all of the required dependencies. The Kafka IO connector is one such example.

3. In the next step, we will parse the input lines into words and apply the window function (with the specified time window). Then, we will count the frequency of each word (as we have already walked through this part, please refer to the previous chapter for a more detailed explanation of it):

```
PCollection<KV<String, Long>> words
   .apply(Window.into(FixedWindows.of(windowLength)))
   .apply(Tokenize.of())
   .apply(Count.perElement());
```

4. Once we have the required counts, we need to get the *K* most frequent words. We do that with the following code:

```
PCollection<KV<String, Long>> output = words
   .apply(
     Top.of(
        params.getK(),
        (Comparator<KV<String, Long>> & Serializable)
        (a, b) -> Long.compare(a.getValue(),
b.getValue()))
        .withoutDefaults())
   .apply(Flatten.iterables());
```

We are using a built-in PTransform Top object, which works exactly as we need.

> **Important note**
>
> Because we must make sure our code can be transferred to another physical machine over the wire, we must make sure that every PTransform object is Serializable. Serializable classes can be turned into byte arrays that can be sent over a network to a remote node for distributed computation. This is why we must explicitly cast the Comparator lambda function to be serializable.

5. Finally, we must store the resulting PCollection object to the output topic. We'll use the same KafkaIO object for that, only with the write transform:

```
output.apply(
  KafkaIO.<String, Long>write()
    .withBootstrapServers(params.getBootstrapServer())
    .withTopic(params.getOutputTopic())
    .withKeySerializer(StringSerializer.class)
    .withValueSerializer(LongSerializer.class));
```

As in the case of KafkaIO.read, we need to specify the bootstrap servers, the output topic, and the serializers for our data elements (for example, string, long).

6. Last but not least, we must not forget to run our pipeline:

```
pipeline.run().waitUntilFinish();
```

Now that we have walked through the code, we need a way to test that what we have done is what we really wanted. Let's test our pipeline!

Testing our solution

We have already seen the use of the TestStream utility in *Chapter 1, Introduction to Data Processing with Apache Beam*, so we will focus on two main differences that apply here:

- As opposed to our previous use of TestStream, we now have input coming from a Kafka topic, and the output is written back to Kafka.

- We want to test that our pipeline correctly outputs data in time windows of the specified duration.

The first requirement for a reasonable test would be to read data from a `TestStream` utility instead of a real Kafka topic. We really don't want to spawn a Kafka cluster for testing a pipeline in a **Continuous Integration** (**CI**) environment.

The second requirement is that we want to be able to provide precise timing for the input data, including watermarks. Luckily, `TestStream` will help us here as well. The test is located in the `com.packtpub.beam.chapter2.TopKWordsTest` test class. The test uses **JUnit 5** for the testing; you will need to get familiar with this tool to understand the complete test. However, we'll walk through the important parts here:

> **Important note**
>
> Beam's testing framework requires the Maven Artifact JUnit 4 (`junit:junit`) and Hamcrest (`org.hamcrest:hamcrest-core`) to run. These dependencies must be added if you are not using them in your tests already.

1. First, we need some generic declarations. We'll test the pipeline in a 10-second fixed window, so we'll prepare some constants for that:

    ```
    Duration windowDuration = Duration.standardSeconds(10);
    Instant now = Instant.now();
    Instant startOfTenSecondWindow = now.plus(
        -now.getMillis() % windowDuration.getMillis());
    ```

2. Next, we'll prepare the input data. Please note how we specify the timestamps using `TimestampedValue`:

    ```
    TestStream lines = TestStream.create(StringUtf8Coder.
    of())
      .addElements(
        TimestampedValue.of(
          "This is the first line.",
          startOfTenSecondWindow),
        TimestampedValue.of(
          "This is second line in the first window",
          startOfTenSecondWindow.plus(1000)),
        ...
      .advanceWatermarkToInfinity();
    ```

3. Next, we need to feed this input to our actual business logic. We have multiple options to do this, but in this first example, we'll introduce the simplest (yet not best) approach. If you take a look at the code for `com.packtpub.beam.chapter2.TopKWords`, you'll see that we wrap the actual logic in a static method (annotated with `@VisibleForTesting`) called `countWordsInFixedWindows`. This way, we can easily test it by calling the logic directly:

```
Pipeline = Pipeline.create();
PCollection<String> input = pipeline.apply(lines);
PCollection<KV<String, Long>> output =
    TopKWords.countWordsInFixedWindows(
        input, windowDuration, 3);
```

We'll see a better-structured coding style for solving this problem when we discuss **Domain Specific Language (DSL)** in *Chapter 4, Structuring Code for Reusability*.

4. The next step will be making an assertion about the output that our pipeline should produce. We need to recall that all streams are intrinsically unordered. Therefore, we don't (without additional tooling) test for some exact outcome of the pipeline. Instead, we declare that we expect a set of outcomes *without any order*. Beam uses a predefined tool for that called `PAssert`:

```
PAssert.that(output)
    .containsInAnyOrder(
        KV.of("line", 3L),
        KV.of("first", 3L),
        KV.of("the", 3L),
        KV.of("line", 3L),
        KV.of("in", 2L),
        KV.of("window", 2L));
```

We encourage you to manually verify that this is the expected outcome from the four lines we fed into the test pipeline in the source of the test class, `com.packtpub.beam.chapter2.TopKWordsTest`.

Once we are reasonably certain that our pipeline produces appropriate outputs, we are ready to deploy our pipeline to a real runner!

Deploying our solution

We will use our running Flink cluster to submit our pipeline. Beam is built on being portable, so there generally should not be any recompilation needed to switch which runner is used to run a pipeline (so far, we have used `DirectRunner`, which is an implementation meant to be used for testing).

To run our pipeline using the Flink Runner, all we have to do is add a few command-line arguments. These arguments will be passed to the constructor of the pipeline as follows:

```
PipelineOptions options = PipelineOptionsFactory.fromArgs(
    params.getRemainingArgs()).create();
```

This will tell our pipeline which runner to use. Each runner can have additional runner-specific arguments, as it is in this case:

```
$ kubectl exec -it packt-beam -- \
    run-class.sh com.packtpub.beam.chapter2.TopKWords \
    10 kafka:9093 input_topic output_topic 5 \
    --runner=flink --flinkMaster=flink-jobmanager:8081 \
    --checkpointingInterval=2000
```

> **Important note**
>
> In order to use a runner, we must include its Artifact (in the case of the Flink Runner, this is `org.apache.beam: beam-runners-flink-1.13`) and possibly all of its other dependencies (`org.apache.flink:flink-streaming-java_2.12`).

Once we run the preceding command, we can point our browser to Flink's web UI (`http://localhost:8001/api/v1/namespaces/default/services/flink-jobmanager:ui/proxy/`; don't forget to run `kubectl proxy`). We'll see a running job with a DAG like the following diagram. Don't worry about reading it; the important part is its shape:

Figure 2.2 – A DAG of the Flink Runner TopKWords job

Note that this resembles *Figure 2.1*. That is, of course, no coincidence! The Flink UI shows interconnections within what is commonly known as the **shuffle phase** – that is, a part of computation that needs to regroup data by a key. This is similar to the **reduce phase** in `MapReduce` mentioned in *Chapter 1, Introduction to Data Processing with Apache Beam*.

You can now connect the consumer to `output_topic` and write some data to `input_topic` the same way we did before (see *Steps 4* and *5* in the *Discussing the problem decomposition* section previously).

Congratulations! You have just successfully deployed a pipeline to a real distributed runner!

Shall we try another task?

Task 2 – Calculating the maximal length of a word in a stream

This is a similar example. In the previous task, we wanted to calculate the *K* most frequent words in a stream for a fixed time window. How would our solution change if our task was to calculate this from the *beginning* of the stream? Let's define the problem.

Defining the problem

Given an input data stream of lines of text, calculate the longest word ever seen in this stream. Start with an empty word value; once a longer word is seen, immediately output the new longest word.

Discussing the problem decomposition

Although the logic seems to be similar to the previous task, it can be simplified as follows:

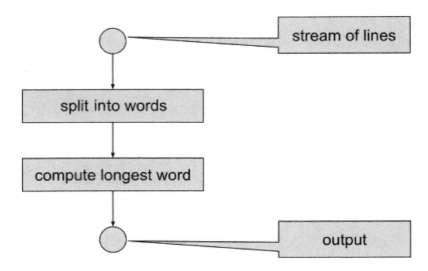

Figure 2.3 – The problem decomposition

Note, there are two main differences from the previous task:

- We must compute the word with the longest length; although this could be viewed as a `Top` transform, with *K* equal to one, Beam has a specific transform for that called `Max`.

- We must compute the maximum in a global window.

Implementing the solution

We will walk through the solution and highlight the key differences from the previous example. The complete source code can be found in the `com.packtpub.beam.chapter2.MaxWordLength` clas:

1. First, we need to specify the global window with appropriate triggering:

```
PCollection<String> windowed = lines
  .apply(Tokenize.of())
  .apply(
    Window.<String>into(new GlobalWindows())
      .triggering(
```

```
     Repeatedly.forever(AfterPane.
elementCountAtLeast(1)))
     .accumulatingFiredPanes())
```

This specification tells Beam to trigger each pane after it has at least one element, and to trigger the pane forever (regardless of whether there is any change or not).

> **Important note**
>
> Triggers in Apache Beam work differently from how you might expect.
> A trigger is not a strict requirement, but rather a recommendation – a runner might apply its own optimization logic to the trigger for better resource utilization. The pane should not trigger *before* a trigger fires but is free to trigger *later* (with a reasonable delay).

2. Next, we need to compute the word with the maximal length:

```
PCollection<String> output = windowed.apply(
  Max.globally(
    (Comparator<String> & Serializable)
    (a, b) -> Long.compare(a.length(), b.length())));
```

Note that as usual, we need to ensure that our `PTransform` object is `Serializable`.

3. Finally, we must write the result back to our output topic. In our previous example, we had a `PCollection` object of the `KV<String, Long>` type, but now, we have only the `String` type. The `KafkaIO` class requires input key-value pairs to be written to Kafka topics, so we need to remap our longest word to `KV`'s prior to feeding them to the output:

```
output
  .apply(
   MapElements
    .into(
      TypeDescriptors.kvs(
        TypeDescriptors.strings(),
        TypeDescriptors.strings()))
     .via(e -> KV.of("", e)))
 .apply(
   KafkaIO.<String, String>write()
    .withBootstrapServers(params.getBootstrapServer())
```

```
            .withTopic(params.getOutputTopic())
            .withKeySerializer(StringSerializer.class)
            .withValueSerializer(StringSerializer.class));
```

The built-in `PTransform` object for one-to-one element-wise transformations is called `MapElements`. As we can see, we need to specify the output's `TypeDescriptor` object. We will talk about why this is needed in the following subsection. For now, we must remember that the specified type descriptor must equal the type of data produced from the mapping function (specified using `via`). The type produced is `KV<String, String>`, which equals `TypeDescriptors.kvs(TypeDescriptors.strings(), TypeDescriptors.strings())`.

The mapping function leaves the key empty for now. We will extend it with something more useful at the end of this section.

Testing our solution

Once we have built the important parts of the implementation, we need to test our solution. The complete test source can be found in the `com.packtpub.beam.chapter2.MaxWordLengthTest` class and, as always, we encourage you to walk through the complete source code and try to run the full test, as we only highlight the important parts here:

1. As always, we need test data to be fed to our pipeline. First, we create a sample input by running the following:

```
TestStream.create(StringUtf8Coder.of())
  .addElements(TimestampedValue.of("a", now))
  .addElements(TimestampedValue.of("bb", now.
plus(10000)))
  .addElements(TimestampedValue.of("ccc", now.
plus(20000)))
  .addElements(TimestampedValue.of("d", now.plus(30000)))
  .advanceWatermarkToInfinity();
```

The first thing you may notice is that we are putting each element in the call to addElements separately. The reason we do this is to ensure that our trigger will be invoked in between each element. Because the trigger invocation is optional, a runner might skip a particular firing. Putting each element separately into addElements makes DirectRunner (our testing runner) invoke a trigger for each input element.

Our goal is then to test that the pipeline behaves as we expect – therefore, we need to test two basic scenarios. First, we will update the previously computed longest word to find the new longest one. We will therefore test a sequence of words: a, bb, and ccc. And second, we want to keep the longest computed word in the presence of shorter ones. Therefore, we add another word, d.

2. The second important part of testing the pipeline is correctly creating the expected output. It would be naïve to expect to immediately see the sequence of longest strings – a, bb, and ccc. Let's have a look at the test code:

```
PAssert.that(output)
    .containsInAnyOrder(
        "a", "bb", "ccc", "ccc", "ccc");
```

We see that the test expects the last word to be *repeated three times*. Why is this? We will dive into a detailed answer of this in the *Understanding default triggers, on time, and closing behavior* section in a few pages. For now, we will give a short explanation, which is that the second repetition of the ccc word is due to the fact that we trigger output panes for every element in the input stream irrespective of whether the content has actually changed. The d word does not change the longest word seen, but our trigger nevertheless causes the longest one to be emitted.

The last occurrence of the ccc word is due to the fact that, as part of our specification for our TestStream input, we advanced the watermark to infinity and, at infinity, all windows reach the end timestamp (even the global window). The contents of each window are, by default, emitted when the window is at the end timestamp to ensure that the last (most accurate) result will be processed.

If we are interested in testing the final outcome only, we can do that by running the following code:

```
PAssert.that(output)
    .inFinalPane(GlobalWindow.INSTANCE)
    .containsInAnyOrder("ccc");
```

Now, we have successfully tested our implementation. So, let's see how it runs.

Deploying our solution

We will run our pipeline with the following command:

```
$ kubectl exec -it packt-beam \
  -- run-class.sh com.packtpub.beam.chapter2.MaxWordLength \
  kafka:9093 input_topic output_topic \
  --runner=flink --flinkMaster=flink-jobmanager:8081 \
  --checkpointingInterval=2000
```

This will create a job in Flink's UI, which we can access as usual. This time, we can see a somewhat more complicated DAG than we would expect:

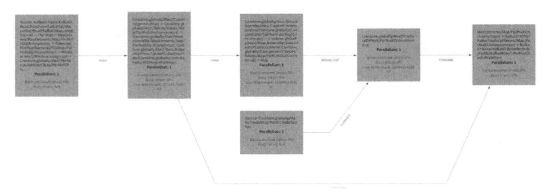

Figure 2.4 – A DAG of the Flink Runner MaxWordLength job

We will explain this decomposition in detail in a section dedicated to the Combine PTransform object later in this chapter (*Introducing the primitive PTransform object – Combine*).

Again, please feel free to experiment with feeding data to input_topic and observe how the output arrives at output_topic.

Before finishing this task and looking at three theoretical aspects related to it, we will add a slight modification to our initial problem definition. We can state the definition as follows:

Given an input data stream of lines of text, calculate the longest word ever seen in this stream. Start with an empty word value, and once a longer word is seen, immediately output the new longest word value. Add a timestamp marking the (rough) validity of this longest word – that is, the (event) time at which the current longest word was emitted.

That is – we would like to extend our output with a timestamp to show when the current longest word was emitted.

As already described in *Chapter 1*, *Introduction to Data Processing with Apache Beam*, a data model of each (meaningful) streaming processing engine must necessarily include a timestamp for each data element. This holds true for every data element that is emitted from a `PTransform` object. In Beam, we can easily access this timestamp via a `PTransform` object called **Reify**. The purpose of this `PTransform` object is to make all implicit parts of the data model accessible. These parts include windows and timestamps, among others. We can easily access the timestamp of each longest word with the following modification to our original `MaxWordLength` class:

```
windowed
  .apply(
    Max.globally(
      (Comparator<String> & Serializable) (a, b) ->
          Long.compare(a.length(), b.length())))
  .apply(Reify.timestamps())
  .apply(
    MapElements
      .into(
        TypeDescriptors.kvs(
          TypeDescriptors.strings(),
          TypeDescriptors.strings()))
      .via(tv -> KV.of(
        tv.getTimestamp().toString(), tv.getValue()))));
```

The `Reify.timestamps()` PTransform object creates a PCollection of `TimestampedValues`. We can access the timestamp with the `getTimestamp()` method and the value with the `getValue()` method.

We can run this modified pipeline by running the `com.packtpub.beam.chapter2.MaxWordLengthWithTimestamp` class:

```
$ kubectl exec -it packt-beam \
  -- run-class.sh \
  com.packtpub.beam.chapter2.MaxWordLengthWithTimestamp \
  kafka:9093 input_topic output_topic
```

We will feed data to input_topic as usual. To observe the output, we must remember to specify the print.key=true object, otherwise, we will not see the key (timestamp). We do that as follows:

```
$ ./env/kafka-consumer.sh --topic output_topic \
    --bootstrap-server kafka:9093 --property print.key=true
```

If we write a line containing a bb ccc to the input_topic object, we'll get the following output:

```
294247-01-09T04:00:54.775Z   ccc
```

We can see that the output timestamp is not what we would expect. The reason for that is hidden in something we have not yet talked about: **TimestampCombiner**.

The TimestampCombiner object is a piece of code that is exactly what we are looking for – given the input timestamp of data in an emitted pane, it will compute the output timestamp of the pane as a whole. Beam does not allow arbitrary computations in there; it has a few predefined combiners. The most useful of these are the following two combiners:

- TimestampCombiner.END_OF_WINDOW
- TimestampCombiner.LATEST

The TimestampCombiner.END_OF_WINDOW object is the default one and – as its name suggests – assigns all output panes to the timestamp that represents the end of the current window. We are using a global window, and the somewhat artificial timestamp chosen to be the maximal timestamp of a global window is, you guessed it, 294247-01-09T04:00:54.775Z.

Therefore, if we want the emitted pane to be assigned a timestamp that represents the maximal timestamp of the actual data elements that produced the pane, we must use the TimestampCombiner.LATEST object:

```
words.apply(
  Window.<String>into(new GlobalWindows())
    .triggering(
      Repeatedly.forever(AfterPane.elementCountAtLeast(1)))
    .withTimestampCombiner(TimestampCombiner.LATEST)
    .accumulatingFiredPanes())
```

The `TimestampCombiner` object is specified as part of the `Window` `PTransform` object and is valid for all subsequent grouping operations. The modified code using `TimestampCombiner.LATEST` can be found in the `MaxWordLengthWithTimestampWithLatestCombiner` class. If we run this class (using `kubectl` and `run-class.sh`, as usual), we can feed the `a  bb  ccc` line again to get a similar output to this:

```
2021-03-07T14:31:08.650Z        ccc
```

> **Important note**
>
> Besides `TimestampCombiner.END_OF_WINDOW` and `TimestampCombiner.LATEST`, there is another one: `TimestampCombiner.EARLIEST`. As its name suggests, it assigns each pane a timestamp that equals the first element that was present in the pane. Although this combiner might be useful in some cases, the author of this book would recommend that you think twice before using it. This is because, usually it suggests that the logic should be rewritten to not rely on `TimestampCombiner` (we will speak about this in *Chapter 3, Implementing Pipelines Using Stateful Processing*), as the `TimestampCombiner.EARLIEST` object might have unexpected side effects when it comes to late data.

The previous two examples have raised some theoretical questions. So, we will now pause our practical examples and give these some attention.

Specifying the PCollection Coder object and the TypeDescriptor object

The *PCollection* name is an abbreviation of *parallel collection*, which suggests that it is a collection of elements that are somewhat distributed among multiple workers. And that is exactly what a parallel collection is. To be able to communicate with the individual elements of this collection, each element needs a *serialized representation*. That is, we need a piece of code that takes a raw (in-memory) object and produces a byte representation that can be sent over the wire. After receiving on the remote side, we need another piece of code that will take this byte representation and recreate the original in-memory object (or rather, a copied version of the original). And that is exactly what **coders** are for.

We have already used `Coder` in our test cases. Recall how we constructed our `TestStream` object:

```
TestStream.create(StringUtf8Coder.of())
```

The reason we need to specify a `Coder` object here is that every `PCollection` object needs a `Coder` object for its data type. The `TestStream` object ultimately creates a `PCollection` object, and it therefore needs `Coder` to be able to assign it to the created `PCollection` object. We can assign `Coder` to any `PCollection` object at any time by calling its `setCoder` method. Take the following example:

```
lines.apply(Tokenize.of()).setCoder(StringUtf8Coder.of());
```

A question that comes to mind would be *why didn't we specify a Coder object for each PCollection object in the previous code examples?* The answer to this question is (you guessed it) **TypeDescriptor**.

The `TypeDescriptor` object is a way to automatically infer `Coder` for a `PCollection` object. This inference works at the level of `PTransform` – if it knows the input type of all its PCollections and it knows the output type of the applied **User-Defined Functions** (**UDFs**), it should be possible to infer the final output type of the `PTransform` object and therefore of the output `PCollection` object. We have already seen this, remember? Consider the following example:

```
output
  .apply(
      MapElements
          .into(
              TypeDescriptors.kvs(
                  TypeDescriptors.strings(),
                  TypeDescriptors.strings()))
          .via(e -> KV.of("", e)))
```

This code tells the `MapElements` `PTransform` object that you are going to write a UDF that will return `KV<String, String>`. There are many predefined `TypeDescriptor` objects in the `TypeDescriptors` class shown in the preceding example. If you need a `TypeDescriptor` object for a type not in the predefined class (for example, for some application class), you can create one as an *anonymous subclass* of the `TypeDescriptor` object:

```
new TypeDescriptor<KV<String, String>>() {}
```

The reason why this has to be an anonymous subclass is due to how the **Java** language specification works with regard to type erasure.

We have described what coders are and what `TypeDescriptors` objects are. Now, we need the last piece of the puzzle – how does Beam connect these two? The answer is **CoderRegistry** and **CoderProvider**.

Pipelines use `CoderRegistry` to retrieve the `Coder` object for a given `TypeDescriptor` object. Each pipeline has a predefined set of `Coder` objects for well-known types (for example, `StringUtf8Coder` for `TypeDescriptor` of string), but we can add our own `Coder` object into the registry with the following:

```
pipeline.getCoderRegistry().registerCoderForType(type, coder);
```

We can also register `Coder` for classes without generic type information using the class object instead of `TypeDescriptor`. This registration is compile-time static. If we want a more dynamic behavior, we can register a `CoderProvider` object, which will resolve the mapping from `TypeDescriptor` to `Coder` at runtime (during the pipeline construction).

Writing a custom coder is most commonly done by the extension of the `CustomCoder` class and implementing the following methods, as shown in the `Coder` example in the `com.packtpub.beam.chapter2.MyStringCoder` class:

```java
public class MyStringCoder extends CustomCoder<String> {
  @Override
  public void encode(
      String value, OutputStream outStream)
      throws CoderException, IOException {
    byte[] bytes = value.getBytes(StandardCharsets.UTF_8);
    VarInt.encode(bytes.length, outStream);
    outStream.write(bytes);
  }

  @Override
  public String decode(
      InputStream inStream)
      throws CoderException, IOException {
    byte[] bytes = new byte[VarInt.decodeInt(inStream)];
    inStream.read(bytes);
    return new String(bytes, StandardCharsets.UTF_8);
  }
}
```

Now that we have taken a deep dive into `Coder`, `TypeDescriptor`, and `CoderRegistry` objects, let's head to another topic we touched on in the first two tasks. That is, *how exactly does Beam handle the triggering of output data in panes?* Let's find out!

Understanding default triggers, on time, and closing behavior

As we have seen, when specifying a `PTransform` window, which is necessary for all grouping operations, we may optionally specify a **triggering**. We explored this concept in the theoretical part of *Chapter 1, Introduction to Data Processing with Apache Beam*. Here, we will focus specifically on understanding how Beam interprets triggers and when the output is triggered.

The simplest trigger we can specify is the `AfterWatermark.pastEndOfWindow()` trigger, which simply means *trigger the output once the window has completed*. That is, once the watermark passes the end timestamp of each particular window. We have already seen that each window has such an end timestamp, including the global window, which has a timestamp set in the very distant future.

A question we might ask is, *which trigger will be used if we create a PTransform window without specifying a trigger?* The answer is `DefaultTrigger`. How should this trigger be defined? If we recall that Beam is a unified model for both batch and streaming data, we will deduce that the default should behave the same way as a batch data processing model would. This is because in batch processing, we do not specify any triggers, yet we receive *exactly one* output at the end of the job (window). But when exactly should this one-and-only triggering occur? Each window has several points in time that are of special importance for that particular window:

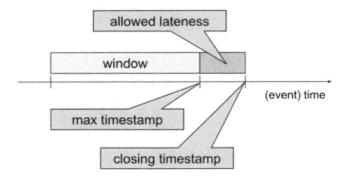

Figure 2.5 – A window max timestamp and closing timestamp

As we can see, there are at least two points in time where we could consider a window to be *complete*. The first one is the time at which the window ends. If we create a fixed window with a duration of 1 hour, it will have a maximal timestamp aligned with the hour boundary (technically, Beam uses a maximal timestamp shifted back by 1 millisecond, so the maximal timestamp of the first window in a day would be `00:59:59.999`, but that is just a technical detail). At the maximal timestamp, the window is finished, without any possible late data accounted for. Once the event time reaches the window closing time, the window can be safely released, as it will not accumulate any more data, as that is how we defined allowed lateness in the first chapter. Putting all this together, we find the answer for the default trigger firing – the only option for `DefaultTrigger` is to trigger exactly once (at the window closing timestamp), after which the window will be closed and accept no more updates.

But wait – does this mean that if we specify a different trigger, we can expect multiple firings per window? The short answer is *yes*. The long answer would be... *well, it depends*. It depends on how we set the allowed lateness for a window, if any data actually arrives between the window max timestamp and the window closing time, and how we set the *window closing behavior*. The options we have should be quite self-explanatory:

- `Window.ClosingBehavior.FIRE_ALWAYS`
- `Window.ClosingBehavior.FIRE_IF_NOT_EMPTY`

The first option fires a pane every time a window is closed, while the second fires if there has been any new data since the last firing. The `FIRE_IF_NOT_EMPTY` option is the default.

The closing behavior of a window is (optionally) specified along with the allowed lateness:

```
input.apply(
  Window.<String>into(new GlobalWindows())
    .triggering(
       Repeatedly.forever(AfterPane.elementCountAtLeast(1)))
    .withAllowedLateness(
       Duration.ZERO, ClosingBehavior.FIRE_ALWAYS)
    .accumulatingFiredPanes())
```

As you might expect, there is very similar logic for the window end timestamp. If there is any firing that precedes the end window timestamp (Beam calls every such firing an *early firing*), we can use the same logic, either to fire every time or only if we have a new update. There is a dedicated class for this called `OnTimeBehavior`, which includes the following options:

- `Window.OnTimeBehavior.FIRE_ALWAYS`
- `Window.OnTimeBehavior.FIRE_IF_NOT_EMPTY`

This looks exactly the same as in the case of `ClosingBehavior`, with one significant difference – the default is exchanged for on-time panes, which is `FIRE_ALWAYS`. The reason is that by default, you would like to have the exactly one on-time pane fired for every pane, irrespective of how often the window has been fired before.

We can pause the theory for a second and try manipulating the `OnTimeBehavior` object in our `MaxWordLength` pipeline. Let's change the `PTransform` window applied to the `computeLongestWord` method to the following:

```
Window.<String>into(new GlobalWindows())
   .triggering(Repeatedly.forever(AfterPane.
elementCountAtLeast(1)))
   .withAllowedLateness(Duration.ZERO)
   .withOnTimeBehavior(OnTimeBehavior.FIRE_IF_NON_EMPTY)
   .accumulatingFiredPanes()
```

Applying this change and running our test with the following code, we can see that there is a failed test with `MaxWordLengthTest.testWordLength`:

```
chapter2$ ../mvnv test
```

We fix this test by removing one occurrence of the `ccc` string from `PAssert` because the on-time firing is no longer generated. The assertion would then look like the following:

```
PAssert.that(output)
   .containsInAnyOrder("a", "bb", "ccc", "ccc");
```

We still get multiple occurrences of the longest word, but that is due to the nature of the `Max PTransform` object. We will describe why in the next section.

> **Important note**
>
> For the test to succeed after we change the `OnTimeBehavior` object, we also need to remove the assertion for the final pane because now we do not get the final pane. We emit only early panes and therefore, the assertion cannot pass.

Introducing the primitive PTransform object – Combine

So far, we have seen three grouping (stateful) transformations: `Count`, `Top`, and `Max`. None of these are actually primitive transformations. A **primitive transformation** is defined as a transformation that needs direct support from a runner and cannot be executed via other transformations. The `Combine` object is actually the first primitive `PTransform` object that we are going to introduce. Beam actually has only five primitive `PTransform` objects, and we will walk through all of them in this chapter. We call non-primitive `PTransform` objects **composite transformations**.

The `Combine` PTransform object generally performs a *reduction* operation on a `PCollection` object. As the name suggests, the transform combines multiple input elements into a single output value per window (`Combine.globally`) or per key and window (`Combine.perKey`). This reduction is illustrated by the following figure:

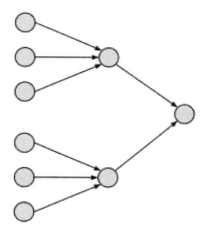

Figure 2.6 – A stream reduction using Combine

As we can see, the reduction is done per part. The reason for this is that such a computation can be easily parallelized, and each sub-reduction can be done on a different worker, thus increasing parallelism and reducing the amount of data that needs to be sent over the network. For this reason, whenever the application logic can be implemented using `Combine`, it should be preferred to any other implementation.

The fact that Combine can be parallelized has an impact on *what* we can actually implement using such a reduction. The formal requirements of the binary function used for reduction are that the function must be **commutative** (independent of the order in which elements are ordered) and **associative** (applicable to partial results). Addition and multiplication are examples of binary functions having such a property. If we have a commutative and associative binary operation (often called a **combinable** operation), we can easily apply such a function on a (properly windowed) stream using the following code:

```
input.apply(Combine.globally((a, b) -> a + b)))
```

This reduces the stream to a single value per window. If we want to reduce it to a single value per key (which would be the case for our example with counting the number of occurrences of a word), we do that via the following:

```
strings
  .apply(
    MapElements
      .into(TypeDescriptors.kvs(
        TypeDescriptors.strings(), TypeDescriptors.longs()))
      .via(s -> KV.o(s, 1L))))
  .apply(Combine.perKey(Long::sum));
```

We first have to create a stream of key-value (KV) pairs, and then use the `Combine.perKey` transform.

The `Combine` transform is a little more generic than using a simple combinable operation, and it allows for a more generic approach using **accumulators**. An accumulator is an object that has two operations: **add element** and **merge**. The combine process using accumulators is depicted in the following figure:

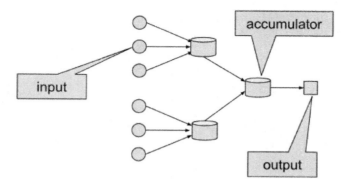

Figure 2.7 – A stream reduction using Combine with accumulators

This generic process uses a `CombineFn` object, which defines the following operations:

1. Create an empty accumulator.

2. Add an element to the accumulator.

3. Merge multiple accumulators into a single accumulator.

4. Convert the accumulator to a final output value.

As we can see, we can get the combinable function from this when we make the accumulator the same type as the input and the output value extraction is identity. This is therefore a special case of the generic approach using `CombineFn`. The `CombineFn` object has to provide a little more than these four functions, namely coders for all types involved, type descriptors, and more.

One more thing worth noting is the ability of the `Combine` transform to perform a **hot key fanout** operation. Let's imagine that the majority of elements in a stream belong to the same key. This would cause a very imbalanced load on individual workers. Some workers who work on the rare keys would have very low usage, while one worker processing the majority of the stream would be overwhelmed. But wait, `Combine` can solve this for us!

It can do this by using the following:

```
input.apply(Combine.perKey().withHotKeyFanout(40))
```

It can also do this by using the following:

```
input.apply(Combine.globally().withFanout(40))
```

We can change the transform to look like the following:

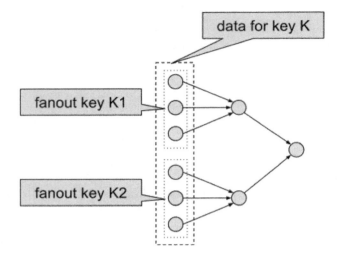

Figure 2.8 – A stream reduction using Combine with accumulators

In this case, the `Combine` object splits keys into disjointed subgroups (the cardinality of each group is determined by the parameter passed to `withHotKeyFanout` or `withFanout`, respectively). These subgroups are combined independently, and the result is finally combined. Note that the definition of `Combine` is exactly what enables this kind of scalability boost.

Now that we have walked through a little theory, let's use what we have learned in something more practical with the use of coders, window closing behavior, and `CombineFn`!

Task 3 – Calculating the average length of words in a stream

In this task, we will investigate how we can use `CombineFn` and accumulators to compute a directly non-combinable reduction and average. Let's see how this works.

Defining the problem

Given an input data stream of lines of text, calculate the average length of words currently seen in this stream. Output the current average as frequently as possible, ideally after every word.

Discussing the problem decomposition

Calculating an average is not a directly combinable function. An average of averages is not a proper average of the original data. However, we can calculate an average using an accumulator. An accumulator would be a pair of (*sum*, *count*) and the output will be extracted using a function that divides the *sum* by the *count*. We can illustrate this with *Figure 2.9*:

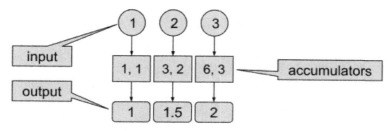

Figure 2.9 – Calculating an average using CombineFn

We will need to create an accumulator object for holding the two values for the count and the sum of the word lengths. For that, we will need to implement a `Coder` object, as the accumulated values might need to be transferred over a network to a different worker. We want to trigger the output as fast as possible, so we will again be using a trigger that fires after each element in a pane. Because of this, we will override the default `OnTimeBehavior` object so that we do not get multiple firings of the same value.

Implementing the solution

The complete implementation can be found in the `com.packtpub.beam.chapter2.AverageWordLength` class. As usual, we will walk through the most important parts here:

1. We create the input `PCollection` object in Kafka as usual. After splitting the lines into words, we need to apply our `Window PTransform` object:

```
words
  .apply(
    Window.<String>into(new GlobalWindows()
      .triggering(Repeatedly.forever(
        AfterPane.elementCountAtLeast(1)))
      .accumulatingFiredPanes()
      .withOnTimeBehavior(OnTimeBehavior.FIRE_IF_NON_
EMPTY))
```

As we have described previously, we need to set the `OnTimeBehavior` object so that we don't receive duplicate firings at the end of a window (which actually affects only tests, as the global window should not close under production use).

2. We need to apply the `Combine PTransform` object, which is straightforward:

```
windowed.apply(Combine.globally(new AverageFn()));
```

As we have described, the `Combine.globally` object creates a single value per window, while `Combine.perKey` creates a single value per each key-window pair. We want a single global value per global window; therefore, we use the `Combine.globally` transform.

3. We will use a `CombineFn` object, for which we need an accumulator. That is the simple value class defined in `AverageWordLength.AverageAccumulator`, which holds the sum of all of the word lengths seen so far in the `sumLength` field, and the total number of words in the `count` field.

4. Next, we need to implement the `AverageFn` object, which is a `CombineFn` object:

```
static class AverageFn extends
    CombineFn<String, AverageAccumulator, Double> {
```

We must define the input type (`String`), the accumulator, and the output type (`Double`).

5. The `CombineFn` object has four mandatory methods when we create an empty accumulator:

```
@Override
public AverageAccumulator createAccumulator() {
    return new AverageAccumulator(0, 0);
}
```

6. Use `addInput` to add a new input value to the accumulator:

```
@Override
public AverageAccumulator addInput(
    AverageAccumulator accumulator, String input) {

    return new AverageAccumulator(
        accumulator.getSumLength() + input.length(),
        accumulator.getCount() + 1);
}
```

7. Next, merge multiple accumulators together and produce a single merged one:

```
@Override
public AverageAccumulator mergeAccumulators(
    Iterable<AverageAccumulator> accumulators) {

  long sumLength = 0L;
  long count = 0L;
  for (AverageAccumulator acc : accumulators) {
    sumLength += acc.getSumLength();
    count += acc.getCount();
  }
  return new AverageAccumulator(sumLength, count);
}
```

8. Finally, we need a way to extract the final value from our accumulator. The average is defined as *sum* divided by *count*, so we get the following:

```
@Override
  public Double extractOutput(AverageAccumulator
accumulator) {
  return accumulator.getSumLength()
    / (double) accumulator.getCount();
}
```

9. This way, we have implemented all the required methods of CombineFn, but running the pipeline like this would result in one last problem. We need a Coder object for the accumulator, as the accumulator is going to be sent over the wire. Specifying the Coder object is optional because if we use a well-known type, the Coder object might be inferred from CoderRegistry. We have defined our own type, so a custom Coder object is mandatory (either directly on CombineFn or using CoderRegistry as well):

```
@Override
public Coder<AverageAccumulator> getAccumulatorCoder(
    CoderRegistry registry, Coder<String> inputCoder) {

  return new AverageAccumulatorCoder();
}
```

10. The last missing piece is the actual implementation of the Coder object. The simplest Coder objects might extend the CustomCoder base class, as we did in this case:

```
private static class AverageAccumulatorCoder
    extends CustomCoder<AverageAccumulator> {

@Override
public void encode(
    AverageAccumulator value, OutputStream outStream)
    throws CoderException, IOException {
  VarInt.encode(value.getSumLength(), outStream);
  VarInt.encode(value.getCount(), outStream);

}

@Override
public AverageAccumulator decode(InputStream inStream)
    throws CoderException, IOException {
  return new AverageAccumulator(
    VarInt.decodeLong(inStream),
    VarInt.decodeLong(inStream));
}
}
```

We use the functionality provided by VarInt to encode the two longs using variable-length encoding for efficient size, as we are going to send the encoded class over a network.

Testing our solution

Testing this new transformation requires no new knowledge, so it is up to you to verify how we tested that the input of a stream containing a, bb, ccc is transformed into a stream of 1.0, 1.5, 2.0.

Deploying our solution

Let's deploy the code using the `run-class.sh` script, specifying our runner via
`-runner`:

```
$ kubectl exec -it packt-beam -- run-class.sh \
  com.packtpub.beam.chapter2.AverageWordLength \
  kafka:9093 input_topic output_topic --runner=flink \
  --flinkMaster=flink-jobmanager:8081 \
  --checkpointingInterval=2000
```

After we run this job, we can look at its web UI by using `kubectl proxy` and pointing
our browser to the already known URL at `http://localhost:8001/api/v1/`
`namespaces/default/services/flink-jobmanager:ui/proxy/#/`
`overview`. We will see the same pipeline DAG as in *Figure 2.4*. The reason is that we are
actually using the same `PTransform` object. The DAG looks a little more complicated
than we would expect because, by default, `Combine PTransform` tries to compute a
default value for a window, which requires adding some complexity to the DAG. We don't
need any default values in this computation, so we can disable them using the following:

```
windowed.apply(
    Combine.globally(new AverageFn()).withoutDefaults());
```

We have prepared this modification for use by adding the (optional)
`--withoutDefaults` argument to the `com.packtpub.beam.chapter2.`
`AverageWordLength` object:

```
$ kubectl exec -it packt-beam -- run-class.sh \
  com.packtpub.beam.chapter2.AverageWordLength \
   kafka:9093 input_topic output_topic \
  --withoutDefaults \
  --runner=flink \
  --flinkMaster=flink-jobmanager:8081 \
  --checkpointingInterval=2000
```

We verify on Flink's web UI that our job's DAG has been simplified to the following:

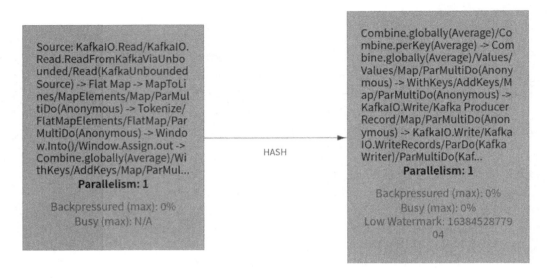

Figure 2.10 – A DAG of Combine.withoutDefaults()

Please note that the --withoutDefaults parameter must precede all other arguments starting with --. We'll send our text file with some *lorem ipsum* placeholder text to the input topic with a delay to be able to watch outputs with the following code:

```
$ cat chapter1/src/main/resources/lorem.txt \
 | ./env/delay_input.sh 0.2 \
 | ./env/kafka-producer.sh --bootstrap-server kafka:9093 \
   --topic input_topic
```

As usual, we'll get the results using the env/kafka-consumer.sh script. We only need to use --value-deserializer org.apache.kafka.common.serialization. DoubleDeserializer, as we are writing double values to the output_topic object.

So far, we have always deployed our pipelines *from scratch* – that is, we deployed a pipeline, ran it for a while, and then terminated it. But stream processing is a continuous process and should therefore be part of a long-running application. Such applications have a life cycle and – besides the necessary ability to recover from various failures – need a way to support the evolution of the application itself. In the following example, we'll explore how to address these requirements.

Task 4 – Calculating the average length of words in a stream with fixed lookback

In this section, we will focus on using a different kind of window – a **sliding window**. Let's see what we can do with them.

Defining the problem

Given an input data stream of lines of text, calculate the average length of the words seen in this stream during the last 10 seconds and output the result every 2 seconds.

Discussing the problem decomposition

This is actually very similar to *Task 3*. However, what we need to do is apply a different `Window` transform. What we need is a sliding window with a length of 10 seconds and a slide interval of 2 seconds, as this will produce the output we want.

Implementing the solution

The solution to this task can be found in the `com.packtpub.beam.chapter2.SlidingWindowWordLength` class.

The modification to the code from the previous task is just the different `Window` transform:

```
words
  .apply(
    Window.into(
      SlidingWindows.of(Duration.standardSeconds(10))
        .every(Duration.standardSeconds(2))))
```

Testing our solution

While testing our solution with sliding windows, we will have to pay more attention to the timestamp we assign to elements in the `TestStream` object. Obviously, to test the behavior of the sliding window, we must include data that spans the complete time interval of the window duration plus at least 1 millisecond. As usual, the complete test can be found in `com.packtpub.beam.chapter2.SlidingWindowWordLengthTest`.

As this will be our first hands-on experience with sliding windows, we will walk through the test to make it clear how exactly we arrived at the solution and what the expected outcome should be:

1. First, we fill our stream with words of different lengths with carefully chosen timestamps:

```
Instant now = Instant.now();
// round this to one minute boundary
now = now.plus(-now.getMillis() % 60000);

TestStream.create(StringUtf8Coder.of())
  .addElements(TimestampedValue.of("a", now))
  .addElements(TimestampedValue.of("bb", now.plus(1999)))
  // add different slide
  .addElements(TimestampedValue.of("ccc", now.
plus(5000)))
  // first non-overlapping set of windows
  .addElements(TimestampedValue.of("dddd", now.
plus(10000)))
  .advanceWatermarkToInfinity());
```

For clarity, we can plot these data points on a time axis, as follows:

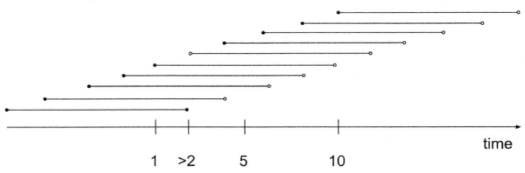

Figure 2.11 – Sliding windows created for the test data of Task 4

We denote by >2 the timestamp of 1 ms before 2 seconds (relative to the starting timestamp of now). Therefore, the four data points correspond to the values a, bb, ccc, and dddd, respectively. The horizontal bars mark the individual windows, which are 10 seconds in length, shifted by 2 seconds between each other.

2. Looking at *Figure 2.11*, we see that we have two windows that contain the a and bb elements, three windows containing a, bb, and ccc, two windows containing ccc and dddd, and three windows with dddd only. Putting this together gives us the following assertion for the result of the pipeline:

```
PAssert.that(averages).containsInAnyOrder(
        1.5, 1.5, 2.0, 2.0, 2.0, 3.5, 3.5, 4.0, 4.0, 4.0);
```

Please note that if we had an empty window, we would not see it in the output (that is, there will be no zero in the output).

Deploying our solution

The following description will be purely theoretical because the successful application of this procedure requires a distributed filesystem (for example, the **Hadoop Distributed File System (HDFS)**), and setting this up is out of the scope of this book. We kindly ask you to look for resources on this in the Flink documentation. We will outline the steps needed to perform such an operation and how this affects the code that needs to be implemented in Beam:

1. We will deploy this pipeline as usual:

```
$ kubectl exec -it packt-beam -- run-class.sh \
        com.packtpub.beam.chapter2.SlidingWindowWordLength \
        kafka:9093 input_topic output_topic --runner=flink \
        --flinkMaster=flink-jobmanager:8081 \
        --checkpointingInterval=2000
```

2. While the job is running, we can send input to input_topic and observe the output in output_topic, as usual. When we are ready, we will cancel the job with **Savepoint**. A Savepoint is how Flink persists its state, which can then be reused by another job. The Savepoint needs a distributed filesystem so that all (distributed) instances of a running Flink **TaskManager** can have access to it.

    In order to create a Savepoint, we first need a JobId object. This is a hash, which can be obtained from the Flink web UI. The job can be canceled with the following command:

```
$ kubectl exec -t flink-jobmanager -- \
        /opt/flink/bin/flink stop <JobId>
```

This will result in a Savepoint being created in the distributed filesystem and the path to that Savepoint should be output to the console.

3. If we want to resume the job from the `savepoint` object, we will add the `savepointPath` parameter with a specified path to the `savepoint` object in the command line:

```
$ kubectl exec -it packt-beam -- run-class.sh \
    com.packtpub.beam.chapter2.SlidingWindowWordLength \
    kafka:9093 input_topic output_topic --runner=flink \
    --flinkMaster=flink-jobmanager:8081 \
    --checkpointingInterval=2000 \
    --savepointPath <PATH>
```

4. As we can see, we are free to run the job with whatever code we want and provide it with the Savepoint path we created. This raises a lot of questions, most importantly – *what are the requirements for the pipeline to be able to load the Savepoint?*

Let's explore that in the following section!

Ensuring pipeline upgradability

First, be aware that Beam (currently, as of version 2.28.0) does not offer an abstraction that would allow us to transfer a pipeline between runners including its state. The code of the pipeline can be transferred, but that means a new pipeline will be created and that any computation done on the previous runner is lost. That is due to the fact that, currently, the processing of pipeline upgrades is a runner-specific task, and details might therefore differ slightly based on which runner we choose.

That is the bad news. The good news is that the pipeline upgrade process is generally subject to the same constraints that are mostly runner independent and, therefore, the chances are high that very similar rules will apply to the majority of runners.

Let's look at the tasks that a runner must perform to upgrade a pipeline:

1. The complete state (including the timers) of all transforms must be stored in a durable and persistent location. This is what Flink calls a Savepoint.

2. Upon restore, the state of every transform needs to be restored and passed as the initial state to the new transforms.

3. The sources need to be reset to a particular position (in the same way as when recovering after a failure).

This process is, of course, significantly simplified. There are many processes that have not been explicitly described, such as how a possible change in parallelism is handled. Those kinds of tasks are purely runner-specific, and Beam does not directly affect them.

On the other hand, the previous simplified description implies what the requirements are for a properly upgradable pipeline:

- Any number of *stateless* transforms (for instance, `MapElements`, `Filter`, `Reify`, and so on) can be added, removed, or changed.

- Every *stateful* operation must be identifiable by its name. A name must be stable, and therefore, it should be assigned manually, as follows:

```
words.apply("CountWords", Count.perElement())
```

This will create a PTransform called `CountWords`. This name is considered stable and is used for matching the operator's state in the Savepoint. Note that we do *not* need to name stateless transformations, but all stateful transformations (implicit or explicit) *should* have a name. If in doubt, it is always safe to add names to all of the transforms we create in a pipeline:

- The element type (and `Coder` object) cannot be changed for any state.

- If we add a completely new stateful transform, its state will be empty.

- Stateful operations can be removed, but it might require additional flags for a runner to allow this because it is a potentially risky operation – that is, the operation implies state deletion, which might cause data loss.

> **Important note**
>
> As you can see, the conditions under which a pipeline can be safely upgraded are somewhat restrictive. It is definitely not possible to upgrade a pipeline with some significant change in its processing logic. Therefore, it is necessary to plan ahead – every pipeline should have a *recovery plan* – that is, a way to replay historical data along with new streaming data. The technical jargon for this is **state bootstrapping**.

Task 5 – Calculating performance statistics for a sport activity tracking application

Let's explore the most useful applications of stream processing – the delivery of high-accuracy real-time insights to (possibly) high-volume data streams. As an example, we will borrow a use case known to almost everyone – calculating performance statistics (for example, speed and total distance) from a stream of GPS coordinates coming from a sport activity tracker!

Defining the problem

Given an input data stream of quadruples (workoutId, gpsLatitude, gpsLongitude, and timestamp) calculate the current speed and the total tracked distance of the tracker. The data comes from a GPS tracker that sends data only when its user starts a sport activity. We can assume that workoutId is unique and contains a userId value in it.

Let's describe the problem more informally. Suppose we have a stream that looks as follows:

```
(user1:track1, 65.5384, -19.9108, 1616427100000)
(user2:track1, 50.0315, 13.8661, 1616427100000)
(user1:track1, 65.5397, -19.9113, 1616427110000)
```

We receive an identifier for the user's track (`user1:track1`) and a GPS location (latitude, longitude) along with a timestamp. We want to create a simplistic performance tracker from this data. We will calculate a speed (in minutes per kilometer) and compute the total distance tracked. The data might be coming in at varying frequencies.

> **Important note**
>
> Calculating a precise position from raw GPS data is a non-trivial task that might require additional data sources (for instance, maps with marked roads) and/or sophisticated (very frequently, probabilistic) calculations. We will not attempt to solve this task; we will assume that the data we have is 100% precise and the diameter of the Earth is a universal constant (6,371 kilometers). Although these assumptions are not 100% correct, we can use them for the purposes of our example.

Discussing the problem decomposition

First of all, we notice that the problem we need to solve requires a state. The only stateful transform we need to know for now is `Combine`. The essential requirement for this transform to work is that the result of the computation does not depend on the order of the input data. That is definitely not the case now, as we can see in the following figure:

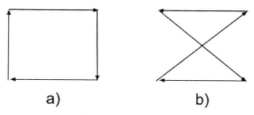

Figure 2.12 – The distance of different trajectories between the same points

As we can see, the distance (and therefore the average speed!) traveled between a set of points in space *depends on the order* in which we pass through them. That means that the (combinable, unordered version of) `Combine` transform itself will not help us on its own.

What we could do is create an accumulator that would hold all of the data points, order them by timestamp, and produce the result using the `extractOutput` method. That would have the correct semantics but wait – Beam has a native transform for that! Say hello to `GroupByKey`. We will discuss the reasons why this is a primitive transform (and is *not* based on `Combine`, as we just suggested).

The following figure shows the final decomposition of our proposed solution:

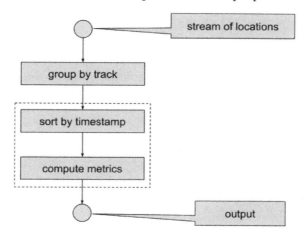

Figure 2.13 – The problem decomposition

As we can see, we need to group all of the data points for a given workout by its key, and then sort the data points by the timestamp at which they happened. After sorting, we can reiterate the data points to compute the distance and speed metrics. We can do that within the same transform, which is why we grouped these two together.

Solution implementation

As always, the complete solution can be found in the `com.packtpub.beam.chapter2.SportTracker` class. Once again, we leave it up to you to walk through the complete source code, and we will highlight only the important parts that need clarification:

1. We will use user-defined types in our pipeline (the `SportTracker.Position` and `SportTracker.Metric classes`). Therefore, we must create and register coders for them. The coders are implemented in `com.packtpub.beam.util.PositionCoder` and `SportTracker.MetricCoder`. There is nothing new about this – the important part is how we register these coders in the pipeline:

```
static void registerCoders(Pipeline pipeline) {
    pipeline.getCoderRegistry().registerCoderForClass(
        Position.class, new PositionCoder());
    pipeline.getCoderRegistry().registerCoderForClass(
        Metric.class, new MetricCoder());
}
```

This way, every time we use either of the two classes inside a `PCollection` object, Beam will know which `Coder` object to use to encode them.

2. We will read and write from Kafka. There is mostly nothing new here, with one important exception. Our data in Kafka contains a custom timestamp – that is, the timestamp for when the data was stored in Kafka does not represent the time the event *occurred*. We must provide this information to the `KafkaIO` object so that it can correctly generate watermarks for us:

```
KafkaIO.<String, String>read()
    .withBootstrapServers(params.getBootstrapServer())
    .withKeyDeserializer(StringDeserializer.class)
    .withValueDeserializer(StringDeserializer.class)
    .withTopic(params.getInputTopic())
    .withTimestampPolicyFactory(newTimestampPolicy())
```

This call is responsible for providing a factory class for a `TimestampPolicy` object that is responsible for reading timestamps from the elements and computing watermarks from the elements flowing through it. The (probably) most commonly used is `CustomTimestampPolicyWithLimitedDelay`, which holds the maximum timestamp seen and subtracts a constant value from it to compute the actual watermark.

> **Important note**
>
> Using a `TimestampPolicy` object generally affects latency, which should be taken into account. The more the watermark is *held back*, the less late data is produced, but the higher the latency. This is a general rule that is worth noting and a proper trade-off is usually necessary.

3. Next, we must assign our data to a window. In our first implementation, we will use a `GlobalWindow` object, which is nothing new. We will specify that it should trigger the output every 10 seconds, as follows:

```
Window.<KV<String, Position>>into(new GlobalWindows())
  .withTimestampCombiner(TimestampCombiner.LATEST)
  .withAllowedLateness(Duration.standardHours(1))
  .triggering(
    Repeatedly.forever(
      AfterProcessingTime.pastFirstElementInPane()
        .plusDelayOf(Duration.standardSeconds(10))))
  .accumulatingFiredPanes())
```

4. After we have assigned our window, we must group the data by the `workoutId` object, which is the key in our input key-value pair. This is as simple as the following transform:

```
windowed.apply(
    "groupByWorkoutId", GroupByKey.create())
```

That's it! We receive a PCollection of the `KV<String, Iterable<Position>>` type, which is exactly what we need!

> **Important note**
>
> There is no specific order in which the elements appear in the `Iterable` object. This is especially important to keep in mind to code accordingly. We will explore this in detail in the following subsection.

5. Finally, we apply a `MapElements` object that will produce our metric (*distance*, *time*, and therefore, *speed*). Producing the metric from the `Iterable` object is pure Java, so we will leave it to you to walk through this in the `SportTracker.computeRawMetrics` method.

As usual, now we have walked through the implementation, we will see how to test our code.

Testing our solution

In order to test our solution, we need input data. We can create this manually or, as we will do now, create a generator for such data. We created a `SportTracker.Generator` class, which can pick a random spot on Earth (probably in the ocean) and create a random path that would resemble a running route. For the purpose of our test, we stored some input data in the test resources in the `chapter2` directory (`chapter2/src/test/resources`) in the `test-tracker-data.txt` file. The rest of the test is similar to the previous examples, with two exceptions:

*   We test more deeply the logic that computes the distance from the GPS coordinates, as this is a non-trivial calculation, and testing such logic separately is always a good idea.

    Do not rely on only black-box testing your pipeline. Wherever possible, test your internal logic independently!

*   Our final `Metric` class contains doubles, which are not easy to compare precisely. Therefore, we apply the common technique of *stringification* to the output:

```
MapElements
    .into(TypeDescriptors.strings())
    .via(
      kv ->
        String.format(
          "%s:%d,%d",
          kv.getKey(),
          Math.round(kv.getValue().getLength()),
          kv.getValue().getTime()))
```

Note that we must also round the double value (or trim it in some other way) for the test to be stable. We then compare the string outcomes:

```
PAssert.that(result)
    .inOnTimePane(GlobalWindow.INSTANCE)
```

```
     .containsInAnyOrder("track1:614,257",
 "track2:5641,1262");
```

After testing the implementation, let's feed it some data and see how it works!

Deploying our solution

Let's run our solution against input_topic and output_topic, as usual:

```
$ kubectl exec -it packt-beam -- \
  run-class.sh com.packtpub.beam.chapter2.SportTracker \
  kafka:9093 input_topic output_topic \
  --runner=flink --flinkMaster=flink-jobmanager:8081
```

As always, we start the consumer from output_topic. We have prepared some test data in chapter2/src/test/resources/test-tracker-data-200.txt.

We will send this data to the input_topic object with the following command:

```
$ cat chapter2/src/test/resources/test-tracker-data-200.txt \
  | ./env/delay_input.sh 0.05 \
  | ./env/kafka-producer.sh --bootstrap-server kafka:9093 \
  --topic input_topic
```

Again, we will use the delay-input.sh command so that we can easily watch the outputs coming from our running pipeline. The data was created so that there are 200 random users with random paths. We can watch the distance of their paths increasing over time, as more and more data arrives in the pipeline.

> **Important note**
>
> The input data has been manually sorted by the timestamp so that it better resembles an actual real-time stream. Remember, as stated in *Chapter 1*, *Introduction to Data Processing with Apache Beam*, real-world streams are never perfectly sorted. We will investigate what happens in these cases at the beginning of *Chapter 3*, *Implementing Pipelines Using Stateful Processing*.

Now that we have created a useful application, let's dive a little deeper into some theory about two more primitive PTransform objects. In the following section we will introduce the first transform - GroupByKey.

Introducing the primitive PTransform object – GroupByKey

As we have seen, a `GroupByKey` transform works in the way illustrated in the following figure:

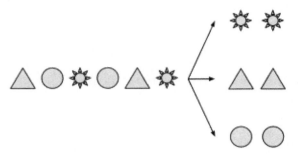

Figure 2.14 – GroupByKey

As in the case of `Combine PTransform` objects, the input stream must be **keyed**. This is a way of saying that the PCollection must have elements of the KV type. This is generally true for any stateful operations. The reason for this is that having a state (which cannot be partitioned) divided into smaller, independent sub-states means that it cannot scale and would therefore lead to scalability issues. Therefore, Beam explicitly prohibits this and enforces the use of keyed PCollections for the input of each stateful operation.

The `GroupByKey` transform then takes this keyed stream (in *Figure 2.14*, the key is represented as the shape of the stream element) and creates something that can be viewed as a *sub-stream* for each key. We can then process elements with a different key (belonging to a different *group*) independently.

We can illustrate how `GroupByKey` works in the following figure:

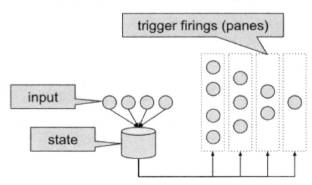

Figure 2.15 – GroupByKey

As we can see, the transform works by caching the entire input (per key and window) into a state. The complete contents of the state are then flushed to the output with each trigger firing. This also illustrates how expensive this transform can become – in cases with frequent trigger firings, it can be as high as *O(N2)* in both space and time complexity.

There are important things to keep in mind when using `GroupByKey`:

- As with every other stream, the order of elements in the group is **undefined**.

- In the Java SDK, the group is represented as an `Iterable` object. It is the responsibility of the programmer to handle this value properly. The biggest concern is that *there is no guarantee that this Iterable object can fit in memory (RAM)*. An obvious example would be if we assigned every element in a stream the same key – the group would then represent the whole stream.

- The `Iterable` object can be re-iterated generally but remember that this can be expensive. It is not even guaranteed that iterating over the group will not involve network communication (the elements might be stored on a remote worker).

- Remember, `GroupByKey` is a very expensive operation and, whenever possible, it should always be replaced with `Combine`. Even applying `Combine` to produce partial results that are then fed into `GroupByKey` is something that can improve the performance significantly.

- Use trigger firings with care. Remember, the more often a trigger fires, the more expensive the transform becomes.

Now that we have walked through a very powerful transform and we are aware of all its caveats, let's look at a different transform – `Partition`.

Introducing the primitive PTransform object – Partition

The `GroupByKey` transform creates a set of *sub-streams* based on a dynamic property of the data – the set of keys of a particular window can be modified during the pipeline *execution time*. New keys can be created and processed at any time. This creates the complexity mentioned in the previous section – we need to store our data in keyed states and flush them on triggers. A question we might have is – *would the task be easier if we knew the exact set of keys upfront, during pipeline construction time?*

The answer is *yes*, and that is why we have a `PTransform` object called `Partition`.

> **Important note**
>
> A pipeline is generally divided into three phases during its life cycle: *pipeline compile time*, *pipeline construction time*, and *pipeline execution time*. Compile time refers (as usual) to the time we compile the source to bytecode. Construction time is the time when the pipeline's DAG of transformations is created. This DAG is then submitted to a runner, which then runs the pipeline – and that is what defines pipeline execution time.

We can apply a `Partition` transform to a `PCollection` object as follows:

```
PCollectionList<String> = input.apply(
  Partition.of(
    10,
    (element, numPartitions) ->
      (element.hashCode() & Integer.MAX_VALUE)
        % numPartitions));
```

The returned `PCollectionList` object is a list of independent PCollections that has the same cardinality as we requested (10 in the case of the preceding code). We can then process these resulting PCollections independently.

The biggest advantage of `Partition`, as opposed to `GroupByKey`, is that the transform is stateless and therefore very cheap. The obvious disadvantage is its static nature. Its typical use cases include cases where we need to split different types of input data and process them using independent paths in a pipeline.

Summary

In this chapter, we first walked through the steps needed to set up our environment to run the code located at this book's GitHub. We created a minikube cluster and ran Apache Kafka and Apache Flink on top of it. We then found out how to use the scripts located on GitHub to create topics in Kafka and publish messages to them, and how to consume data from topics.

After we walked through the necessary infrastructure, we jumped directly into implementing various practical tasks. The first one was to calculate the *K* most frequent words in a stream of text lines. In order to accomplish this, we learned how to use the `Count` and `Top` transforms. We also learned how to use the `TestStream` utility to create a simulated stream of input data and use this to write a test case that validates our pipeline implementation. Then, we learned how to deploy our pipeline to a real runner – Apache Flink.

We then got acquainted with another grouping transform – Max, which we used to compute the word with maximal length in a stream. We saw what TypeDescriptor objects are and how they relate to Coder objects.

After that, we saw how *composite* PTransform objects expand into *primitive* ones, and we saw the first primitive object of great practical value: Combine. Although Combine is not exactly a primitive transform, due to its extreme importance, it is often implemented by runners. We will get into the details of that in *Chapter 8, Understanding How Runners Execute Pipelines*. We have seen how the transform works and how it can have a significant performance benefit to another quite similar primitive PTransform object: GroupByKey.

We have walked through the reasons why it is necessary to name all stateful PTransform objects with stable, unique names in order to ensure the upgradability of a streaming application during its life cycle.

Finally, we used the GroupByKey PTransform object to implement a sport activity tracker that computed the distance and speed of a runner along a route. We also introduced the last primitive PTransform object of this chapter: Partition.

In this chapter, we walked through the basics of coding, testing, and deploying some of the simple pipelines in Beam, and this didn't require any low-level coding. But what if our requirements mean that we are no longer able to meet them with the Combine or GroupByKey transforms? In the next chapter, we will explore how to solve such cases with **stateful processing**, where we have access to user-defined states and therefore can create any application logic.

3

Implementing Pipelines Using Stateful Processing

In the previous chapter, we focused on implementing pipelines that used *high-level* transformations. Such transforms tend to have low numbers of parameters and/ or methods that need to be implemented in order to use them, and this comes at the expense of somewhat limited usability. Let's demonstrate this using the example of the GroupByKey transform. This is quite simply defined as a transform that wraps elements with the same key into an Iterable object. This Iterable object (essentially, nothing more than a bag of elements) is then *triggered* based on a **windowing strategy**. Nothing more, nothing less. But what if we need finer control? What if we want to control *exactly* when we emit the output for a particular input element? In that case, these high-level transformations will not do anymore.

In this chapter, we will first (nearly) complete the picture of the primitive PTransform objects that **Apache Beam** has in the model, and then we will focus on how to implement low-level stateful processing via a user-defined state and timers.

In this chapter, we will discuss the following topics:

- Task 6 – Using an external service for data augmentation
- Introducing the primitive transform – stateless `ParDo`
- Task 7 – Batching queries to an external RPC service
- Task 8 – Batching queries to an external RPC service with defined batch sizes
- Introducing the primitive transform – stateful `ParDo`
- Using side outputs
- Defining droppable data in Beam
- Task 9 – Separating droppable data from the rest of the data processing
- Task 10 – Separating droppable data from the rest of the data processing, part 2
- Using side inputs

After completing these topics, we will have covered the complete model of Beam – with one exception. There is one more flavor of the `ParDo` transform, which makes use of **Splittable DoFn**. This is the last transform that will still be ahead of us, and we will describe it in *Chapter 7, Extending Apache Beam's I/O Connectors*.

Technical requirements

We will use the same tools as in the previous chapter, so, for a detailed description of how to get set up, please refer to *Chapter 2, Implementing, Testing, and Deploying Basic Pipelines*. If you already have everything working, then there is nothing new needed. Please make sure that you have cloned the book's GitHub repository from `https://github.com/PacktPublishing/Building-Big-Data-Pipelines-with-Apache-Beam`.

Now that we have everything set up, we can jump directly to solving our next puzzle!

Task 6 – Using an external service for data augmentation

All of the tasks we solved so far in the previous chapter had all of their data readily available in the input `PCollection` object. That might not be the case in all situations. Imagine a situation in which you need to augment your input data with some metadata that is located behind an external service. This external service is accessible via a **Remote Procedure Call** (**RPC**), as illustrated in the following figure:

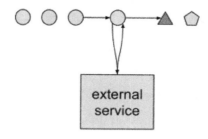

Figure 3.1 – Augmenting data with an external service

We feed our input data to a (stateless) operation, which performs an RPC call for each input element (possibly doing some caching) and uses this outcome to somehow modify the input element and output (or discard) it to downstream processing. From this description, we will create a definition of the task problem.

Defining the problem

Given an input stream of lines of text (coming from Apache Kafka) and an RPC service that returns a category (an integer) for each input word, use the integers returned from the RPC service to convert the stream of lines of text to a stream of pairs comprising the words with their respective integers.

To rephrase this, our goal is to turn the `hello, world!` input string into two pairs, (`hello`, 1) and (`world`, 2), given that the result of the RPC call of the `hello` word is 1 and the result for `world` is 2

Discussing the problem decomposition

A naive implementation would use either `MapElements` or `FlatMapElements` (if we wanted to output *exactly* one element per single input element, or we wanted to output zero or multiple elements, respectively). Therefore, the solution would look as follows (in pseudocode):

```
input.apply(
  MapElements
    .into(
      TypeDescriptors.kvs(TypeDescriptors.strings(),
      TypeDescriptors.integers()))
    .via(input -> KV.of(input, callRpc(input))))
```

The `callRpc` method does all the magic – it takes the input element and produces the output based on the return value from the RPC service.

This approach has an obvious drawback – we either have to create a new connection for each element (which is going to be extremely expensive in terms of wasted CPU time), or we must resort to some static caches, which are error-prone and hard to debug.

A better solution is to couple the life cycle of the necessary connection to the RPC service with the life cycle of the operator. And – to come to the rescue – Beam has a *primitive* transform called `ParDo`. The name stands for *parallel do*, and – as the name suggests – it allows you to apply a rather generic work on elements of an input `PCollection` object in parallel. All other element-wise transforms (for example `MapElements`, `FlatMapElements`, `Filter`, and so on) are just wrappers around this generic transformation. The transformation has a defined life cycle, which enables exactly what we need – *setup* and *teardown* methods that enable us to create and gracefully close any ephemeral resources. In our case, this resource is the connection to the RPC service.

We will discuss various aspects of the life cycle of the `ParDo` transform in the following section. For now, we have enough information to jump directly to the implementation.

Important note

The implementation will use a built-in RPC service based on **gRPC**, which is a framework for remote procedure calls based on **protocol buffers** and **HTTP/2**. If you are not familiar with these technologies, don't worry, as they are not important for the discussion and are used only as a handy tool for the easy creation of an RPC server and client. In our example, the server will be a basic one and simply return the length of the input words as the output.

Implementing the solution

The task does not differ in how it reads input from **Apache Kafka**, or how it stores the results. The biggest concern here is how to ensure the correct life cycle of the connection to our RPC server, so let's get straight into that. Please see the full code in the `com.packtpub.beam.chapter3.RPCParDo` clas:

1. The `ParDo` transform is applied in the `applyRpc` method, and this is quite straightforward:

```
String hostAddress =
    InetAddress.getLocalHost().getHostAddress();
input
```

```
.apply(Tokenize.of())
.apply(ParDo.of(new RpcDoFn(hostAddress, port)));
```

We already know the `Tokenize` transform, so what is new here is the `ParDo.of()` call, which is an instantiation of the `ParDo` transform. The transform takes an instance of a class that extends `DoFn<InputT, OutputT>`, which actually does all the work.

2. First, you might notice that the API that Beam uses for expressing various features of a `DoFn` object looks extraordinary. It uses annotations for methods of instances of a class instead of the *standard* way of overriding methods. The reasons for this are purely practical – it gives much higher flexibility regarding the various (optional) arguments these methods can take. The declaration of the `DoFn` object looks as follows:

```
private static class RpcDoFn
        extends DoFn<String, KV<String, Integer>>
```

The arguments of the `DoFn` object define which type the resulting `PTransform` object takes as its input and which type is the resulting type of the `PCollection` object. Thus, if we define the `DoFn` object like this, the resulting `PTransform` object takes `PCollection<String>` and creates `PCollection<KV<String, Integer>>`. These types will be checked at compile time.

3. Next, we define which fields of our `DoFn` object we will use:

```
private final String hostname;
private final int port;


private transient ManagedChannel channel;
private transient RpcServiceBlockingStub stub;
```

What is notable is that some fields are marked as `transient`. As we know, `transient` fields in **Java** are fields that are not serialized using Java serialization. The key insight here is that our `DoFn` object is being used in `ParDo` (parallel do), and therefore, it needs to be distributed among multiple workers. Beam's **Java SDK** uses Java serialization for this purpose, and therefore, any non-serializable fields of any class that needs to be sent over the wire need to be marked as transient and handled appropriately – that is, initialized at proper places after deserialization.

The non-transient fields are what we are actually going to use to create the transient fields because the transient fields are what gRPC uses to represent a connection. The details of this are out of the scope of this example and can be found online in the documentation for gRPC.

4. Once we have defined a port and hostname to connect to, we want to create the connection once we have transferred our class to the target **Java Virtual Machine (JVM)**. For this purpose, Beam defines a @Setup life cycle annotation:

```
@Setup
public void setup() {
    channel = ManagedChannelBuilder
        .forAddress(hostname, port)
        .usePlaintext()
        .build();
    stub = RpcServiceGrpc.newBlockingStub(channel);
}
```

This ensures that we correctly create the channel and stub for the gRPC communication that will be used during processing.

5. If we create a transient resource, it is always a good idea to free it once it is not needed. The DoFn life cycle defines a @Teardown method for exactly this purpose:

```
@Teardown
public void tearDown() {
    if (channel != null) {
        channel.shutdownNow();
        channel = null;
    }
}
```

This code will close the channel once the DoFn object is no longer needed. It is always a good idea to implement methods like this to be **idempotent** – that is, calling them multiple times should have the same effect as calling them once.

6. Finally, we can get to the actual business logic of our transformation, which is processing elements and outputting the results of an RPC call:

```
@ProcessElement
public void process(
    @Element String input,
```

```
    OutputReceiver<KV<String, Integer>> output) {
      Response = stub.resolve(
        Request.newBuilder().setInput(input).build());
      output.output(KV.of(input, response.getOutput()));
  }
```

Here, the important parts are highlighted. We must annotate our processing method with the `@ProcessElement` annotation. The method then takes a broad range of arguments; Beam uses both type inference and explicit annotations for these arguments to actually know which parameters to pass to which variables of the method. Therefore, a method argument annotated with `@Element` will receive the input element (and the type will be checked during *pipeline build time*). The output is written to the downstream processing using an instance of `OutputReceiver<OutputT>`, which is passed as an argument to the `@ProcessElement` method.

The method annotated using `@ProcessElement` can take many different arguments – we will discuss some of them throughout this chapter and additional ones in *Chapter 7, Extending Apache Beam's I/O Connectors*.

Testing our solution

Please walk through the complete test source code in the `com.packtpub.beam.chapter3.RPCParDoTest` class. The test is quite straightforward, much like the other tests we previously carried out. One notable difference is that we must not forget to start our RPC server. An appropriate place to do this is `@BeforeAll`, which is the **JUnit 5** way of running code that is supposed to be run once for all test cases:

```
@BeforeAll
public static void setup() throws IOException {
  server = AutoCloseableServer.of(runRpc(PORT));
  server.getServer().start();
}
```

If we run the server, it is polite to stop it once finished:

```
@AfterAll
public static void teardown() {
  server.close();
}
```

Instead of actually running and stopping the server, we could use a different approach – wrap the RPC functionality in a (`Serializable!`) interface that would create a mock implementation of the RPC server and provide this interface to the `RpcDoFn` object. Because we want to be able to deploy our solution to a real (distributed) runner, we actually need a working RPC server, so we could just use that for the tests as well.

Deploying our solution

As always, we deploy the built pipeline using the `run-class.sh` script:

```
$ kubectl exec -it packt-beam -- run-class.sh \
    com.packtpub.beam.chapter3.RPCParDo \
    kafka:9093 input_topic output_topic \
    --runner=flink --flinkMaster=flink-jobmanager:8081
    --checkpointingInterval=2000
```

We then send any input to the `input_topic` object using `./env/kafka-producer.sh`. We can see that the output is as expected (observing `output_topic` via `./env/kafka-consumer.sh`).

Now that we have successfully applied our first `ParDo` object, let's look into a bit of theory about what to expect from this `PTransform` object!

Introducing the primitive PTransform object – stateless ParDo

As we have already noted, the `ParDo` PTransform is the most basic primitive transform that we can use to do a variety of useful work. The name is an abbreviation of *parallel do*, and that is what it does. As already noted, there are multiple versions of this PTransform with different requirements and different behaviors. But, in essence, the basics of stateless `ParDo` remain valid for the other cases as well.

The essential parts of a `ParDo` object are illustrated in the following figure:

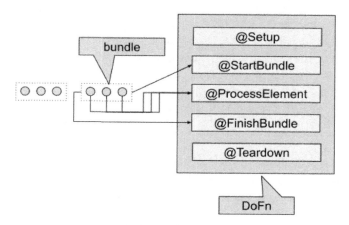

Figure 3.2 – A DoFn object life cycle

The first thing we notice is that the stream is split into *chunks* called **bundles**. The size of bundles or other runtime parameters are runner-specific – that is, each runner can choose its preferred way of assigning elements in a stream into bundles. The important thing to remember is that *bundles are considered atomic units of work*. The processing of a bundle is either successful as a whole or failed (and retried) as a whole. This does not necessarily mean that the bundle will be completely the same, as the runner might choose to re-bundle the stream.

So, the life cycle of a `DoFn` object (the processing logic inside the `ParDo PTransform`) is as follows:

1. A method annotated with `@Setup` is called. The method cannot accept any arguments and therefore cannot output any data. Its purpose is to initialize transient resources that will be needed during the processing.

2. When a new bundle arrives, a method annotated with `@StartBundle` is invoked. This method does not take any input yet – it just notifies the `DoFn` object that there is a new bundle available for processing. A typical use case would be to initialize any caching mechanisms that will be used during processing and (probably) then during the finishing of the processing of the bundle.

3. After that, each input element inside the bundle is fed to a method annotated with `@ProcessElement`. This method accepts various arguments, most notably, an argument annotated with `@Element` (which will receive the input element), an argument annotated with `@Timestamp` (for the element's timestamp), or an argument of the `BoundedWindow` (sub-)type, which will receive a window associated with the element and `OutputReceiver` for outputting outputs of a computation. The full list of arguments can be found in the online **javadoc** for the `DoFn.ProcessElement` annotation.

> **Important note**
>
> Always use the smallest set of arguments that the method actually needs in order to complete the processing. Some of the arguments, when specified, may have an impact on performance – for instance, passing the window parameter to the `@ProcessElement` object results in actually invoking the `DoFn` object multiple times for the same input element when there are multiple windows associated with it (as is the case for sliding windows).

4. Once all of the elements in a bundle are successfully processed, a `@FinishBundle` method is called. The most important argument to this method is of the `FinishBundleContext` type, which enables us to output values before the bundle is *committed*. A bundle commit is a (runner-dependent) way to acknowledge the processing of the whole bundle and persist its output or any other modifications to the `DoFn` object. There is usually no need to worry about this process, apart from when inputs are to be committed to (usually) external systems in **I/Os**. We will discuss this in *Chapter 7, Extending Apache Beam's I/O Connectors*.

5. Once the `DoFn` object is ready to be released, a `@Teardown` method is called. The only purpose of this method is to clean up transient resources (typically) created in the `@Setup` method. The instance of a `DoFn` object is destroyed when the pipeline terminates or in cases when processing fails and is restarted. In the latter case, a new instance of `DoFn` will be created and initialized using the `@Setup` method, as would be expected.

Note that we call this `PTransform` object a *stateless* `ParDo` object. There is a very significant distinction between this and a *stateful* `ParDo` object. Although there might be an illusion that even the stateless version actually can hold a state – at least between `@StartBundle` and `@FinishBundle` – this approach is unreliable and non-deterministic due to the fact that bundling itself is not deterministically defined. We will describe the way to do a useful stateful computation soon, but before that, let's use our new understanding of the life cycle of `DoFn` to enhance our RPC example from the previous section.

Task 7 – Batching queries to an external RPC service

Let's imagine that the RPC service we used in *Task 6* supports the *batching* of RPC queries. **Batching** is a technique for reducing network overhead by grouping multiple queries into a single one, thus increasing throughput. So, instead of querying our RPC service with each element, we would like to send multiple input elements in a single query.

Defining the problem

Given an RPC service that supports the batching of requests for increasing throughput, use this service to augment the input data of a PCollection object. Be sure to preserve the timestamp of both the timestamp and window assigned to the input element.

Discussing the problem decomposition

The first thing to notice is that unlike in *Task 6*, where we queried our RPC service with each element separately (and therefore, simply kept the timestamp and the window of the element untouched), in this case, we can have multiple elements with multiple timestamps and multiple windows present in the batch. That is certainly something that we need to resolve. Our first attempt will then be to use ParDo and hook it to the start and end of the bundles to perform the batching.

The solution will then look like the diagram in the following figure:

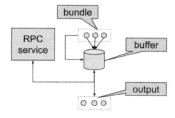

Figure 3.3 – A batched RPC service using stateless ParDo

The idea is to use a buffer that will be initialized at the start of each bundle, which is filled with input data and then flushed to the RPC service when the bundle finishes.

Implementing the solution

We used the solution for *Task 6* as a base and changed the necessary parts to create `com.packtpub.beam.chapter3.RPCParDoBatch`. We will walk through the important changes now:

> **Important note**
>
> The `RPCParDoBatch` object is mostly copied from `RPCParDo`. That is not a good engineering practice and should be avoided whenever possible. We have used this copy and paste approach here to keep the important things together for learning purposes. Production code should be better structured, and you should reuse code as much as possible.

1. The first change to the previous code example is that we have to use a modified `DoFn` object:

   ```
   input
     .apply(Tokenize.of())
     .apply(ParDo.of(new BatchRpcDoFn(hostAddress, port)));
   ```

2. All of the other changes relate to the `BatchRpcDoFn` object itself. As in the previous case, we still initialize and tear down our RPC channel (connection) in the `@Setup` and `@Teardown` methods, respectively. What is new is that we add our buffer:

   ```
   private transient
   List<ValueWithTimestampAndWindow<String>> elements;
   ```

   Note that we don't want to serialize this, so it is a good idea to make the field `transient`.

3. The type inside the buffer is `ValueWithTimestampAndWindow`, which is a simple `@Value` (**lombok**) class holding the data we will need to output the correct results. As we can see, we will buffer the value, including its timestamp and associated window. Note that all windows in Beam are bounded:

   ```
   @Value
   private static class ValueWithTimestampAndWindow<T> {
     T value;
     Instant timestamp;
     BoundedWindow window;
   }
   ```

4. Next, we need to initialize our buffer, which is best done in the `@StartBundle` method, as follows:

```
@StartBundle
public void startBundle() {
  elements = new ArrayList<>();
}
```

Although the `@StartBundle` method generally accepts some arguments (the most usable are the `PipelineOptions` arguments), we don't need it here.

5. We then need to fill our buffer, which will be done in the `@ProcessElement` method:

```
@ProcessElement
public void process(
    @Element String input,
    @Timestamp Instant timestamp,
    BoundedWindow window) {

    elements.add(new ValueWithTimestampAndWindow<>(
        input, timestamp, window));
}
```

We need to declare that we will use the timestamp and window of each input element, which we do with the highlighted code.

6. The last part is to flush our buffered elements to the RPC service and output the results. We do this in the `@FinishBundle` method, which we will walk through in a few steps. First, we declare the method, which mainly takes a `FinishBundleContext` argument, which we will use for the data output:

```
@FinishBundle
public void finishBundle(FinishBundleContext context)
```

7. Next, because we know that our RPC service takes only the input word and always produces the same answer for the same input (this should probably hold true for essentially all meaningful RPC services – at least when we query it at the same time), we want to pick only distinct words and store the timestamps and windows of all possible duplicates:

```
Map<String, List<ValueWithTimestampAndWindow<String>>>
distinctElements =
```

```
elements
   .stream()
   .collect(
       Collectors.groupingBy(
           ValueWithTimestampAndWindow::getValue,
           Collectors.toList()));
```

8. After that, we are ready to send our batched RPC request and wait for the answer:

```
RequestList.Builder builder = RequestList.newBuilder();
distinctElements
   .keySet()
   .forEach(r ->
       builder.addRequest(Request.newBuilder().
setInput(r)));
RequestList requestList = builder.build();
ResponseList responseList = stub.
resolveBatch(requestList);
```

9. We have received the list of responses, so now we create our output KV object and flush it to the output with the following code:

```
for (int i = 0; i < requestList.getRequestCount(); i++) {
   Request request = requestList.getRequest(i);
   Response response = responseList.getResponse(i);
   List<ValueWithTimestampAndWindow<String>>
   timestampsAndWindows =
       distinctElements.get(request.getInput());
   KV<String, Integer> value = KV.of(
       request.getInput(), response.getOutput());
   timestampsAndWindows.forEach(v ->
       context.output(value, v.getTimestamp(),
v.getWindow()));
}
```

Now that we have our batched RPC pipeline, we can run it as usual. We will skip this here because it is the same as in the case of the original RPCParDo object. The same goes for the tests, which will be exactly the same (this is to be expected, as we did not change the functionality, we just changed the way we query our RPC service).

> **Important note**
>
> Do not forget to add the `-checkpointingInterval` option to the `run-class.sh` command. Without that specified, **Apache Flink** disables checkpointing, which affects the way the input stream is split into bundles. For a deeper explanation of what this parameter does, please refer to *Chapter 8, Understanding How Runners Execute Pipelines*.

We should ask ourselves another question – *what if our bundles are either too small or too large?* We would probably need to flush the buffer inside `@ProcessElement` if its size exceeded some boundary. That can be solved quite easily, but what if the size of the bundle is too small? The size of bundles is outside the control of user code, as it is the runner that decides how exactly to split the stream into bundles. Although runners may provide configuration settings to tune this, what if we need stricter control of the size of the bundles? The answer is that in that case, we can no longer do with *stateless* `ParDo`. So, let's use this as a motivating example for our first exploration of *stateful* `ParDo`, shall we?

Task 8 – Batching queries to an external RPC service with defined batch sizes

Let's suppose that our RPC server works best when it processes about 100 input words in a batch. A real-world requirement would probably look different and would be the result of measurements rather than an arbitrary number. However, for the present discussion, let's suppose that this performance characteristic is given. We can then summarize the task as follows.

Defining the problem

Use a given RPC service to augment data in an input stream using batched RPCs with batches of a size of about K elements. Also, resolve the batch after a time of (at most) T to avoid a (possibly) infinitely long wait for elements in small batches.

As we can see, we extended the definition of the problem with the introduction of a parameter, *T*, which will guard the time for which we can buffer the elements waiting for more data.

Discussing the problem decomposition

As already mentioned, we cannot do with a state held only between bundles (inside DoFn), because a runner can create small-sized bundles arriving at a high rate. What we need is access to a state that can hold the input elements for us. We can illustrate this with the following figure:

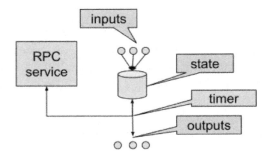

Figure 3.4 – A batched RPC service using stateful ParDo

As we can see, this image is not too different from *Figure 3.3*, which illustrated the case of batches per bundle. The main differences are as follows:

- We have access to a state that can span multiple bundles.
- We need a timer to signal the flush of the state (if this flush does not occur due to achieving the necessary size of the batch).

Now that we have discussed the differences, let's jump to the implementation and see how it needs to change.

Implementing the solution

The complete implementation located at `com.packtpub.beam.chapter3.RPCParDoStateful` might look a little long first, but don't worry, we'll walk through it to make the relevant parts as clear as possible:

1. The first significant change from the previous stateless version is how the DoFn object itself is defined:

```
class BatchRpcDoFnStateful
    extends DoFn<KV<Integer, String>, KV<String, Integer>>
```

We might notice that the input is no longer a plain `String` input but a `KV<Integer, String>` input. A detailed explanation of this will be covered in the next section, which is dedicated to a deep explanation of the stateful `ParDo` transform. For now, what we need to know is that every `DoFn` object that uses a state must take a KV on its input. All elements with the *same key* part of the KV are routed to the same instance of a `DoFn`.

Trying to apply a stateful `ParDo` transform on a `PCollection` object that is not of the KV type results in the following error:

```
java.lang.IllegalArgumentException: ParDo requires its
input to use KvCoder in order to use state and timers.
```

2. Therefore, we to assign a key to each of our input words. It would be nice if the same words ended up on the same instance of `DoFn` – that could lower the pressure on our RPC because the same word could be present in the same batch multiple times, and thus it would be resolved only once. We do that before we actually apply the stateful `ParDo` transform:

```
MapElements
    .into(
        TypeDescriptors.kvs(
            TypeDescriptors.integers(),
            TypeDescriptors.strings()))
    .via(e -> KV.of(
        (e.hashCode() & Integer.MAX_VALUE) % 10, e)))
```

We use a `hashCode` of our input word and bucket it into 10 distinct keys. Note that a production use would use a higher value. The total number of distinct keys determines the maximal parallelism of the processing, so this would depend on the total volume of data that is flowing through the pipeline.

3. Next, we apply our stateful `ParDo` transform , which is not different from the stateless variant we already know, apart from the added parameters that are needed for our computation (that is, the size of the batch and the maximal wait time for the batch before being flushed, even when not complete):

```
.apply(
    ParDo.of(
        new BatchRpcDoFnStateful(
            params.getBatchSize(),
            params.getMaxWaitTime(),
```

```
            hostAddress,
            params.getPort())))
```

4. Let's now focus on the `BatchRpcDoFnStateful` object. We can see several additions to the previous version. First, we have two declarations of a `StateSpec` object:

```
@StateId("batch")
private final
StateSpec<BagState<ValueWithTimestamp<String>>>
batchSpec = StateSpecs.bag(
    ValueWithTimestampCoder.of(StringUtf8Coder.of()));


@StateId("batchSize")
private final StateSpec<ValueState<Integer>>
batchSizeSpec =
    StateSpecs.value();
```

A `StateSpec` object is a way for Beam to declare that a particular `DoFn` object is going to use some form of state. We see two types of state in the preceding code: `BagState` and `ValueState`. A `BagState` defines a state that holds an unordered collection of elements, while `ValueState` defines a state that holds a single value. There are other types of states besides these two – the most important of which is `MapState`. The state type defines how elements are stored in the state and what the access (read/write) complexities are for the state. This is similar to how **Java** defines `List`, `Set`, `Map`, and so on.

Each state needs a unique name, which we then use to create an actual instance of an object that can be used to access the state. The name is specified as an argument to the `@StateId` annotation that must annotate each `StateSpec` field. Each `StateSpec` field has to be final in order to prevent it from being modified and avoid any ambiguity.

Finally, each state needs a `Coder` object, because data elements are stored in serialized form. The `Coder` object can be either specified manually (as in the case of `ValueWithTimestampCoder` in the `batchSpec` object) or inferred automatically from the pipeline's `CoderRegistry` object (as in the case of `batchSizeSpec`).

5. Another two declarations refer to `TimerSpec`. This is pretty much analogous to the declaration of `StateSpec`, with the exception that there a `TimerSpec` object only needs two parameters – that is, its `TimeDomain`:

```
@TimerId("flushTimer")
private final TimerSpec flushTimerSpec =
    TimerSpecs.timer(TimeDomain.PROCESSING_TIME);


@TimerId("endOfTime")
private final TimerSpec endOfTimeTimer =
    TimerSpecs.timer(TimeDomain.EVENT_TIME);
```

Processing time timers are used to set a timer that fires after a specified duration in the processing time of the operator that executes the `ParDo` transform, while **event time timers** are fired based on **watermarks**. We'll explain the purpose of both of these timers now.

6. The timer named `flushTimer` is set whenever we insert the first element in the `batch` state. The timer is set for the duration of `maxBatchWait`, which defines how long we can wait before flushing the batch, even when there are fewer elements than `maxBatchSize`. This is done with the following code:

```
flushTimer.offset(maxBatchWait).setRelative();
```

We'll see the definition of the `flushTimer` variable in a few moments. The call to `offset(Duration).setRelative()` tells Beam to offset the timer from the current value to fire after the specified duration.

7. We set up the `endOfTime` timer to fire at the end of a global window. The reason for this is that when using stateful `ParDo`, there are no triggers to ensure that we fire each window at the end of its scope. We must do all of this manually. If we don't fire at the end of our window, we would get a data loss, as data buffered at the state might not get flushed:

```
endOfTimeTimer.set(GlobalWindow.INSTANCE.maxTimestamp());
```

8. Whenever we set a timer, we need to associate a callback method with it. This callback is defined as follows:

```
@OnTimer("flushTimer")
public void onFlushTimer(
    @StateId("batch") BagState<ValueWithTimestamp<String>>
        elements,
```

```
    @StateId("batchSize") ValueState<Integer> batchSize,
    OutputReceiver<KV<String, Integer>> outputReceiver)
```

This statement defines a callback for the flushTimer firing. This method is analogous to @ProcessElement, with the difference that it does not have any @Element object to process. The @StateId annotation declares a method argument that corresponds to the StateSpec object defined with the same name. The type of the argument must match the parameter defined in the corresponding StateSpec object (for instance, ValueState<Integer>). As usual, we can use OutputReceiver to output data from the @OnTimer methods.

9. The last (but most important) change is in the @ProcessElement method. This declaration changed to the following:

```
@ProcessElement
public void process(
    @Element KV<Integer, String> input,
    @Timestamp Instant timestamp,
    @StateId("batch") BagState<ValueWithTimestamp<String>>
        elements,
    @StateId("batchSize") ValueState<Integer> batchSize,
    @TimerId("flushTimer") Timer flushTimer,
    @TimerId("endOfTime") Timer endOfTimeTimer,
    OutputReceiver<KV<String, Integer>> outputReceiver)
```

We see the same @StateId definitions as in the case of the @OnTimer method. The difference is that we have a @TimerId declaration, which gives access to the timers declared using our TimerSpecs object. We reference them by name – exactly the same as in the case of state declarations.

10. Once we have declared the states and timers that we will be using in the @ProcessElement method, we only need to implement its body. First, we need to set the timer for end-of-time. We need to do that for each element, but that should not be a problem, as setting a timer should be cheap under normal circumstances:

```
endOfTimeTimer.set(GlobalWindow.INSTANCE.maxTimestamp());
```

11. Next, we need to read the current size of the batch. Although we could read the complete contents of the batch and count the number of elements inside it, that would be expensive because it would have to load the state, with many items being sent back and forth:

```
int currentSize = MoreObjects.firstNonNull(
    batchSize.read(), 0);
```

Keep in mind that the state need not be initialized (for instance, when we add the first element in a batch). Therefore, we have to check for `null` values.

12. Another step is to flush the batch if the size is big enough. Note that we don't need to put the current element in the bag state, because that might introduce avoidable I/O operations. Therefore, we flush a concatenation of the current element and the contents of the current element (wrapped in `ValueWithTimestamp`):

```
ValueWithTimestamp<String> value = new
ValueWithTimestamp<>(
    input.getValue(), timestamp);
if (currentSize == maxBatchSize - 1) {
    flushOutput(
      Iterables.concat(
        elements.read(), Collections.
singletonList(value)),
      outputReceiver);
    clearState(elements, batchSize, flushTimer);
}
```

After we flush the batch to output (using our RPC service), we clear the state and get to the same state as before the first element arrived.

13. The final part is to put elements in the bag state if there are not enough elements present yet:

```
else {
  if (currentSize == 0) {
    flushTimer.offset(maxBatchWait).setRelative();
  }
  elements.add(value);
  batchSize.write(currentSize + 1);
}
```

The most important part in this code block is setting the `flushTimer` object to fire after `maxBatchWait` (as discussed in *Step 6*) and adding elements into the bag state.

Note that adding elements into a bag state (via the `add` method) is quite cheap compared to reading the complete bag state back. That is why we should use the `ValueState` holding size of the batch.

14. The `clearState` method is straightforward, with the exception of clearing the `flushTimer` object:

```
private void clearState(
    BagState<ValueWithTimestamp<String>> elements,
    ValueState<Integer> batchSize,
    @Nullable Timer flushTimer) {

    elements.clear();
    batchSize.clear();
    if (flushTimer != null) {
        flushTimer.offset(maxBatchWait).setRelative();
    }
}
```

Beam currently does not support clearing (canceling) timers in its Java SDK, so what we do instead is reset the timer to fire again after the `maxBatchWait` time. By that time, the bag will either be empty (because no other element was added) and therefore, there will be nothing to flush, or a new element will arrive and the timer will be reset (in `@ProcessElement`).

15. The last part of this is the `flushOutput` method, which is pretty much pure Java (creating a batch of elements, sending them over gRPC and reading the result back, and outputting it to the `OutputReceiver` object with the `outputWithTimestamp` method).

And that's it – we have walked through the implementation of our first stateful `ParDo` transform! There are two main caveats to this implementation:

- It assumes we are only using the global window in our pipeline. A generic implementation without this assumption would have to be a little more complex.

- There is a possible problem with elements being output from the transform that might turn into *late* elements. This, again, is not a concern in our use case, but we'll explain what exactly can happen with this scenario in the following section when we will be doing a deep dive into the stateful processing solutions that Beam offers.

Last but not least, we would like to note that Beam offers a reusable transform that does exactly what we did here and it is named `GroupIntoBatches`. This transform should obviously be used whenever we need to use batching, instead of implementing it on our own. This is a typical scenario – many problems have already been solved, so Beam (or some library) might contain a solution for that.

We will skip the deployment and testing subsections for this task, as there would be no difference from the previous examples. Now, let's deep dive into stateful processing!

Introducing the primitive PTransform object – stateful ParDo

This section will focus on a theoretical description of the stateful `ParDo` transform, which is the most complex transform that a typical user of Beam needs to understand. We will divide this section into two subsections. First, we will describe its theoretical properties and the differences from the stateless version of `ParDo`. Then, we will see how this theoretical knowledge applies to API changes.

Describing the theoretical properties of the stateful ParDo object

As we have seen, the main difference between a *stateful* ParDo object and a *stateless* ParDo object is – as the name suggests – the presence of user state or timers. This alone brings one important requirement: every meaningful access to a state must be **keyed**. That is to say, the PCollection object we apply to a stateful ParDo object must be of the KV<K, V> type. We must assign a key to every element of a PCollection object (or use an already assigned key, which some sources might provide). Every state access is then within the *context of the key and window*. Two different keys cannot share the same state or timer and are completely independent of each other. The reason for this is obvious: *scalability*. The key defines only a unit of parallelism, otherwise, the partitioning of data among multiple instances of workers would be somewhat arbitrary and it would be very complicated to implement meaningful logic on top of such a model. The following figure illustrates how stateful processing works:

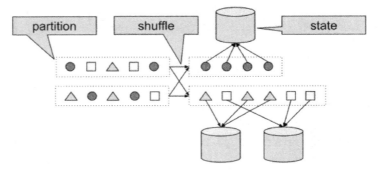

Figure 3.5 – The stateful ParDo transform

As we can see, the first phase of the stateful ParDo transform is a **shuffle**. Each distributed stream consists of **partitions**. A partition is a physical division of the input stream into parallel sub-streams. These sub-streams are typically managed by a single node of a parallel system. Together, these partitions form a complete stream. A shuffle is a process of rearranging these partitions of the input stream to co-locate elements with some common characteristics (in our case, the key, which is represented by the shapes in *Figure 3.5*).

Once the input data is reshuffled, the stateful ParDo operation can be applied by creating the required state (declared via StateSpec and @StateId, as we have already seen) and/or timers (declared via TimerSpec and @TimerId) *for each key independently*. Each state is then scoped within the window of each input element.

The shuffling once again puts emphasis on the fact that the elements processed by the DoFn object inside the ParDo object are **unordered**. The order in which the four elements appear – represented as circles to the first partition after the shuffle – is completely **non-deterministic** and will vary over different attempts to run the same pipeline. The application logic needs to account for that. And what can you use in Beam to come to the rescue? You guessed it: **watermarks** and **event time timers**. As we defined in *Chapter 1, Introducing Data Processing with Apache Beam*, watermarks are a way to measure progress in data processing inside an unordered stream. We can imagine a watermark as a marker in data that tells us that there is a sufficiently low probability (but not zero!) that we will ever encounter an element with a timestamp lower than the value of the watermark. This is obvious for a single partition of a stream, but how does this information propagate through the shuffle? We can illustrate that in the following figure:

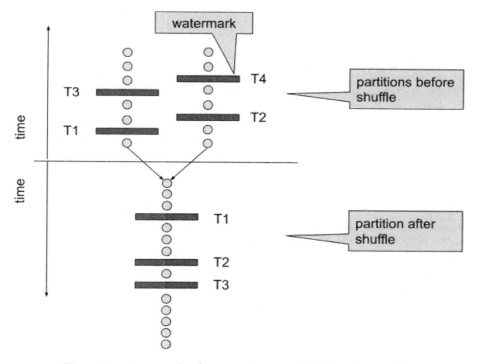

Figure 3.6 – An example of watermark propagation through a shuffle

The preceding figure (*Figure 3.6*) shows one of the possible outcomes of a shuffle consisting of two partitions before the shuffle and one partition after the shuffle. As already mentioned, the shuffle is not a deterministic operation, so the order of the elements and watermarks may differ. The important thing to note is that *the watermark of the downstream (after shuffle) partition is always a minimum of the watermarks received from all of the upstream (before shuffle) partitions.* This is dictated by the definition of a *watermark* – that is, the downstream partition can be (reasonably) sure that it will not receive an element with a timestamp lower than T after it receives a watermark with a value of at least T from all of the upstream partitions. This is also the reason why the downstream partition cannot contain a watermark for a time of $T4$, as it would have to first receive a watermark with a higher timestamp from the left upstream partition. This behavior is dictated by the correctness of the computation but results in the following caveat.

> **Important note**
>
> In any stateful (or grouping) operation, the watermark on the input of the transform is always at most the minimum of the watermarks received from all of the upstream partitions. This means that if – for whatever reason – a *single* partition stops sending watermarks, the computation cannot proceed, and it looks *stalled* from an outside perspective. Whenever your computation seems not to be able to make any progress, watermarks are the first place to check.

This section deals with stateful processing, so a legitimate question one might ask is – *does the stateful computation in any way affect the watermarks being emitted to the output stream?* The answer is – as we would expect – *yes*. Every stateful transform actually has two watermarks – one is called the **input watermark** and is computed as described previously, while the other is called the **output watermark** and defines the watermark that has been emitted for downstream processing. Let's once again illustrate this graphically for clarity:

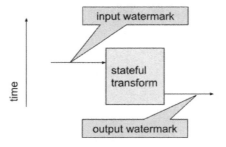

Figure 3.7 – The input and output watermarks of a stateful transform

As one would expect, stateful processing can introduce a delay. Note that this is not the case for stateless processing, because in this case, there is no buffering that could cause elements to be delayed in their processing until some condition is met. In the case of a stateless transform, each element is processed and emitted immediately (in event time), so there is no delay possible, and the output watermark of a stateless transform should always be – for all practical purposes – equal to the input watermark.

The situation changes when we allow the elements to be buffered. Once we do that, it is natural that the watermark being output might be *delayed* after the input watermark. This naturally defines a requirement, which can be stated as – *the output watermark of a stateful transform is always less than or equal to the input watermark.* Normally, user code does not directly deal with output watermarks but rather defines them indirectly through triggers and timestamp combiners. We will describe one more way to affect output watermarks when we describe timer output timestamps later in this section.

To recap what we have learned so far in this section, stateful `ParDo` differs from the stateless version in the following ways:

- It always requires a keyed `PCollection` object on its input.
- It uses state and/or timers.
- Grouping elements with the same key into the same partition (nearly always) results in a shuffle phase.
- It can introduce a delay to the output watermark propagation due to internal buffering.

The runner might – under very specific circumstances – prevent the adding of the shuffle phase, as long as it is certain that the elements are already shuffled correctly as a result of the upstream processing. However, this happens rather sporadically.

The rest of the properties of the `ParDo` transform remain valid for the stateful version, and these include the following:

- Bundling
- The life cycle of the `DoFn` object (`@Setup`, `@StartBundle`, `@FinishBundle`, `@Teardown`)

Now that we have walked through the theoretical properties of the stateful `ParDo` transform, let's see how these properties apply to the required changes on the API side.

Applying the theoretical properties of the stateful ParDo object to the API of DoFn

First, we should note that there is no difference in how a stateful or stateless `ParDo` object is applied to a `PCollection` object. In both situations, this is exactly the same:

```
input.apply(ParDo.of(new MyDoFn()));
```

Therefore, the difference is hidden in the implementation of the `DoFn` object only. We speak about stateful or stateless `DoFn`, but what we mean by that is whether the resulting `ParDo` object is going to be executed as stateful or stateless.

A `DoFn` object is considered to be stateful if one of the following conditions is met:

- It contains a definition of the state via `@StateId` in one of its final fields.
- It contains a definition of the timer via `@TimerId` in one of its final fields.

It is very often the case that the `DoFn` object uses both, as flushing a state typically requires at least one timer – as otherwise, it would be possible to flush the element only with incoming data and that might last forever – and at the same time, having a timer without a state feels weird, because there is nothing the timer can *trigger*.

Let's walk through the main API changes compared to the stateless `DoFn` object:

- One or more `final` fields of the `StateSpec` type can be annotated using a `@StateId` annotation. This annotation requires a name as a parameter. This name must be unique and must not change during pipeline upgrades, as renaming a state is equivalent to creating a new state and discarding the old one. The `StateSpec` object then defines the type of the state (`BagState`, `ValueState`, `MapState`, combining). The description of these can be found online and it is likely that more state types (with different runtime characteristics) will appear in the future. An example we have already seen would be as follows:

```
@StateId("batchSize")
private final StateSpec<ValueState<Integer>>
batchSizeSpec =
    StateSpecs.value();
```

- One or more `final` fields of the `TimerSpec` type can be annotated using an `@TimerId` annotation. As with `@StateId`, `@TimerId` also needs a unique and stable name. The `TimerSpec` object defines the `TimeDomain` object of the timer – that is, if it is an event-time or processing-time timer. We have also already seen this:

```
@TimerId("endOfTime")
private final TimerSpec endOfTimeTimer =
    TimerSpecs.timer(TimeDomain.EVENT_TIME);
```

- When a timer fires, it calls a method that is annotated by `@OnTimer` with the given timer name. Therefore, each timer needs its own method, though it is common practice to call a private shared method from there. The parameters for the method are the same as for `@ProcessElement` (see the next bullet point), with the exception of `@Element` and `@Timestamp`. A very useful feature is that the `@OnTimer` method can annotate an argument with `@Key`, and this argument will receive the key associated with the timer. Its type must match the type of the key part of the KV input. As opposed to `@ProcessElement`, the `@OnTimer` method can contain a parameter of the `OnTimerContext` type that can give access to the firing timestamp, as shown in the following example:

```
@OnTimer("myTimer")
public void onFlushTimer(
  OnTimerContext context,
  @Key Integer key,
  @StateId("size") ValueState<Integer> sizeState,
  @TimerId("myTimer") Timer myTimer,
  IntervalWindow myWindow,
  OutputReceiver<KV<String, Integer>> outputReceiver)
```

- The `@ProcessElement` method can take the same arguments as `@OnTimer` (plus `@Element` and `@Timestamp` and without `OnTimerContext`). As of the time of writing, there are two more annotations that can be used on a `@ProcessElement` method itself, namely `@RequiresStableInput` and `@RequiresTimeSortedInput`. While the first one is handy mostly when implementing I/O connectors (and we will get into that in *Chapter 7, Extending Apache Beam's I/O Connectors*), the latter declares that the runner should make sure that the order in which the `DoFn` object observes the contents of a `PCollection` object is time-sorted (as opposed to the default, which is unordered). In this case, the declaration might look like this:

```
@RequiresTimeSortedInput
@ProcessElement
public void process(
  @Element KV<Integer, String> input,
  @Timestamp Instant timestamp,
  @StateId("size") ValueState<Integer> sizeState,
  @TimerId("myTimer") Timer myTimer,
   OutputReceiver<KV<String, Integer>> outputReceiver)
```

Though the annotation might look appealing, there is a big warning needed.

> **Important note**
>
> **Warning**: The `@RequiresTimeSorted` object is (as of the time of writing) considered an experimental feature and should be used with extreme caution. First of all, it has performance implications in terms of both CPU usage and increased latency. Second, it has implications for the handling of late data (discussed later in this chapter). Finally, its support is not very widespread among runners. As a rule of thumb, this annotation should be used only as a last resort when there is no other solution to the problem, and every time it must be thoroughly tested that it works as intended.

- A stateful `DoFn` object can take one additional method, annotated using `@OnWindowExpiration`, which gets called before a window is going to be cleared and discarded. It is a place where the application logic can perform a last access to the state and flush what is (for whatever reason) left over. The method can take the same arguments as `@OnTimer` (without `OnTimerContext`), but setting timers essentially equals to no-op because they will be cleared immediately. An example might look like this:

```
@OnWindowExpiration
public void onWindowExpiration(
  @Key Integer key,
  @StateId("size") ValueState<Integer> sizeState,
  IntervalWindow myWindow,
  OutputReceiver<KV<String, Integer>> outputReceiver)
```

As we can see, we have already seen the majority of this in our example with batching RPCs. We have purposefully left out one last note – both stateful and stateless `ParDo` objects can have side inputs and side outputs added to their main input and output. What are these, what are they good for, and how do we use them?

Using side outputs

As the name suggests, side inputs are something that is added to the main input *from the side*, while side outputs are something that is output from the `DoFn` object *outside* of the main `PCollection` output. Let's start with the side outputs, as they are more straightforward.

As an example, let's imagine we are processing data coming in as **JSON** values. We need to parse these messages into an internal object. But what should we do with the values that cannot be parsed because they contain a syntax error? If we do not do any validation before we store them in the stream (topic), then it is certainly possible that we will encounter such a situation. We can silently drop those records, but that is obviously not a great idea, as that could cause hard-to-debug problems. A much better option would be to store these values on the side to be able to investigate and fix them. Therefore, we should aim to do the following:

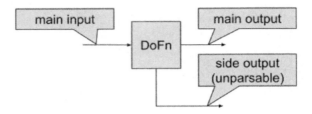

Figure 3.8 – Main and side outputs

One option we have would be to create a wrapping value that could carry both the main input and side output and **tag** these values to identify them as the main or side output. We could then apply a `Partition` transform to separate these two parts into two separate PCollection objects and then handle them separately. This would be a lot of work and luckily (because this use case is very common), Beam offers tools that can help us with this.

What we need first is to create an instance of `TupleTag` that will distinguish various side outputs. Once we are able to support a single side output, there is no reason not to enable many of them. A `TupleTag` object carries type information for `Coder` inferences and an (optional) name. Because of how Java works with type erasure, we need to create an anonymous subclass from a `TupleTag` object that we want to use for side outputs, as follows:

```
TupleTag<String> errorOutput = new TupleTag<String>() {};
```

This way, Beam will be able to infer that the type of `PCollection` object that should result from the side output tagged with this tag should be `PCollection<String>` and correctly set `Coder` for us.

When using side outputs, Beam also needs a `TupleTag` object for the main output:

```
TupleTag<Parsed> mainOutput = new TupleTag<Parsed>() {};
```

This will declare a `TupleTag` object of the `Parsed` type, which is an object that holds the parsed JSON value after successful parsing.

Now, we need to provide our `TupleTag` objects to the `ParDo` transform with the following code:

```
input.apply(ParDo.of(new MySideOutputDoFn())
    .withOutputTags(mainOutput, TupleTagList.
of(errorOutput)));
```

In order to tell Beam which tag our output belongs to, we need to change `OutputReceiver` to `MultiOutputReceiver` and then output this with the following:

```
@ProcessElement
public void processElement(
    @Element String jsonValue, MultiOutputReceiver output) {
  @Nullable Parsed parsed = parse(jsonValue);
  if (parsed == null) {
    output.get(errorOutput).output(jsonValue);
  } else {
    output.get(mainOutput).output(parsed);
  }
}
```

Because we declared that we will be using side outputs (by calling `withOutputTags` on the `ParDo` object), we will now receive an object of the `PCollectionTuple` type instead of a plain `PCollection` object. The reason for this is to provide a way to split the tuple into individual `PCollection` objects, as follows:

```
PCollectionTuple tuple =
    input.apply(ParDo.of(...).withTupleTags(...));
PCollection<Parsed> parsed = tuple.get(mainOutput);
PCollection<String> errors = tuple.get(errorOutput);
```

We can then use these individual `PCollection` objects to apply any transform we need on them individually. For instance, we can process the correct main output and store the errors somewhere else. We will investigate this more deeply in an example later in this chapter, and learn about using side inputs too!

Defining droppable data in Beam

This section will be a short return to the material we covered in *Chapter 2, Implementing, Testing, and Deploying Basic Pipelines*, where we already defined what **late data** means. To recap – *late data* is every data element that has a *timestamp* that is behind the *watermark*. That is to say, the watermark tells us that we should not receive a data element with a timestamp lower than the watermark, but nevertheless, we do receive such an element. This is perfectly fine, and as already described in *Chapter 1, Introduction to Data Processing with Apache Beam*, a perfect watermark would introduce unnecessary – or even impractical – latency. However, what we left unanswered is the following question – *what happens to data elements that arrive too late?* We know that we can define **allowed lateness**, but what if any data arrives even later? And as always, the answer is – *it depends*. Luckily, some of the concepts relating to streaming processing are very natural to our everyday life, so we can illustrate this in a way that is easy to grasp.

Imagine you run a mobile gaming application. The game might be something really simple, like finding a solution to some puzzle within a specified time interval. Let's say that users are free to solve the puzzle, even when being offline, and what matters is that the application can later submit their solution and the time that was taken to solve the puzzle. You would like to keep a sorted table of the *K* best results.

This sounds perfectly reasonable, but let's imagine the following situation:

1. A user starts solving the puzzle, prior to boarding a plane.
2. Before take-off, the user is forced to switch off their data connection but keeps solving the puzzle.
3. After some time, the user solves the puzzle while still on the plane.
4. The results get submitted once the plane lands and the user is able to re-establish the data connection.

We can see that the time that can pass between *Step 3* and *Step 4* can take many hours. What if we publish a scoreboard every hour and the time needed by this particular user was actually the (currently) best one? In that case, our approach would probably depend on our policy. The most polite way of solving this would be to try hard to accept as many solutions as we can. Therefore, we could recompute our scoreboard and publish a new one for the affected hours that changed due to the late submission. That is exactly what allowed lateness does.

On the other hand, what if the solution from our user traveling on a plane comes so late that we already announced a final winner? We might have even performed an official presentation of the results. If we have made a clear statement that we have a final submission date, we are free to drop any submissions after that date. And this is exactly what happens in the case of the GroupByKey or Combine transforms – the data is silently dropped. On the other hand, these transforms do their best to accept any late data element that can be accepted if there is no cost associated with this acceptance. Let's see this illustrated in the following figure:

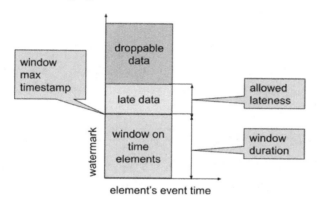

Figure 3.9 – An illustration of droppable data

Figure 3.9 shows the relation between the event time timestamp of a particular data element, the current position of the (input) watermark of a stateful transform, and the resulting classification of that particular data element. As we can see, elements are actually allowed to be behind the watermark, but can even be processed as on-time elements if the watermark has not yet passed the timestamp that marks the maximum timestamp of a window. After the watermark passes that timestamp, all of the data elements are handled as late data up to a point of (window max timestamp + allowed lateness). When the watermark passes this point (often referred to as window **Garbage Collection** (**GC**) time), all data that would otherwise belong to the particular window gets dropped. The reason for this is that there is actually nothing else left to do with it – the state of the window has already been deleted, which means there is no state that could accumulate the data element.

> **Important note**
> The notion of late data is a concept only of `GroupByKey` and `Combine`.
> When using stateful `ParDo`, the only strict point in time relevant is the
> *window GC time*. From the perspective of the stateful `DoFn` object, the end of
> the window timestamp no longer plays any significant role, and how the logic
> handles this data is defined entirely by the application logic.

Dropping data is generally unfortunate. If someone sends data in, silently discarding it is
definitely not polite. If we receive data from a user, what we would like to do instead is let
them know that we received the data but, unfortunately, it is too late for their submission.

We will use these last two concepts (*side outputs* and the definition of *late data*) to create
a system that will split droppable data from the processing logic and process it so that we
will be notified of the situation. Let's solve this in the following task!

Task 9 – Separating droppable data from the rest of the data processing

Under normal circumstances, data flowing in a pipeline does not change its status
regarding being late, droppable, or on time. However, the exceptions to this are as follows:

- Data could change its status if we change our `WindowFn` object and re-window our
  stream, thereby producing different points in time that define the window GC time.

- Data could change its status if we apply logic with a more sensitive definition of
  droppable data – this specifically applies to `@RequiresTimeSortedInput`,
  where droppable data becomes every data element that is – at any point in time –
  more behind the watermark than the defined allowed lateness.

We can rephrase these conditions so that as long as we do not change the window
function and do not apply logic with specific requirements, the droppable status of an
element should not change between transforms. We will use this property to solve the task
with the following definition.

Defining the problem

Create a pipeline that will separate droppable data elements from the rest of the data. It will send droppable data into one output topic and the rest into another topic.

Therefore, we will need to configure *three* topics in total: one input topic and two output topics.

Discussing the problem decomposition

The logic is quite simple – write a stateful `ParDo` object to separate the droppable elements from the others by using side outputs. So far, the problem looks simple, but we'll soon run into trouble for the following reasons:

- Beam provides no way to explicitly monitor the watermark of a transform. This is a design decision, and the only way to be able to *hook* on a watermark's progress is using a `Timer` object.

- We cannot use a window function that is specified on the input (for instance, a fixed window with a duration of 1 minute) because we need to set the timer for the window GC time to start marking elements as droppable. However, once we pass the window GC timer, all of the input data is silently dropped and our logic will not be able to process it. Therefore, we must re-window the provided `PCollection` object using `GlobalWindow` and then return the window function for the main output.

- Finally, as we know, a stateful `DoFn` object must have a KV on its input – so, what should be used as a key? The best option would be to use the window itself as a key, because that way, we only have to set a single timer per key. This raises some additional potential challenges that we will discuss later in this section.

So, our pipeline should look like the illustration in the following figure:

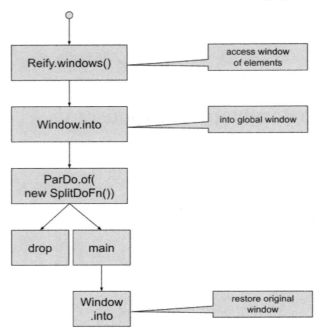

Figure 3.10 – The problem decomposition

Let's see how to implement this in the Beam Java SDK.

Implementing the solution

As always, we strongly encourage you to walk through the complete source code located in the `com.packtpub.beam.chapter3.DroppableDataFilter` class in the book's GitHub repository. We'll now walk through the most important parts:

1. First, we need to read the input, which as always is as follows:

```
PCollection<String> input =
  readInput(pipeline, params)
  .apply(Window.<String>into(
       FixedWindows.of(Duration.standardMinutes(1))
      .withAllowedLateness(Duration.standardSeconds(30))
     .discardingFiredPanes());
```

For the sake of this example, we hard code the window to fixed windows of 1 minute with an allowed lateness value of 30 seconds.

2. The rest of the main method is also quite self-explanatory:

```
PCollectionTuple outputs = splitDroppable(
    mainOutput, droppableOutput, input);

storeResult(
    outputs.get(mainOutput),
    params.getBootstrapServer(),
    params.getOutputTopicMain());

storeResult(
    outputs.get(droppableOutput),
    params.getBootstrapServer(),
    params.getOutputTopicDroppable());

pipeline.run().waitUntilFinish();
```

Here, the most important part is to pass the TupleTag object associated with the main or droppable output, respectively, to the DoFn object and then retrieve the individual PCollection objects from the PCollectionTuple object.

3. We will skip the details of the readInput and storeResult methods, as there is nothing new for these. Instead, we will focus on the splitDroppable method, as this is what performs all the magic. We will need to access the actual windowing strategy that is applied on the input PCollection object before we change the window to GlobalWindow. We need this in order to be able to re-window the main output as necessary after we finish:

```
@SuppressWarnings("unchecked")
WindowingStrategy<String, BoundedWindow> strategy =
    (WindowingStrategy<String, BoundedWindow>)
    input.getWindowingStrategy();

Coder<BoundedWindow> windowCoder =
    strategy.getWindowFn().windowCoder();
```

The `WindowingStrategy` object holds everything needed to restore the window after we are done. We will also need the `Coder` of the window because we will use `BoundedWindow` as a key in our input KV object.

4.   Next, we need to create the KV object that will be passed to our stateful `DoFn` object:

```
input
  .apply(Reify.windows())
 .apply(
   MapElements
     .into(
       TypeDescriptors.kvs(
         TypeDescriptor.of(BoundedWindow.class),
         TypeDescriptors.strings()))
     .via(v -> KV.of(v.getWindow(), v.getValue())))
   .setCoder(
     KvCoder.of(windowCoder, StringUtf8Coder.of()))
```

We must either set `Coder` for the KV object by using `setCoder` or register a `Coder` object for all possible window types, as these are not registered automatically. A `WindowFn` object always has an associated `Coder` object, so it is safe to set it manually.

5.   Next, we re-window the input to `GlobalWindows` and apply our stateful `DoFn` object:

```
 .apply(Window.into(new GlobalWindows()))
 .apply(
   ParDo.of(
     new SplitDroppableDataFn(
       strategy.getAllowedLateness(),
       mainOutput,
       droppableOutput))
     .withOutputTags(
       mainOutput, TupleTagList.of(droppableOutput)));
```

We must pass the `DoFn` object the actual allowed lateness applied on the input windowing strategy because that is what defines the window GC time.

6. The last thing to do before we get to the implementation of the DoFn itself is restore the windowing on the main output as follows:

```
return PCollectionTuple
  .of(mainOutput, rewindow(result.get(mainOutput),
strategy))
    .and(droppableOutput, result.get(droppableOutput));
```

The reason why we cannot restore the windowing strategy on the droppable output as well is that that output is produced when the watermark reaches the window GC time. Therefore, in a PCollection object with a restored window function, all of this data would again be immediately droppable and any stateful operation would drop it. Therefore, it makes no sense to return such windowing on this output. Please investigate the details of the rewindow function yourself – it is fairly straightforward.

7. The last part is the DoFn object itself. For this, we will need one state and one timer, as follows:

```
@StateId("tooLate")
private final StateSpec<ValueState<Boolean>> tooLateSpec
=
  StateSpecs.value();


@TimerId("windowGcTimer")
private final TimerSpec windowGcTimerSpec =
  TimerSpecs.timer(TimeDomain.EVENT_TIME);
```

The ValueState object will hold a flag indicating that we have already passed the time of the window GC.

8. We will then need to implement our @ProcessElement method. It will use our Timer and ValueState objects, but it will also need a MultiOutputReceiver object, which will be used to output data to the main or droppable output:

```
@ProcessElement
public void processElement(
  @Element KV<BoundedWindow, String> element,
    @StateId("tooLate") ValueState<Boolean> tooLate,
    @TimerId("windowGcTimer") Timer windowGcTimer,
  MultiOutputReceiver output)
```

9. Next, we need to read the current value of our `tooLate` state, and if not already too late, we will set up the `Timer` object for the window GC time:

```
boolean tooLateForWindow =
  MoreObjects.firstNonNull(tooLate.read(), false);
if (!tooLateForWindow) {
  windowGcTimer.set(
    element.getKey().maxTimestamp().
plus(allowedLateness));
}
```

It is good to recall that reading the state can return `null`, and that we need to handle that appropriately. Also note that for better clarity, we have ignored a detail: we cannot set a `Timer` object for a time that is after the end of `GlobalWindow`. Therefore, we should add a check that the `element.getKey().maxTimestamp().plus(allowedLateness)` term does not exceed `GlobalWindow.INSTANCE.maxTimestaamp()`.

10. After reading the state of `tooLate`, we are left with simply outputting the input element to the appropriate `TupleTag` object:

```
if (tooLateForWindow) {
  output.get(droppableOutput).output(element.getValue());
} else {
  output.get(mainOutput).output(element.getValue());
}
```

11. The last part is to handle when our `Timer` object fires – marking the time when the watermark crosses the GC time for a window:

```
@OnTimer("windowGcTimer")
public void onTimer(
    @StateId("tooLate") ValueState<Boolean> tooLate) {
  tooLate.write(true);
}
```

Now that we have discussed various aspects of the implementation, let's test our solution!

Testing our solution

We need to be sure that our solution works, but how do we test the progress of watermarks? Again, `TestStream` comes to the rescue! The complete test code is in the `com.packtpub.beam.chapter3.DroppableDataFilterTest` class. We already know how to use the testing utility, so we'll just rapidly walk through the main parts:

1. We will need a reference time (we'll call that reference time now). This should be aligned with the window boundary because that way we can be sure that now and `now.plus(1)` belong to the same window (provided the window is longer than 1 millisecond). We align this reference time with a minute boundary like this:

    ```
    Instant rawNow = Instant.now();
    Instant now = rawNow.minus(rawNow.getMillis() % 60000);
    ```

2. Next, we need to specify the input of the test pipeline. We'll do that as follows:

    ```
    TestStream.create(StringUtf8Coder.of())
      .advanceWatermarkTo(now)
      .addElements(ts("a", now.plus(1)))
      .advanceWatermarkTo(now.plus(1999))
      .addElements(ts("b", now.plus(999)))
      .advanceWatermarkTo(now.plus(2000))
      .addElements(ts("c", now))
      .advanceWatermarkToInfinity();
    ```

    We will use the `advanceWatermarkTo` method to explicitly manipulate the watermark within our testing input. That way, we can produce one input element (a) that is on-time, another input (b) that is delayed after a watermark for one second, and a final input element (c) that is delayed for two seconds. The `ts` function is just a helper that creates a `TimestampedValue` object from the provided arguments.

3. We then window our input stream in 1-second windows with an allowed lateness of 1 second. Note that the window end times are always shifted by 1 millisecond (to ensure that the window maximum timestamp belongs to the window itself), which makes the c element the only droppable one.

4. We apply our logic as usual:

```
PCollectionTuple split =
    DroppableDataFilter.splitDroppable(
    DroppableDataFilter.mainOutput,
    DroppableDataFilter.droppableOutput,
    input);
```

5. We then test that the outcome is as expected on the main input. We also test that the main input is correctly windowed, that is, the windowing is preserved:

```
PAssert.that(split.get(DroppableDataFilter.mainOutput))
    .inWindow(new IntervalWindow(now, now.plus(1000)))
    .containsInAnyOrder("a", "b");
```

6. The last assertion is about the droppable output, as follows:

```
PAssert.that(split.get(DroppableDataFilter.
droppableOutput))
    .inWindow(GlobalWindow.INSTANCE)
    .containsInAnyOrder("c");
```

Everything seems to be working as expected. But wait – what if the very first element that arrives at our window is droppable? What if even the very first input data element is droppable? Our state would then be empty and our timer would not be set up, so how could we recognize this data as droppable? The answer is somewhat complex, and we will get into that in the next section. We will ignore this minor misbehavior for now and see how our solution works when it is implemented as is.

> **Important note**
>
> **Scalability of the solution**: There is one additional notable issue. Using the window as a key in the KV object that is fed into our stateful DoFn object might be good for the simplicity of the solution, but it raises questions about the scalability of the solution. In our current implementation, all of the elements of a single window will have to pass through one instance of the DoFn object, and this can seriously limit scalability. We can overcome this with a technique called **key salting**. Instead of using the plain window as a key, we would use a tuple of (window, salt), where salt is something added to the window to create multiple copies of the same window. Some runners might have problems with non-deterministic mapping functions, so the best option to create a salt of a cardinality of N is to use a hashCode object of the associated value with something like (value.hashCode() & Integer.MAX_VALUE) % N. This way, we can increase parallelism up to N.

Deploying our solution

Finally, we can deploy our solution and see how it works:

1. We will need to add a topic for the delayed data. We will do this by running the following command:

```
$ ./env/kafka-topics.sh --bootstrap-server kafka:9093 \
    --create --topic output_topic_droppable
```

2. As always, we will run our code as follows:

```
$ kubectl exec -it packt-beam -- run-class.sh \
  com.packtpub.beam.chapter3.DroppableDataFilter \
  kafka:9093 \
  input_topic output_topic output_topic_droppable \
  --runner=flink --flinkMaster=flink-jobmanager:8081 \
  --checkpointingInterval=2000
```

3. Our pipeline supposes that we will write the timestamp of a message into the key of a record stored in Kafka. We have created a tool that will help us create records in a valid format by running the following command:

```
$ ./env/format-stamp.sh | \
  ./env/kafka-producer.sh --topic input_topic \
  --property "parse.key=true" \
  --property "key.separator=;" \
  --bootstrap-server kafka:9093
```

We can then send a message as follows:

```
+1 second;message
```

Or we can send a message as follows:

```
-1 minute;another message
```

These commands will send messages containing message and another message, the first with a timestamp shifted by 1 second to the future and the second with a timestamp shifted by 1 minute to the past. The timestamp is written into the key of the published message.

4. We can now run the `kafka-consumer.sh` command for both of the output topics, each in a different terminal window:

```
$ ./env/kafka-consumer.sh \
  --topic output_topic_droppable \
  --bootstrap-server kafka:9093
$ ./env/kafka-consumer.sh --topic output_topic \
  --bootstrap-server kafka:9093
```

5. We can now experiment with sending various messages with their timestamps shifted to the future and the past. Most notably, try something like the following:

```
-20 minutes;first
-20 minutes;second
```

You should be able to observe the effect of the first element in a window, which is (wrongly) marked as non-droppable and output to the main output topic. The second message will be (correctly) output to the droppable topic.

As we can see, our solution works under the assumption that the droppable data elements do not appear *too often*, and so the chances that the first element in a particular window is droppable are low. That might or might not be good enough for our use case. Let's suppose we need to implement a solution that will work more reliably – we'll walk through some examples of this in the following two sections.

Task 10 – Separating droppable data from the rest of the data processing, part 2

First, let's rephrase our problem definition from *Task 9*.

Defining the problem

Create a pipeline that will separate droppable data elements from the rest of the data elements. It will send droppable data to one output topic and the rest to another topic. Make the separation work even in cases when the very first element in a particular window is droppable.

Discussing the problem decomposition

The main problem of our previous approach was that we were not able to distinguish a data element as late in the case when it was the very first data element in that particular window. Therefore, we need to be able to generate window labels *prior to receiving* any data for that particular window. We can do that using a technique called **looping timers** – that is, we set a timer and then reset it for a fixed duration in an infinite loop. If possible, we would like to align this timer with the starting boundary of a WindowFn object. On every timer firing, we will compute and output all of the windows for that particular timestamp, thus ensuring we receive all of the window labels within the scope of the on-time data. This approach will work well for all WindowFn objects that are *time-based* and **non-merging**. A WindowFn object is time-based if *the window assignment does not depend on the data element*. Non-merging windows are such WindowFn objects, which generate a window label that *cannot change in the future*. Some WindowFn objects violate this constraint (for example, session windows) and we will exclude them explicitly.

Therefore, our solution will look like the following:

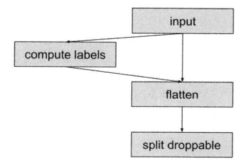

Figure 3.11 – A droppable data filter with label computation

We must compute the labels from the input data (although it would seem possible to compute them independently) because we need to make sure that the *Compute labels* and *Split droppable* steps *share a watermark*. We can actually drop the input data before we run the *Compute labels* step (by filtering them out using a `Filter` transform), but only the direct connection of the edges in the computation DAG ensures a shared watermark. On the other hand, if we filter out all of the data, there is nothing that would start the *Compute labels* step. In Beam, everything reacts to input elements, so we need at least one input element. Luckily, Beam has a transform that is used precisely for these purposes, and it is called `Impulse`. The `Impulse` transform generates a single empty byte array and then terminates. That is exactly sufficient, so our DAG will look like the following:

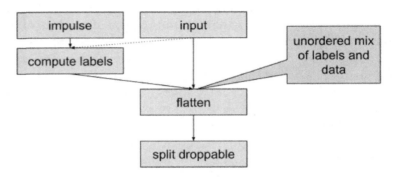

Figure 3.12 – A droppable data filter with label computation and an Impulse transform

We can set up a timer and compute labels for our `WindowFn` object from the element coming from the `Impulse` transform, but the resulting union of the elements and the window labels will be unordered (as with everything in distributed stream processing). This means we can receive droppable data elements prior to receiving the appropriate window label that would enable us to set a timer for the end of the window. We can solve this using a buffer – we insert an element into the buffer and remove and flush it once a timer has fired, and this way we can know what the real timing is. So, let's look into the code, shall we?

Implementing the solution

The complete solution is available in the `com.packtpub.beam.chapter3.`
`DroppableDataFilter2` class. We will skip all the boilerplate code that we have
already seen in the previous examples and focus on what is really important, as the
solution has several possible head-scratching spots:

1. At first, we will focus on our reimplementation of `SplitDroppableDataFn`.
    As in the previous task, it takes a `KV<BoundedWindow, String>` object in its
    input and produces a tagged output depending on whether an input `String` object
    is droppable or not. The most important part of the contract of this transform is
    that *once an element is marked as not-droppable, it must not be viewed as droppable
    at any place in the downstream processing*. At the same time, we obviously want to
    mark as many elements as we can as non-droppable. Therefore, we declare a buffer
    that will hold the input data elements (and their timestamps) until a timer is fired,
    thus giving us an estimation of the watermark:

    ```
    @StateId("buffer")
    private final StateSpec<BagState<KV<Instant, String>>>
      bufferSpec =
        StateSpecs.bag(
          KvCoder.of(InstantCoder.of(), StringUtf8Coder.
    of()));
    ```

2. Next, we will need a timer that will ensure we hold the elements inside this buffer
    for as short a time period as possible to reduce latency:

    ```
    @TimerId("bufferFlush")
    private final TimerSpec bufferFlushTimer =
      TimerSpecs.timer(TimeDomain.EVENT_TIME);
    ```

3. Finally, we have the same state and timer as in the previous implementation – a
    `windowClosed` object, a boolean `ValueState` object, and a `windowGcTimer`
    object marking the time after which the elements in our particular window become
    droppable. We make use of the fact that the boolean `ValueState` object is in fact
    potentially three states – it can be set to `true`, `false`, or not set at all. Therefore,
    we can use that to signal if any timer has already fired or not:

    ```
    buffer.readLater();
    Boolean isWindowClosed = windowClosed.read();
    if (isWindowClosed == null) {
    ```

Note the `buffer.readLater()` call. Remember, any state access can involve non-trivial I/O operations and is by nature blocking. When we need access to multiple states during one call to `@ProcessElement`, `@OnTimer`, or any other method, it is always a good idea to prefetch the values of the state so that we do not block the state access sequentially. And that is exactly what the `readLater()` method is for.

4. If the value of the `windowClosed` state is `null`, it means we haven't written it yet. That is a signal that we need to set up timers (we can do that multiple times, which should be cheap) and start buffering the input until any timer is fired:

```
Instant lastNotDroppable =
   element.getKey().maxTimestamp().plus(allowedLateness);
Instant gcTime = lastNotDroppable.plus(1);
windowGcTimer
   .withOutputTimestamp(lastNotDroppable).set(gcTime);
bufferFlush.offset(Duration.ZERO).setRelative();
buffer.add(KV.of(ts, element.getValue()));
```

The trickiest part to understand is the `withOutputTimestamp` setting of the `windowGcTimer` object. When we set a timer, it is supposed to be that the timer will output data (if any) with the same (output) timestamp as that of the timer set for (fire timestamp). That is not the case in our situation, though. We store elements in a buffer and need to output them with their original timestamp. The buffer can contain elements that are not supposed to be droppable – we must make sure that we output them before the output watermark moves past the maximum allowed time for non-droppable elements. That is exactly what the `withOutputTimestamp` object does – it holds output watermarks at the output timestamp.

The second part is setting the flush timer. We want it to fire as soon as possible, but we also want it to still give us an estimation of the current input watermark – a **relative timer** is what is useful for us here. Relative event time timers are relative to the input watermark, which fires timers, so offset the input watermark of zero duration tells Beam to fire as soon as the watermark moves.

> **Important note**
>
> The most technically correct solution would be to first set the timer for
> `window.maxTimestamp()` and, only after this timer fires, set it to the
> `gcTime` object with a `lastNotDroppable` output timestamp. This would
> ensure that elements that arrive `ON_TIME` (that is to say, before the watermark
> reaches the end of the window without any added lateness) would remain
> `ON_TIME` even in downstream processing. We don't want to complicate the
> implementation with this part, so just make a note of it.

5. The rest of the `SplitDroppableDoFn` object should be self-explanatory, with the
    exception of the following:

```
@Override
public Duration getAllowedTimestampSkew() {
    return Duration.standardHours(1);
}
```

This method tells Beam that the `DoFn` object is allowed to output data that is shifted
to the past up to the value of the `skew` object. The best option would be to be able
to avoid using this directive, but that would require the even more precise working
of the timers and their output timestamps than that required to achieve our goal.
Using this directive is not harmful if we are sure that we hold the watermark at the
boundaries of late and droppable data. On the other hand, every time you need to
use this option, always ask yourself if you know the consequences (for example, if
you cannot output droppable data).

6. Having our implementation of `SplitDroppableDoFn` would technically be
    enough to solve our droppable data problem. However, one performance issue
    would remain. At least every first element in each window would have to be
    buffered at the beginning of each window. That is something we might be fine with,
    but if not, we have sketched the solution to that. We need to be able to generate the
    window labels upfront and send them to the `SplitDroppableDoFn` object so
    that it is able to set timers and not have to buffer input data when it arrives.

7. The implementation of the window label generator is in
    `LoopTimerForWindowLabels`. The trickiest part here is figuring out the seed
    duration (the best option would be to specify that explicitly). We used a **heuristic**
    like this:

```
final Duration loopDuration;
if ((WindowFn) strategy.getWindowFn()
        instanceof FixedWindows) {
```

```
FixedWindows fn = (FixedWindows) (WindowFn)
    strategy.getWindowFn();
loopDuration = fn.getSize().getMillis() > 5000
    ? Duration.standardSeconds(5) : fn.getSize();
} else {
  loopDuration = Duration.standardSeconds(1);
}
```

The best option is when the loopDuration object is aligned with the real window duration. It can fire more frequently than once per window, but it should fire as close to the window start time as possible.

8. Next, we don't want to push all of our input data through our window label generator (as there is no reason for that), but we need the watermark, so we create an empty PCollection object from the input as follows:

```
PCollection<String> inputWatermarkOnly =
  input
    .apply(Window.into(new GlobalWindows()))
    .apply(Filter.by(e -> false));
```

9. We will then union this with the Impulse source using Flatten. pCollections(), and then pass this input to LoopTimerForWindowLabels DoFn.

10. The most interesting part of LoopTimerForWindowLabels is the @OnTimer method. We need to store the timestamp of the last firing so that we know the range of timestamps for which to generate the labels. We cannot set a looping timer for an absolute time, because that would result in (nearly) infinite loops when the watermark shifts to TIMESTAMP_MAX_VALUE. Therefore, we need to use a relative timer setting and shift it for the loopDuration:

```
Instant lastFired =
    Objects.requireNonNull(lastFireStamp.read());
Instant timestamp = context.fireTimestamp();
lastFireStamp.write(timestamp);
if (timestamp.isBefore(
    GlobalWindow.INSTANCE.maxTimestamp())) {
  loopTimer.withOutputTimestamp(timestamp)
    .offset(loopDuration).setRelative();
```

```
outputWindowsWithinInterval(output, lastFired,
timestamp);
  }
```

Again, we have to specify the output timestamp because otherwise, we might generate the labels as late data.

Testing our solution

The test can be found in the `com.packtpub.beam.chapter3.DroppableDataFilter2Test` class. The first important thing to note is that – due to how we generate labels and merge them with the actual data – in general, the watermark propagation is not that straightforward (as in the case of *Task 9*). Testing a specific scenario is actually more complex because, sometimes, something that comes from the source as droppable might actually arrive before the watermark that would mark it as droppable, and therefore, it would actually become non-droppable. But that is not a problem; if this is preserved for all downstream processing, then it is okay if droppable data becomes non-droppable. A problem would be if the opposite happened – that is, non-droppable data becoming droppable. We want to avoid that, and that is what we focus on in `DroppableDataFilter2Test.testContract`. Here, we generate quite a large bunch of data and then test the post-conditions. That is to say, anything that is marked as non-droppable should not be dropped in downstream processing. Therefore, we do the following:

1. We generate some input data:

```
for (int i = 0; i < numElements; i++) {
   Instant currentNow = now.plus(100 * i);
   TimestampedValue<String> value = newValue(currentNow,
i);
   builder = builder.addElements(value)
      .advanceWatermarkTo(currentNow);
}
```

2. Then, we compute the result:

```
PCollectionTuple result =
   DroppableDataFilter2.splitDroppable(
      DroppableDataFilter2.mainOutput,
      DroppableDataFilter2.droppableOutput,
      input);
```

3. Next, we compute something in the main input using the original windowing we used to identify the droppable data and then aggregate everything up to the global window:

```
result
    .get(DroppableDataFilter2.mainOutput)
    .apply(Combine.globally(
        Count.<String>combineFn()).withoutDefaults())
    .apply(
        Window.<Long>into(new GlobalWindows())
        .triggering(AfterWatermark.pastEndOfWindow())
        .accumulatingFiredPanes()
        .withAllowedLateness(Duration.ZERO))
    .apply(Sum.longsGlobally());
```

4. We then sum all of the droppable elements together:

```
PCollection<Long> allElements =
    PCollectionList.of(mainCounted)
        .and(droppableCounted)
        .apply(Flatten.pCollections())
        .apply(Sum.longsGlobally());
```

5. The resulting sum must be precisely equal to the number of input elements, which we verify as follows:

```
PAssert.that(allElements)
    .containsInAnyOrder((long) numElements);
```

6. And because that would be trivially satisfied, if our pipeline somehow held the output watermark, we would also want to be sure that we had seen some droppable data. We could not be sure about the exact number, but it should be non-zero:

```
PAssert.that(droppableCounted)
    .satisfies(e -> {
    assertTrue(Iterables.size(e) > 0);
    return null;
    });
```

We can use arbitrarily complex test logic inside the PAssert. that(..).satisfies() predicate.

Deploying our solution

We can deploy and run the solution in exactly the same way as in *Task 9*, but we must not forget to add --checkpointingInterval. The reason for this is that without this object, Flink seems to have some problems propagating the watermark from the Impulse source downstream. So, consider the following example:

```
$ kubectl exec -it packt-beam -- \
    run-class.sh com.packtpub.beam.chapter3.DroppableDataFilter2 \
    kafka:9093 input_topic output_topic output_topic_droppable \
    --runner=flink --flinkMaster=flink-jobmanager:8081 \
    --checkpointingInterval=2000
```

We can then use the same tools as in *Task 9* to write data with various timing characteristics and see the output in output_topic and output_topic_droppable.

We will conclude this chapter with a theoretical note about side inputs.

Using side inputs

We have already seen how to use side outputs, and **side inputs** are analogous to them. Besides the single main input, a ParDo transform can have multiple additional side inputs, as shown in the following figure:

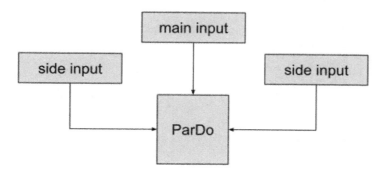

Figure 3.13 – Side inputs

We have multiple ways of declaring a side input to a `ParDo` object. For instance, consider the following example:

```
ParDo.of(new MyDoFn())
```
Analogous to side outputs is also the way how we declare a side input – we must provide it to the ParDo by call to withSideInput as follows:
```
input.apply(ParDo.of(new MyDoFn())
    .withSideInput("side-input", sideInput));
```

Because we may have multiple side inputs, we need a way to distinguish them – if we assign a name to the side input, we can later access it easily in `DoFn` using a `@SideInput` annotation:

```
@ProcessElement
public void processElement(
    @Element .. element,
    @Stateid(...),
    @SideInput("side-input") ...)
```

What remains unanswered is what exactly are the `sideInput` variable and the associated type of `@SideInput` annotation in the preceding code example? The answer can be found in the declaration of the `withSideInput` method – it has to be a `PCollectionView` object. A `PCollectionView` object is a reduced form of a `PCollection` object. That is, if a `PCollection` object can be viewed as a stream, we can imagine a `PCollectionView` object as an accumulated portion of the stream with random access.

We have multiple options for accumulating a part of a stream:

- We can always take the last (most recent) value.
- We can gather all of the elements of a stream into memory and provide them as a `List` object.
- We can gather all of the elements in some external storage and provide them as an `Iterable` object.
- If the input `PCollection` object is keyed (that is, it is of the KV type), we can take the most recent value of each key and provide the associated values as a `Map` object.
- If the input `PCollection` object is keyed, we can store all of the values of a key and provide all its associated values as `MultiMap`.

The reduction of a PCollection object into PCollectionView is done by applying a View transform, as follows:

```
PCollection<String> input = ...
PCollectionView<String> view = input.apply(View.asSingleton());
```

The View transform has five versions corresponding to the five respective options we just listed – View.asSingleton(), View.asList(), View.asIterable(), View. asMap(), and View.asMultimap().

Therefore, we can update our first illustration of side inputs as follows:

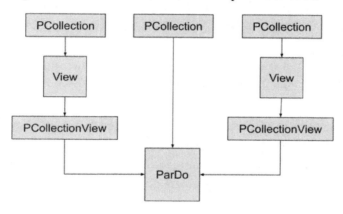

Figure 3.14 – Side inputs created from PCollection objects

When using side inputs, we obviously need to care about memory requirements. If the PCollection object that backs the view is too large, processing the pipeline might either completely fail (due to insufficient memory), or become impractically expensive in terms of CPU usage (for instance, if we use View.asIterable() – which need not necessarily fit into memory – but process the whole Iterable object with each element in the main input).

On the other hand, if we know that the cardinality of the PCollection object that produces the PCollectionView object is rather limited – for example, if we produce the PCollection object from a Combine transform with a reasonable number of keys, or when we use the View.asSingleton() object, which will always give the most recent value – the use of side inputs may be a very efficient choice.

But wait! We already know that every stream is unordered in terms of event time, so how can we know which element of the side input will be matched to each element in the main input? The answer is that we do know that *if we apply the same windows to both the main and side input*. In that case, the elements in the main input wait for the side input window to be ready (and produce output that can be served to the processing logic during the processing of the main input elements). If we use a trigger for the side input, the main input stops waiting when the first triggered pane from the side input arrives and then processes the updates in the **processing time** (defined by the order in which the elements arrive). This is very important to remember when working with side inputs, as it often leads to design patterns of *slowly changing side inputs* (that is, the side inputs are either computed once per window or should be updated with a period that gives the pipeline reasonable time to process one update at a time).

To rephrase this, the elements from the main PCollection input will wait for a side input if there is no side input data for a corresponding window. Once there is at least *some* data in the side inputs, the elements get processed and the side input can be updated asynchronously from the perspective of the main input elements.

The typical use case for side inputs is when there is a need to either inject some per-window data computed inside our pipeline or some external *configuration* that might change over time.

Let's sum up what we have learned in this chapter!

Summary

In this chapter, we learned about all the remaining **primitive** transforms. We now know the details of both the **stateless** and **stateful** ParDo objects. We know the basic life cycle of DoFn and understand the concept of **bundles**. We understand why input to stateful ParDo objects has to be in the form of **keyed** PCollection objects. We have seen and understood the details of how states and timers are managed by Beam and how they are delegated to runners in order to ensure **fault tolerance**. We know how a watermark propagates in transforms in general and what the (stateful) transform's **input watermark** and **output watermark** are. We have successfully used our knowledge to create our version of the GroupIntoBatches transform, which stores data into states before delegating them to an external RPC service.

Next, we focused on handling late and droppable data to be able to avoid data loss. We created one simple and one sophisticated version of a transform process to filter (split) data into two parts – that is, to divide it into the *droppable elements* and the *rest of the elements*. We also learned how the DoFn object works with watermarks, timers, and their **output timestamps**.

We have learned to use **side inputs**, **side outputs**, and TupleTag objects, which is information we will use in the following chapter. We learned a lot in this chapter, so let's not slow down – now, we'll dive into writing **Domain-Specific Languages (DSLs)**!

Section 2
Apache Beam: Toward Improving Usability

This section focuses on improving usability and productivity when implementing Apache Beam pipelines. It defines how to implement reusable PTransforms, how to use and/ or implement your own DSLs, and how to use SQL. It also covers the Apache Beam portability layer, which enables the use of a variety of alternative programming languages besides Java, focusing mostly on the Apache Beam Python SDK.

This section comprises the following chapters:

- *Chapter 4, Structuring Code for Reusability*
- *Chapter 5, Using SQL for Pipeline Implementation*
- *Chapter 6, Using Your Preferred Language with Portability*

4
Structuring Code for Reusability

We have already walked through a great deal of the Apache Beam programming model, but we haven't investigated one of its core primitives – **PTransform**. We have seen many particular instances of PTransforms, but what if we wanted to implement our own? And should we even do that in the first place? In this chapter, we will explain how exactly Apache Beam builds the **Directed Acyclic Graph (DAG)** of operations, and we will use this knowledge to build a **Domain Specific Language (DSL)** to solve a specific use case that uses less boilerplate code than just by using plain Apache Beam. Then, we will introduce some of the built-in DSLs of Apache Beam. Last, but not least, we will learn how to view a stream of data as a **time-varying relation**, which is a fancy term for a table changing in time, which will help us establish a base to introduce one additional DSL – SQL. That will be the topic of *Chapter 5, Using SQL for Pipeline Implementation.*

This chapter will cover the following topics:

- Explaining PTransform expansion
- Task 11 – Enhancing SportTracker by runner motivation using side inputs
- Introducing composite transform – CoGroupByKey
- Task 12 – Enhancing SportTracker by runner motivation using CoGroupByKey
- Introducing the Join library DSL
- Stream-to-stream joins explained
- Task 13 – Writing a reusable PTransform – StreamingInnerJoin
- Table-stream duality

Technical requirements

There is nothing new regarding the technical requirements for this chapter; we will continue to use the same toolset that we used in the previous two chapters. As always, please make sure that you have the current `main` branch cloned from this book's GitHub repository.

Because setting everything up was so quick, let's head directly to our first topic – explaining how PTransform expansion works!

Explaining PTransform expansion

A `PTransform` is a short name for parallel transform – an Apache Beam primitive for transforming `PInput` into `POutput`. `PInput` is a labeling interface that marks objects as suitable as input to `PTransform`, while `POutput` marks objects as suitable as outputs. We already know these objects quite well – a typical one that's used for both input and output is `PCollection`. But there are others as well – most notably `PCollectionTuple` and `PCollectionList`. There are also two special objects – `PBegin` and `PDone`. As we already know, an Apache Beam program – a pipeline – is a DAG whose edges represent PCollections and whose nodes represent PTransforms. PTransforms in the DAG that take `PBegin` as input are **roots**, while PTransforms that produce `PDone` are the **leaves** of the DAG.

This can be seen in the following diagram:

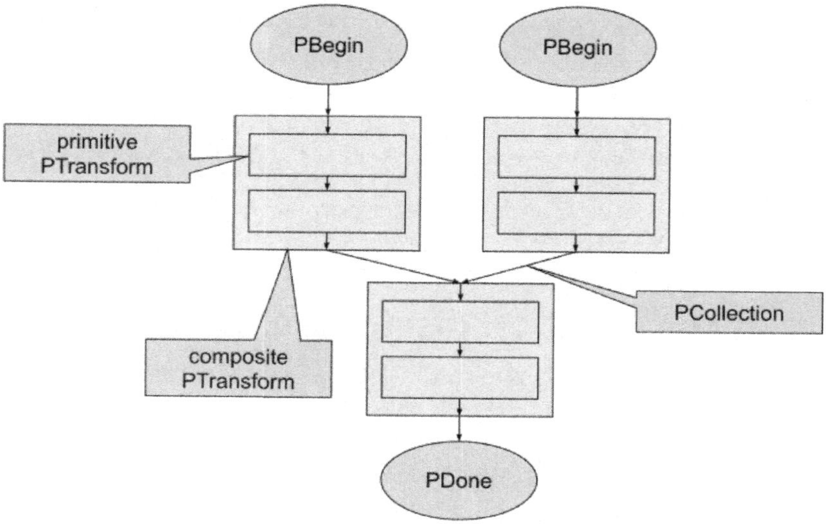

Figure 4.1 – DAG of PTransforms and PCollections

A PTransform is a recursive structure that can contain different PTransforms, and these can be made up of further PTransforms. We call the process of removing composite PTransforms a **PTransform expansion** – a composite PTransform can be recursively expanded to primitive PTransforms that have no further expansion and have to be executed directly.

This way of *top-down* PTransform structuring lets us encapsulate common tasks as high-level transforms that can be used as singular building blocks. We will use this approach in the following example.

Task 11 – Enhancing SportTracker by runner motivation using side inputs

In our first task for this chapter, we will enhance the SportTracker application we used in *Task 5*. We want to create motivating push notifications for users who are currently on track. Users will be notified every minute with information on whether their running performance over the last minute was better than their average pace over the last 5 minutes. Let's look at this problem in more detail.

Problem definition

Calculate two per-user running averages over the stream of artificial GPS coordinates that we generated for Task 5. One computation will be the average pace over a longer (5-minute) interval, while the other will be over a shorter (1-minute) interval. Every minute, for each user, output information will be provided regarding whether the user's current 1-minute pace is higher or lower than the longer average if the short average differs by more than 10%.

We will use our `output_topic` and write this information there, thus simulating push notifications that would be sent.

Problem decomposition discussion

The biggest head-scratching problem in this task turns out to be converting timestamped location data into speed at *defined time intervals*. We cannot (should not) rely on the source device that's sending us notifications at the given timestamp as that might not be possible for that device at all – for instance, when we're moving through an area without a mobile network. The data might be buffered and sent once the device is brought online, but we cannot wait for that data forever. We will choose an alternative approach instead and transfer the location data that's received at arbitrary timestamps into positions at defined time intervals via interpolation. This can be seen in the following diagram:

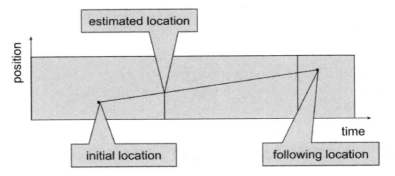

Figure 4.2 – Position interpolation on window boundaries

Here, we can see that linear interpolation can give us approximate locations in an arbitrary time, given that we know two successive locations on the track. So, we will keep the last known location of every user (and track) and generate *two* positions at *two* distinct timestamps. The first one will be at the millisecond of each 1-minute interval, while the other will be 1 millisecond less, which is going to be the maximal timestamp (the end of the window) of the preceding window. Due to this, we will receive (at least) a position at the start and at the end of each 1-minute interval (plus any additional data in-between if we receive the location data more frequently than once per minute, which should be desirable). Then, we can turn these `boxed` locations into speeds over these minute intervals and then calculate two averages, as shown in the following diagram:

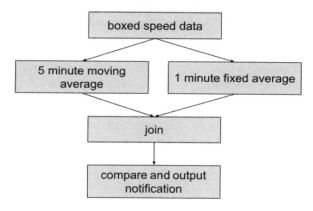

Figure 4.3 – Long and short average join

We can immediately see that we have two problems to solve:

1. We want to compute two averages (over different windows, but the logic seems identical); can we somehow reuse that logic?

2. How do we implement the join?

The answer to the first question is – as would be expected – yes, we can. We will implement our own `PTransform` for that! The answer to the second question has been answered in this section's heading – we will use **side inputs**. In the following tasks, we will look at other options we might have to perform the join operation. So, let's walk through the solution.

Solution implementation

The complete implementation can be found in the `com.packtpub.beam.chapter4.`
`SportTrackerMotivationUsingSideInputs` class. We can immediately spot
the first main difference – it is in the definition of the class itself. As usual, we will walk
through all the important parts in the following steps:

1. As we've already mentioned, the class extends a `PTransform`:

    ```
    public class SportTrackerMotivationUsingSideInputs
        extends PTransform<
          PCollection<KV<String, Position>>,
          PCollection<KV<String, Boolean>>>
    ```

    Here, we have defined a `PTransform` that will take a
    `PCollection<KV<String, Position>>` (the user track and GPS locations)
    and produce a `PCollection<KV<String, Boolean>>` (the user and an
    increase/decrease flag).

2. When a class extends `PTransform`, it must implement the `expand` method,
    which takes `PInput` defined in the definition of `PTransform` and returns the
    defined `POutput`:

    ```
    @Override
    public PCollection<KV<String, Boolean>>
    expand(PCollection<KV<String, Position>> input)
    ```

3. In the `expand` method, we must receive the input we need. For this, we need to
    produce the `"boxed"` speed metrics, like so:

    ```
    PCollection<KV<String, Metric>> metrics =
        input.apply("computeMetrics", new ToMetric());
    ```

    Again, here, `ToMetric` is our user-defined `PTransform`, so we can immediately
    see the recursive expansion. We will return to the implementation of this
    `PTransform` in a few moments.

4. Next, we need to create our side input view. We need to compute the longer,
    5-minute sliding window average. For reusability, we created a `CountAverage`
    `PTransform`, which takes the metrics and computes the average distance over the
    defined window:

    ```
    PCollectionView<Map<String, Double>>
    longRunningAverageView =
      metrics
    ```

```
.apply(
    Window.into(
        SlidingWindows.of(Duration.standardMinutes(5))
            .every(Duration.standardMinutes(1))))
.apply("longAverage", new ComputeAverage())
.apply(
    Window.into(
        FixedWindows.of(Duration.standardMinutes(1))))
.apply("longMap", View.asMap());
```

We need to create the view-compatible windows with the short average, so before we apply `View.asMap()`, we must change the window function.

5. In the last part of the `expand` method of our main `PTransform`, we need to compute the short speed average and compare it to the long one. We will use `FlatMapElements` here, which can gain access to side inputs using the `Contextful` function, as follows:

```
return metrics
    .apply(
        Window.into(
            FixedWindows.of(Duration.standardMinutes(1))))
    .apply("shortAverage", new ComputeAverage())
    .apply(
        FlatMapElements
            .into(...)
            .via(
                Contextful.fn(
                    (elem, c) -> {
                        double longPace =
                            c.sideInput(longRunningAverageView)
                                .get(elem.getKey());
                        // skipped, see the code
                    },
                    Requirements
.requiresSideInputs(longRunningAverageView))));
```

We could have used a standard `ParDo`, but using `FlatMapElements` gives us a little more concise code in this case. In the case of `ParDo`, side inputs would have been defined by `ParDo.withSideInput`, as we mentioned in *Chapter 3, Implementing Pipelines Using Stateful Processing.*

6. Next, we will look at the implementation of the `ToMetric` PTransform. We briefly explained the implementation details of linearly estimating positions on 1-minute boundaries in the previous paragraph, so let's look at this implementation. The `expand` method is straightforward, as shown in the following code block:

```
@Override
public PCollection<KV<String, Metric>>
expand(PCollection<KV<String, Position>> input) {
  return input
    .apply("globalWindow", Window.into(new
GlobalWindows()))
    .apply(
      "generateInMinuteIntervals",
      ParDo.of(new ReportInMinuteIntervalsFn()))    .
setCoder(KvCoder.of(
      StringUtf8Coder.of(), new MetricCoder()));
}
```

7. As shown in the preceding code block, the complete logic reduces to a single (stateful) `ParDo` that's applied via `ReportInMinuteIntervalsFn`. The implementation of this `DoFn` should also not be new to us – it uses the looping timer technique to fire every minute. Until the timer fires, we hold input data in a `BagState` called `positions`, and then remove all the elements from the state with a timestamp lower than the fire timestamp of the timer.

> **Important note**
>
> A more efficient implementation of the `positions` state would be to use a state that can hold data sorted by timestamp. There is such a state called `OrderedList`, but unfortunately, its support is currently limited and, for instance, `FlinkRunner` does not support it. Hopefully, this will change in a future release. The state is supported by `DirectRunner`, so you may wish to swap it in the implementation and test it yourself.

8. We must remove the elements from the state by iterating over the elements and splitting them into a `PriorityQueue` called `queue` and a `List` called `keep`. After that, we must clear the state and reinsert everything from the `keep` list. We always need to include the last known position as well so that when a new update arrives, we can compute the newly projected positions.

9. Note how we set a new timer in the `setNewLoopTimer` method. If we have any unemitted data in our `positions` state, we must ensure that we hold the output watermark of our transform. Otherwise, we risk emitting data behind the watermark, and such data could then be dropped by downstream transform. So, we must compute a minimal timestamp from all the positions stored in our `positions` state and pass this to the `setNewLoopTimer` method via the `minTsToKeep` parameter. Then, we have two main options – either our state is empty (which means our `minTsToKeep` parameter has a value of `BoundedWindow.TIMESTAMP_MAX_VALUE.getMillis()`) or there is some data and the timestamp is lower.

10. In the case of an empty state, we simply set the looping timer to the next 1-minute boundary to be able to flush any newly added data. We do that by using the `align` method, which will align a relative timer to the given boundary:

```
timer
    .offset(Duration.ZERO)
    .align(Duration.standardMinutes(1))
    .setRelative();
```

11. If our state is not empty, we must make sure that we hold the output watermark so that it does not progress past the minimal timestamp in our state. As we already know, we can hold the watermark by specifying the output timestamp of a timer. Doing so will make the timer expect that the data that's emitted when the timer fires will have the given timestamp. So, we must set the timer the same way as we did in *Step 10*, except we specify the output timestamp instead:

```
timer
    .withOutputTimestamp(
        Instant.ofEpochMilli(minTsToKeep))
    .offset(Duration.ZERO)
    .align(Duration.standardMinutes(1))
    .setRelative();
```

12. The last notable detail in this implementation is the (hardcoded) limit on the maximal age of a data point in the `positions` state. We can do this by using the code in `setNewLoopTimer`:

```
if (currentStamp.getMillis()
    > minTsToKeep + 300000) {

    minTsToKeep = currentStamp.getMillis();
}
```

Here, without any limit, a single user that would (for whatever reason) stop sending the location data (probably without sending a track termination) would *stop the watermark from progressing for all users*. The reason for that is that the watermark is not a per-key (user) instance but global, so it is always equal to the minimum from all (per-key) watermark holds. For simplicity, we decided not to deal with late data in this task. If we wanted to solve that, we would hold the watermark for a (quite short) period and then allow the late data to be emitted. We would also have to set allowed lateness in downstream processing appropriately and handle the late data explicitly. We have skipped this here because we wanted to focus on other parts of the problem.

13. After computing the "boxed" 1-minute aligned positions, we are ready to apply the `ComputeAverage` PTransform. Let's see its expansion:

```
@Override
public PCollection<KV<String, Double>>
expand(PCollection<KV<String, Metric>> input) {
    return input.apply(
        Combine.perKey(new AveragePaceFn()));
}
```

14. Here, we can see that it only reduces to the `Combine` PTransform. It would require a little more work here to be able to handle (possible) late data correctly, as noted in *Step 12*.

15. The rest of the `ComputeAverage` PTransform should be familiar – we need to create a `CombineFn`, an accumulator, and an associated `Coder`. All of this is then wrapped into a single `PTransform` and does not leak into the code that wants to use this transform.

16. The final step is to use our `SportTrackerMotivationUsingSideInputs` transform. We can do this in its `main` method, alongside parsing the input arguments, as follows:

```
pipeline
  .apply(
    "ReadRecords",
    new ReadPositionsFromKafka(
      params.getBootstrapServer(), params.
getInputTopic())))
  .apply(
    "computeTrackNotifications",
    new SportTrackerMotivationUsingSideInputs())
  .apply(
    "createUserNotification",
    new WriteNotificationsToKafka(
      params.getBootstrapServer(), params.
getOutputTopic()));
```

Here, we have created the `ReadPositionsFromKafka` and `WriteNotificationsToKafka` PTransforms so that we can reuse them in different implementations of similar tasks. The `WriteNotificationsToKafka` PTransform formats `KV<String, Boolean>` into a more readable form, which we will see after we deploy our pipeline. What is worth explaining is our custom `TimestampPolicy`, which we applied to `KafkaIO.read()`. Due to how we feed our pipeline, we need it to be able to progress into the future. That is why we implemented our custom `TimestampPolicy`, which only derives the watermark from the timestamps of the records that are read from Apache Kafka. You can see the details in the `ReadPositionsFromKafka.newTimestampPolicy()` method.

Testing our solution

In our previous cases, we tested our code by publishing a package-private (`@VisibleForTesting`) method, which returned our output `PCollection`. We will take a different approach here; we will test every `PTransform` independently, which is very handy as it reduces the number of tests needed to test complex pipelines. We have three PTransforms that we can test individually – `ToMetric`, `ComputeAverage`, and `SportTrackerMotivationUsingSideInputs`. The tests for these transforms can be found in `ToMetricTest`, `ComputeAverageTest`, and `SportTrackerMotivationUsingSideInputsTest`, respectively.

We will briefly walk through all these three tests. Let's begin with `com.packtpub.beam.chapter4.ToMetricTest`:

1. We need to test that the transform correctly outputs a `Metric` that represents speed – at least at the 1-minute boundaries – if we do not receive any data with a higher frequency. We created two similar tests – `testComputationBatch` and `testComputationStream`. We feed both tests with the same data; we just work differently with the watermark. The batch case uses the `Create` transform to create a bounded input, which moves the watermark from `BoundedWindow.TIMESTAMP_MIN_VALUE` to `BoundedWindow.TIMESTAMP_MAX_VALUE` in one step after the end of the input.

2. The data simulates a single key (user track) and a single hop from some arbitrary initial point to a point located 360 meters away. The second point is reached in 2 minutes, which should give 3 meters per second. The important part is that we need to fix our initial data point to a fixed position within a 1-minute time interval. Leaving it arbitrary would make the test non-deterministic and therefore probably unstable. We chose the following timestamp:

```
Instant now = Instant.ofEpochMilli(1234567890000L);
```

This gives us the position that's in the middle of a 1-minute interval.

3. Then, we must apply our transform and –to be able to retrieve the timestamps associated with each metric – apply `Reify.timestamps()`, as follows:

```
PCollection<TimestampedValue<KV<String, Metric>>> result =
    input.apply(new ToMetric()).apply(Reify.
timestamps());
```

4. The last interesting part of these tests is that we cannot test the metric for equality, which means we cannot apply `PAssert.that(result).containsInAnyOrder()` as usual. This is due to the floating-point rounding errors. Here, we need to use the following code:

```
PAssert.that(result)
    .satisfies(
        values -> {
```

5. Then, we must iterate over the values and verify that we have the correct values up to a certain small delta, like so:

```
if (val.getTimestamp().equals(now.plus(30000))) {
    assertEquals("foo", val.getValue().getKey());
    assertEquals(
        90, val.getValue().getValue().getLength(), 0.0001);
    assertEquals(
        30000, val.getValue().getValue().getDuration());
}
```

Breaking down the complete pipeline into smaller user-defined PTransforms gives us this option to test that our building blocks behave as expected. Testing this on a complex pipeline would require putting together far more test cases and far more corner cases.

Similar to `ToMetricTest`, we must implement `ComputeAverageTest`. We have already seen tests like this, so there is nothing new here. You can walk through the complete sources in your cloned version of this book's GitHub repository. We will skip this here and focus on the last part, which is to test the complete transform in the `com.packtpub.beam.chapter4.SportTrackerMotivationUsingSideInputsTest` class.

6. Do not forget to fix the initial timestamp so that the output will be fully deterministic and predictable. As we did previously, we chose the following value:

```
Instant.ofEpochMilli(1234567890000L);
```

However, any fixed value would work as well, it just may result in different outcomes, which would have to be accounted for. This also happened in the `ToMetric` transform – we divided the test into two parts called `testComputationBatch` and `testComputationStream`. `testComputationStream` focuses on working with the watermark, while `testComputationBatch` focuses on working on the overall logic. Here, we can see that since we were able to test the sub-transform separately, the overall complexity of the resulting test is quite low.

Deploying our solution

We can deploy the pipeline as usual:

```
$ kubectl exec -it packt-beam -- run-class.sh \
  com.packtpub.beam.chapter4.
SportTrackerMotivationUsingSideInputs \
  kafka:9093 input_topic output_topic \
  --runner=flink --flinkMaster=flink-jobmanager:8081 \
  --checkpointingInterval=2000
```

Then, we need to feed the pipeline with the data written in `input_topic`. We created a script to generate sample data, which is located at `chapter4/bin/emit_tracks.py`. This script generates a new position for a set of users. Every 2 seconds, it generates 1 minutes' worth of random data. We can generate data for 20 users and write this data to our `input_topic` to see the outputs by running the following command:

```
$ ./chapter4/bin/emit_tracks.py 20 \
  | ./env/kafka-producer.sh --topic input_topic \
  --bootstrap-server kafka:9093
```

Then, we can view the output in `output_topic`, as shown here:

```
Looks like you are slowing down user user18. Go! Go! Go!
Great job user user15! You are gaining speed!
```

With that, we have successfully solved our runner motivation problem. However, using the side inputs to put the long and short averages together might hit some limits. Mostly, it must fit into memory. In the next section, we will explore a transform that can help us overcome this.

Introducing composite transform – CoGroupByKey

In *Task 11*, we solved the tracker motivation problem by using side inputs. The actual operation that's involved can be described as a **join**. We want to join two streams – that is, a 5-minute average with a 1-minute average – to compare them and then output a notification. Using side inputs is handy and efficient, provided they fit in memory. If we have enough users, we will likely run into trouble with this approach. What other options do we have to solve our problem? Fortunately, Apache Beam has a composite transform called **CoGroupByKey** for this purpose. The transform is composite because it wraps around `GroupByKey` and `PCollectionTuple`, where each element of two or more input PCollections is *tagged* using `TupleTag` and then processed using `GroupByKey` to produce a `CoGbkResult` – a wrapper object that holds all the values from each of the input PCollections with the same key and same window. This can be seen in the following diagram:

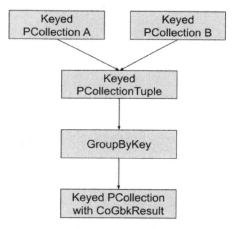

Figure 4.4 – CoGroupByKey expansion

The `CoGbkResult` object is a wrapper around the `Iterable`, which was provided as the output of `GroupByKey`. It provides grouped values for the input PCollections based on `TupleTag`. This implies that this transform has the following requirements and resulting properties:

- All input PCollections must have *compatible* window functions. Though this requirement is not as strict as having the same window functions, it is often similar in practice. Technically, the requirement is that the windows are of the same type and have the same **merging strategy**. We will discuss merging strategies in *Chapter 8, Understanding How Runners Execute Pipelines*. We can assume that the requirement is to have the same window functions for now.

- The resulting `CoGbkResult` is created and sent for downstream processing according to the same rules as in the case of `GroupByKey` – a trigger defines when the result will be emitted. Note that the result might not be complete until we reach the window garbage collection time – that is, the window's maximal timestamp plus the allowed lateness.

Some runners might require that `CoGbkResult` fits in memory per key, as opposed to the side input approach, where the requirement might be to fit the complete side input into memory for all keys.

Now that we have explained how `CoGroupByKey` works, let's use it in our next task!

Task 12 – enhancing SportTracker by runner motivation using CoGroupByKey

In *Task 11*, we solved the problem of sending motivating push notifications to users currently on track using side inputs. We already know that this approach might suffer from the problem of forcing the side input to fit into memory for all users, which might become restrictive once we have many users. The chances are pretty high that we will not ever hit the memory limit in such a use case, but let's assume that we want to avoid using side inputs and use `CoGroupByKey` instead.

Now, let's redefine *Task 11* so that we can reimplement it by using `CoGroupByKey`.

Problem definition

Implement Task 11 but instead of using side inputs, use CoGroupByKey to avoid any possible memory pressure due to forcing side input to fit into memory for all keys (user-tracks).

Problem decomposition discussion

We will reuse as much code from *Task 11* as we can. Our discussion of the problem remains, so our solution will use our ToMetric and ComputeAverage transforms. What will change is the way we put our long-term average and the short-term average together.

Solution implementation

Let's jump straight into the implementation, which will be short for this task. We will compare it to the previous implementation for *Task 11*. The complete implementation can be found in the com.packtpub.beam.chapter4. SportTrackerMotivationUsingCoGBK class:

1. The first thing that changes is that we no longer use the View.asMap() PTransform as that is used for side inputs. So, we only need to compute the long average in the sliding window, and then re-window it back to 1-minute fixed windows, as follows:

```
PCollection<KV<String, Double>> longAverage =
  metrics
    .apply(
      Window.into(
        SlidingWindows.of(Duration.standardMinutes(5))
          .every(Duration.standardMinutes(1))))
    .apply("longAverage", new ComputeAverage())
    .apply(
      Window.into(
        FixedWindows.of(Duration.standardMinutes(1))));
```

2. Then, we need to create our TupleTags, which we will use to distinguish between the long-term and short-term average:

```
TupleTag<Double> shortTag = new TupleTag<>("short");
TupleTag<Double> longTag = new TupleTag<>("long");
```

> **Important note**
>
> We have already seen `TupleTag` when using side outputs. When using it
> to tag outputs, we must create it as an anonymous class using something like
> `TupleTag<Double> tag = new TupleTag<>() {};`. This is
> not required here; we can use the standard instantiation. The reason for this is
> that when we're using it for outputs, we need to be able to retain an output data
> type at runtime for coder inference. When using `TupleTag` for inputs,
> we already know the data type and coder from the previous `PTransform`,
> so we don't need to retain it. Although it is an error not to use an anonymous
> class for outputs, it is not an error to use an anonymous class for input. So,
> a *safe* approach is to use the anonymous class whenever you're in any doubt.

3. Now, we need to create a `KeyedPCollectionTuple`, which is of the `PInput` type, for `CoGroupByKey`:

```
PCollection<KV<String, CoGbkResult>> grouped =
  KeyedPCollectionTuple.of(longTag, longAverage)
    .and(shortTag, shortAverage)
    .apply(CoGroupByKey.create())
```

4. Once we apply `CoGroupByKey`, we get `PCollection<KV<K, CoGbkResult>>` on output. Then, we can retrieve both the long-term and short-term average using the following code:

```
grouped.apply(
  FlatMapElements
    .into(...)
      .via(
      elem -> {
        double longPace = elem.getValue()
          .getOnly(longTag, 0.0);
        double shortPace = elem.getValue()
          .getOnly(shortTag, 0.0);
    ...
```

Because we are outputting a single value per key and window in our aggregation, both for the long term and the short term, we can use the `getOnly()` method to retrieve it. If there was more than one value per key and window, we would have to retrieve them using the `getAll()` method, which returns all values as an `Iterable`.

We will skip the deployment and testing part as it is the same as in *Task 11*. Instead, we'll jump into another topic. By using `CoGroupByKey`, we can derive several join types that are consistent with the relational definition of SQL JOIN. Let's see that next!

Introducing the Join library DSL

Before we proceed, let's recall what a relation JOIN is. A relation can be viewed as a table. This table can have an arbitrary number of columns, but for the sake of this discussion, only three of them matter, as shown in the following table:

Primary Key	Gender	Value
alice	female	foo
bob	male	bar

Table 4.1 – A sample relationship between individuals

This table defines a relation of a set of individuals (*alice, bob*), a set of different genders (*female, male*), and a set of some other properties with values of *foo* and *bar*. If the table contained more than three columns, we could view all the other values in the table as a single *value*. The actual structure and data type of the value column are not relevant to the discussion, so we can assume that we only have a single value in the table.

Let's assume we have another table:

Primary Key	Average Height
female	163 cm
male	176.5 cm

Table 4.2 – A relationship of average heights based on gender

This table is a relationship between gender and an expected average height over the population. Let's assume that we want to answer the following question: *What is the expected average height of individuals from Table 4.2?* We would answer this question by using a JOIN operation – we would find the average height in *Figure 4.2* based on a *join key* – the gender – from *Figure 4.1*.

In some situations, there can be multiple matches of a join key in both relations. In such cases, we do a mathematical operation called the **Cartesian product** – we create every possible pair of objects from the two respective sets. For instance, if we have a set, A, of numbers – A = (1, 2) – and a set, B, of characters – B = (a, b, c) – the Cartesian product (denoted by A x B) equals A x B = ((1, a), (1, b), (1, c), (2, a), (2, b), (2, c)). An important question arises here – what should be the outcome when one of the sets is empty? The classical mathematical definition implies that the resulting set is empty as well. The relational algebra somewhat extends this definition and allows for three possible outcomes, as follows:

- If one side (either left or right) of the join is empty, the result will be empty as well. This is the default behavior and is called an **inner join**.

- If the left-hand side is not empty but the right-hand side is, the result is a tuple, (X, null), for each element, X, on the left-hand side. If the left-hand side is empty, the result is empty. This is called a **left (outer) join**.

- If either side is empty and the other is not empty, the result is either (X, null) or (null, X), depending on which side was empty and which was not empty. This is called a **full (outer) join**.

Now that we've covered the relational theory, let's see how this applies to streaming data!

In the classical relational world, relations are considered to be *static*, which means they don't change over time – at least not concerning the query. We query our data at a given moment in time and we want to find an answer that is valid at that time. Do we have a concept in our definition of a streaming world that can match this? Yes, we do – a **global window**. A global window places all our data in a single *bucket*, just as it would in the classical relational world. But we have other window types as well; can we generalize the classical approach a little? Yes, we can, as shown in the following diagram:

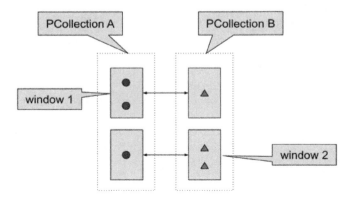

Figure 4.5 – Windowed join

If we split both our input, PCollection A (often called the **left-hand side** of the join), and PCollection B (often called the **right-hand side** of the join), into windows, we can only match the elements in *matching windows*. So, to implement this type of windowed join, we need a transform that groups elements with a matching join key in the same windows and then outputs a Cartesian product of these elements. Do we have such a transform? Sure – this is what CoGroupByKey does! And because a join is a common operation, Apache Beam has a library – a DSL – that can use it for us. This DSL is located in a maven artifact called org.apache.beam:beam-sdks-java-extensions-join-library. We can use it to replace the CoGroupByKey transform from *Task 12* with the following code:

```
PCollection<KV<String, KV<Double, Double>>> joined =
    Join.innerJoin("joinWithShort", longAverage, shortAverage);
```

The resulting KV<String, KV<Double, Double>> is exactly what we need to instantly compare the long, short average pace, and output a notification. You can walk through the simplified code by referring to the com.packtpub.beam.chapter4.SportTrackerMotivationUsingJoinLibrary class. The tests remain the same as in *Task 11* and *Task 12*.

Important note

We can use arbitrary triggering on the window function of the inputs of the arbitrary join. We must not forget that the underlying implementation is GroupByKey with a union of values from the Pcollections input, so a correctness condition is that we must use the accumulatingFiredPanes accumulation mode. Otherwise, we will get an arbitrary subset of the real join's output. Another implication is that any trigger that can fire multiple times, which includes DefaultTrigger in case we have non-zero allowed lateness, will result in duplicates because values will be emitted multiple times, which the downstream logic must account for – for instance, by distinguishing the outputs by PaneInfo.

Though the join library is quite simple, it can be very handy and can help us avoid writing boilerplate code for windowed joins. The obvious question immediately follows – are there situations where the windowed join is not enough to solve a practical problem? The answer is, unfortunately, yes. We'll explore what would happen if we were to take the window join and minimize the window's duration to the extreme in the next section.

Stream-to-stream joins explained

Let's look at *Figure 4.6* but modify it a little. Let's say that we want to get the results from the join as quickly as possible. Currently, the latency is defined by the length of the window – because the join is delegated on CoGroupBeyKey, which, in turn, relies on GroupByKey, we can only get results when a trigger that's associated with our window function fires. This typically happens at the end of the window (though it can happen sooner, which would then result in duplicates). If we want to avoid deduplication downstream and increase efficiency, because the duplicates can become a performance issue, we have no other option than to decrease the size of the window. At the limit, we end up with a situation like this:

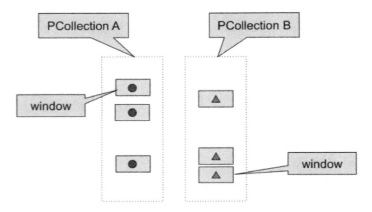

Figure 4.6 – Degenerated windowed join

The smaller we make our window, the less data we can join. If the window's duration is zero, will not be able to join any data at all. This is not going to work. This motivating example shows us that what we want is to *perform the join on a global window*, or at least on as large a window as possible. But how do we do that? What are the required semantics?

To answer these questions, we need to return to the relational data model, because we want our definition of a join to be consistent with the classical relational one. The invariant of relational data models is that a *primary key is unique*. No two distinct rows can have the same type of primary key (for the relation). We cannot write a new row with a primary key that already exists – we must *update the old row*. If we perform the join after the update, the old data will not be part of the join; we will only see the new data. Our complete stream-to-stream join semantics must respect that. So, we end up with a data model that consists of a triple *(primary_key, join_key, value)* on both sides of the join. As always, because we are talking about streaming systems, each data point has an implicit timestamp associated with it. A simplified version of the join could look as follows:

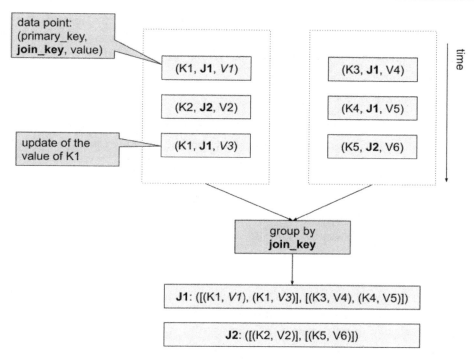

Figure 4.7 – Simplified stream-to-stream join

Let's explain what we can see in this diagram. As always, we have two input PCollections – the left-hand side and the right-hand side. Both contain three triples – for instance, *(K1, J1, V1)* denotes a triple consisting of a primary key, *K1*, a join key, *J1*, and a value, *V1*. As the name of the middle term suggests, we want to join on the common join key – that is, we want to select all the elements with the same join key on both sides and group them. As we already know, values and join keys can be updated, which is the case for the third element on the left-hand side's input – it updates the value of the element with the primary key, *K1*, from *V1* to *V3*.

Our goal is to perform a shuffling operation and group – not necessarily via `GroupByKey` – all the elements with the common join key on the same worker. By using the example shown in the preceding diagram, we will end up with two groups – one for the *J1* join key and the other for the *J2* join key. So far, everything seems fine. But how do we produce the final Cartesian product pairs from the groups? The answer to this question is that we must *order the elements inside the group by timestamp*. The reason for this is that for each data element on both sides, we need to know about all the data elements on the other side with lower timestamps; that is, we need to know about all the data elements with common join keys that existed at the time the new element was created. For all practical intents and purposes, this equates to sorting by time.

So, we need to keep both sides sorted. Every time a new data element arrives from either side, we must match it to all the elements from the other side with a lower timestamp and output the joined pairs by using the Cartesian product of the values with different primary keys.

We still have two unresolved issues, as follows:

1. The join key might be a derived property, it might be computed from the value, or it can be updated on its own – how do we handle change in the join key?

2. As we've mentioned multiple times in *Chapter 1, Introduction to Data Processing with Apache Beam*, distributed streams are inherently unsorted, so although we can keep values sorted, they will arrive out of order. This means that if some data element arrives later than its joined counterpart, we might output an incorrect match – a value that was changed (or deleted!) but we didn't know about it at the time we output it.

Surprisingly, both these problems have one common solution – we need a way to *retract data elements* from a stream. A retraction is a way of notifying downstream processing that some previous output should be removed. The complete generic implementation of this concept is tricky and is not currently supported by Apache Beam but hopefully will be in the future. But that should not stop us from solving the first problem. Here, we can implement our own *custom* simplified version of the retraction – the only thing we need to do is allow a value in our triple to be null with the semantics of a delete operation. Then, we must break down a change of join key into two data elements – the first will be the delete on the old join key, while the second will be the actual value for the new join key. Let's illustrate this for clarity:

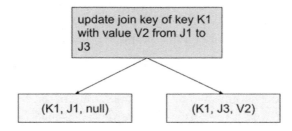

Figure 4.8 – Retraction and update for the changed join key

This way, we can ensure that the downstream group processing join key, *J1*, will be notified that the primary key, *K1*, is no longer part of the group.

But how do we know that a join key has been updated? The answer is that we must prepend one stateful operation (a stateful `ParDo`) that will be keyed by our primary key and will hold the last seen value of the join key. Once the new value arrives, it will compare it with the last value. If it changes, it will output the retraction to the old join key. Sounds simple, right? But, as always, and the same as in the second problem we mentioned previously, we have the problem of unordered data, which may cause us to output the wrong data.

So, how do we solve this? You've guessed it – we will use watermarks and buffer data up to allowed lateness, as shown in the following diagram:

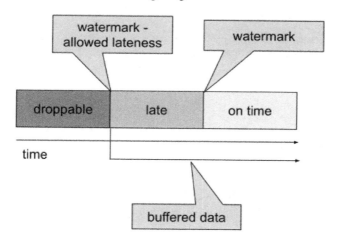

Figure 4.9 – Buffering up to allowed lateness

As we can see, we can only process data that does not arrive after the allowed lateness after the watermark. We buffer all the elements until the watermark passes their timestamp, plus the allowed lateness. If an element arrives delayed for more than the allowed lateness, it has to be dropped immediately, as opposed to the standard definition of droppable data, which can only be dropped at the boundary of a window. The reason for this is that we have already emitted the results downstream and do not have a fully universal way to retract data right now. This approach also significantly increases latency since any output will have to be delayed for the duration of the allowed lateness.

The low-latency fully universal solution for this would require holding several (at least two) copies of the state at each stateful operator – one at the current watermark and the other at the watermark – so that we can allow lateness and the ability to replay the input data when we receive a retraction. The full explanation is somewhat out of the scope of this book, but we hope that the full implementation will be supported by Apache Beam sometime in the future. Until then, we need to resort to somewhat suboptimal solutions.

The good news is that once we can accept the increased latency, we don't have to implement the buffering and sorting ourselves. We can use the (experimental) `@RequiresTimeSortedInput` annotation on the `@ProcessElement` method of a stateful `DoFn` to get this behavior.

Let's recap on our discussion of a fully unwindowed stream-to-stream relational join semantics-compatible solution by looking at the following diagram:

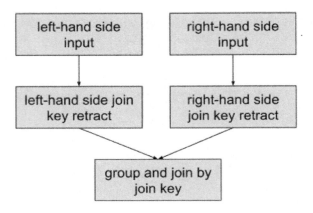

Figure 4.10 – Parts of full stream-to-stream join semantics

With that, we have walked through a transform that provides unwindowed stream-to-stream join semantics, but how about actually implementing it on our own?

Task 13 – Writing a reusable PTransform – StreamingInnerJoin

Our goal in this task is to create a reusable `PTransform` that will do the fully stream-oriented join. For simplicity, we will constrain ourselves to the inner join as the implementation of the full outer join would become a little lengthy. We will mention the differences at the end of this section, though.

Problem definition

Implement a `PTransform` that will be applied to a `PCollectionTuple` with exactly two TupleTags (`leftHandTag` and `rightHandTag`) and will produce a streaming join operation on top of them. The transform needs to take functions to extract join keys and both sides' primary keys. The output will contain the (inner) joined values and any retractions.

Problem decomposition discussion

We described the theoretical properties of a streaming join in the previous section, so we will focus on describing the semantics in practical examples. We will then use these examples to test our solution.

To recap once again, we will introduce the concept of an **upsert** – shorthand for *update or insert* – which is, semantically, an operation that either creates a new record with a given primary key, if one doesn't exist, or updates an already existing one. Let's explain this while looking at the following stream:

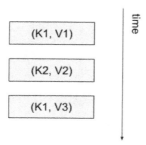

Figure 4.11 – Upsert stream

The preceding diagram shows three upserts. The first one creates a row with a key, *K1*, and a value, *V1*; the second adds a new row with a key, *K2*, and a value, *V2*; and the third one replaces the value, *V1*, of *K1* with a value of *V3*. Note that the absolute time does not matter here. What matters is the time when these upserts occur – namely, that the value of the *K1* key was *V1* before it was updated to *V3*. We will use this property in the following discussion. Upserts that happen concurrently (without any influence or any causality) will be denoted as being on the same line.

We will need one more graphical aid here. The following diagram denotes a retraction:

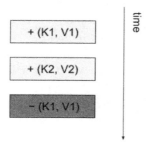

Figure 4.12 – Retract stream

The preceding diagram shows a stream that consists of two additions and one retraction – *(K1, V1)* had the semantics for removing the previously present value, *(K1, V1)*, which was added by the first value, + *(K1, V1)*. The result will be a single row containing *(K2, V2)*. The reason why we need a retraction is that a stream might not have a primary key. In such a case, using an upsert of something like *(K1, null)* would have different semantics – it would result in both *(K1, V1)* and *(K1, null)* being present in the output. Only the retraction makes it possible to remove rows from a stream without a primary key – which might be the case for the output of a join operation if the left or right key (or both) are projected away from the resulting stream. We will see that shortly.

Let's look at the first example of streaming an inner join and its expected output:

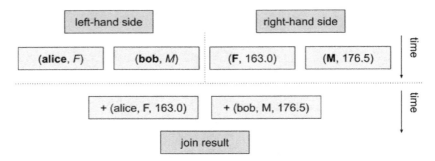

Figure 4.13 – Simple join using a foreign key

We will explain this diagram thoroughly to ensure that you understand other, more complex examples. What we can see here is two upsert streams – a left-hand side containing pairs, *(alice, F)* and *(bob, M)*. We denote the primary key in bold, while the join key is written using *italics*. The right-hand side of the join contains pairs, *(F, 163.0)* and *(M, 176.5)*, which represent average heights, with *F* and *M* being the respective primary keys. All the upserts are put on the same line, meaning that they have the same timestamp. Below the horizontal dotted line is the result of the join – as expected, we should get the two triples; that is, *(alice, F, 163.0)* and *(bob, M, 176.5)*. The result of a join should always be a retract stream (because if we were to only take the average height instead of the full triple, there would be no primary key). Note that the result of the join is equal to the result of a windowed join. That is exactly what we want – *a windowed join is a special case of the streaming join, where all the data is shifted (projected) to window.maxTimestamp()*. The differences will start to become apparent once we move to a case where the data is not timestamp aligned.

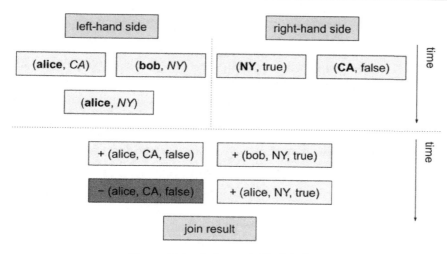

Figure 4.14 – A change in the join key

As we can see, we now expect a completely different result than a classical windowed join would produce. We have two individuals (*alice* and *bob*) with associated states (*CA* and *NY*). Next, we have a Boolean value associated with each state, the meaning of which is not important to the discussion currently. What the preceding diagram represents is a change in the state associated with *alice* from *CA* to *NY*. As a result, the joined stream reflects this by *retracting* the previous value, *(alice, CA, false)*, and *adding* the new value, *(alice, NY, true)*.

A very similar case is when we change a value associated with a joined key. Let's see what happens:

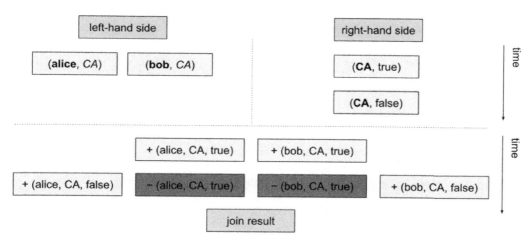

Figure 4.15 – A change in the joined value

In this case, the result should be that all the data previously associated with the changed joined key is retracted and replaced with the new value.

The last most complex example will help us understand the last missing pieces of the join semantics. Let's suppose we have our two individuals (*alice* and *bob*) and a set of cities associated with a state (*CA*). We will denote each city in the list with an index. So, the primary key of the first city in the list for *CA* would be *CA.1*. The following diagram depicts a situation where we add a new city to the list and then replace a city with an empty value. This empty value may effectively mean deletion, but for simplicity, we will treat it as updating to an empty string. This could be solved with downstream processing, if necessary.

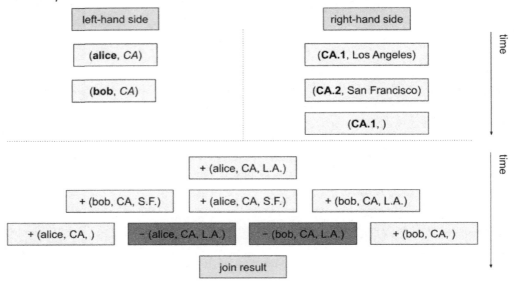

Figure 4.16 – A change in a list of joined values

These examples define how our join should work, so let's go and implement it!

Solution implementation

The solution can be broken down into two main pieces. The first is caching the primary key of both the left-hand side and the right-hand side, while the second part is the actual join. The complete implementation can be found in the `com.packtpub.beam.chapter4.StreamingInnerJoin` class, as well as a few associated classes (`JoinRow` and `JoinResult`) that hold the internal data (key, join key, and value) and the joined result. These two classes are pure data (lombok `@Value`) classes and are associated with `Coder`, so they should not bring us anything new, so we will skip them here. Instead, we will focus on the more important parts. First, we will explore the `expand` method of our join's `PTransform`:

1. We need to extract the left-hand and right-hand inputs from our `PCollectionTuple` input:

    ```
    PCollection<L> leftInput = input.get(leftHahdTag);
    PCollection<R> rightInput = input.get(rightHandTag);
    ```

2. Then, we must create our internal data format, `JoinRow`, which will hold the triple (PrimaryKey, JoinKey, Value). We need to apply the same transform to both sides of the join; we've only shown the left-hand side here. Note that we are building a completely reusable transform, so the actual data types are type parameters (`K`, `J`, `L`, and `R`):

    ```
    PCollection<JoinRow<K, J, L>> leftRow =
        leftInput
        .apply(mapToJoinRow(
            leftKeyExtractor, leftJoinKeyExtractor))
        .setCoder(JoinRow.coder(
            keyCoder, joinKeyCoder, leftInput.getCoder()))
    ```

3. Then, we must apply an internal PTransform that will cache and retract any changes in the join key. Note that the output is the same because we implemented our `JoinRow` to be able to include retractions (by having a value of `null`):

    ```
    leftRow = leftRow
        .apply("retractLeftUpdates", new JoinKeyRetract<>())
        .setCoder(
        JoinRow.coder(
            keyCoder, joinKeyCoder, leftInput.getCoder()));
    ```

4. Now, we need to make both sides of the join the same type – we will need to create a single `PCollection` from them. Our `PCollection` must contain elements of the same type. Apache Beam has a helper value class called `RawUnionValue` that takes a list of coders and creates an object that can hold a single value of any of these types. First, we must create a `UnionCoder`:

```
UnionCoder unionCoder = UnionCoder.of(
    Arrays.asList(leftRow.getCoder(), rightRow.
getCoder()));
```

5. Then, we must use it to create a `PCollection` of `RawUnionValues`:

```
PCollection<RawUnionValue> leftRawUnion =
  leftRow
 .apply(
  MapElements
    .into(TypeDescriptor.of(RawUnionValue.class))
    .via(e -> new RawUnionValue(0, e)))
 .setCoder(unionCoder);
```

Note the index, 0, which refers to the index of the associated coder in the coder. So, 0 represents the left-hand side, while 1 represents the right-hand side.

6. Once we have the same type on both sides, we can flatten them into a single `PCollection`:

```
PCollection<RawUnionValue> union = PCollectionList.
of(leftRawUnion)
  .and(rightRawUnion)
  .apply(Flatten.pCollections())
```

7. Because we will apply a stateful `DoFn`, we need to create a keyed `PCollection` as input. The key must be our join key because we need to process all the elements with the same join key on the same instance:

```
PCollection<KV<J, RawUnionValue>> withJoinKey = union
  .apply(
   WithKeys.of(
    val ->
       ((JoinRow<K, J, ?>) val.getValue()).
getJoinKey()))
    .setCoder(KvCoder.of(joinKeyCoder, unionCoder))
```

8. The last step is to apply our stateful join, `DoFn`:

```
withJoinKey.apply(
  "innerJoin",
  ParDo.of(
    new StreamInnerJoinDoFn<>(
      keyCoder,
      leftInput.getCoder(),
      rightInput.getCoder())))
  .setCoder(
    JoinResult.coder(
      keyCoder,
      joinKeyCoder,
      leftInput.getCoder(),
      rightInput.getCoder()));
```

There is a lot of hidden magic here, so let's uncover the details of the `JoinKeyRetract` transform.

9. The `expand` method is straightforward and reduces to a simple expansion:

```
JoinRowCoder<K, J, V> coder =
  (JoinRowCoder<K, J, V>) input.getCoder();

return input
  .apply(WithKeys.of(JoinRow::getKey))
  .setCoder(KvCoder.of(coder.getKeyCoder(), coder))
  .apply("cachePrimaryKey", ParDo.of(
    new CacheAndUpdateJoinKeyFn<>(coder)));
```

10. `CacheAndUpdateJoinKeyFn` is a `DoFn` that has a single state, which is declared as follows:

```
private static final String STATE_ID = "cache";

@StateId(STATE_ID)
private final StateSpec<ValueState<JoinRow<K, J, V>>>
cacheSpec;
```

11. For `ValueState`, we need a coder that is passed in as a constructor:

```
CacheAndUpdateJoinKeyFn(Coder<JoinRow<K, J, V>> rowCoder)
{
    this.rowCoder = rowCoder;
    cacheSpec = StateSpecs.value(this.rowCoder);
}
```

12. The last missing piece is the `@ProcessElement` method, which is declared as follows:

```
@RequiresTimeSortedInput
@ProcessElement
public void processElement(
    @Element KV<K, JoinRow<K, J, V>> element,
    @StateId(STATE_ID) ValueState<JoinRow<K, J, V>> cache,
    OutputReceiver<JoinRow<K, J, V>> output) {
```

Once again, it is worth emphasizing that the `@RequiresTimeSortedInput` annotation is still considered experimental and might not be supported on all runners. The alternative would be to implement the buffering and sorting ourselves, but that would add additional non-trivial complexity.

Last but not least, this annotation can optimize itself in the case of batch processing. Another caveat is that this annotation changes the semantics of droppable data, as we mentioned in *Chapter 3*, *Implementing Pipelines Using Stateful Processing*.

13. The body of the `processElement` method is straightforward: it compares the current value of the join key and if it differs, it outputs a retraction to the old join key via the following command:

```
output.output(cached.toDelete());
```

The last part is the implementation of `StreamInnerJoinDoFn`.

14. We will need two `MapStates` – the key is the primary key of elements on both sides, while the value is the respective element:

```
@StateId(LEFT_STATE)
final StateSpec<MapState<K, L>> leftStateSpec;
```

```
@StateId(RIGHT_STATE)
final StateSpec<MapState<K, R>> rightStateSpec;
```

15. A `MapState` can efficiently store and look up a value for a key. To create it, we need a `Coder` for both the key and value, so we will create `StateSpec` in the constructor:

```
StreamInnerJoinDoFn(
  Coder<K> keyCoder,
  Coder<L> leftValueCoder,
  Coder<R> rightValueCoder) {
    leftStateSpec = StateSpecs.map(keyCoder,
leftValueCoder);
    rightStateSpec = StateSpecs.map(
      keyCoder, rightValueCoder);
}
```

16. Our `@ProcessElement` method is declared as follows:

```
@RequiresTimeSortedInput
@ProcessElement
@SuppressWarnings("unchecked")
public void processElement(
  @Element KV<J, RawUnionValue> element,
  @StateId(LEFT_STATE) MapState<K, L> left,
  @StateId(RIGHT_STATE) MapState<K, R> right,
  OutputReceiver<JoinResult<K, J, L, R>> output) {
```

17. If we are processing an element from the left-hand or the right-hand side, by a tag in the `RawUnionValue`:

```
boolean isLeft = element.getValue().getUnionTag() == 0;
```

18. Next, we must extract all the other relevant pieces of data:

```
JoinRow<K, J, Object> value =
  (JoinRow<K, J, Object>) element.getValue().getValue();
K primaryKey = value.getKey();
J joinKey = element.getKey();
@Nullable Object inputValue = value.getValue();
```

Note that `inputValue` might be `null`, which means the previous value (`delete`) will be retracted. Also, note that the type of the value is `Object` because it might be either the left or right type. We don't know this yet, but we will decide this based on the tag (the `isLeft` Boolean flag).

19. The logic for the left and right parts is symmetric, except we exchanged the roles of `inputValue` and its associated `MapStates`. So, here, we created a method and interface that help us reuse the code. Note the symmetry between both `if` branches. We've only included the first part here; you can easily find the other in the source code:

```
if (isLeft) {
  handleProduct(
    left,
    right,
    primaryKey,
    joinKey,
    (L) inputValue,
    (j, lk, lv, rk, rv, r) ->
      output.output(JoinResult.of(
        j, lk, (L) lv, rk, (R) rv, r)));
}
```

20. The `handleProduct` method creates the outputs. We will not walk through the code here as it is more or less pure Java. Instead, we will describe the logic. If we receive an element from the left- or right-hand side, we must pair it with all the values present in `MapState` of the other side. That way, we can produce a correct Cartesian product, even though the values arrive one by one. If we have a previous value associated with the key, we need to do the same (pair the old value with all the contents of the other side's `MapState`) but output each pair as a retraction since it should be removed and replaced with the new value.

And that's it – we have implemented a fully functional streaming inner join. Congrats! Let's now see how to test it and how to use it in our SportTracker motivation task.

> **Important note**
>
> If we wanted to implement an outer join, we would have to complicate the code by adding a timer. We would not be able to emit a one-side result as this would result in either the left or right value being missing from the @ProcessElement method. This is because the missing element may still arrive. We would have to use a timer, which will tell us that there will be no more data within the given timestamp. We didn't want to complicate the already not so straightforward code here, so we left this as an open exercise for you.

Testing our solution

As we mentioned while discussing the problem, we will use our four examples of joins, run our transform against those exact inputs, and verify that we received the expected output. The complete tests can be found in com.packtpub.beam.chapter4. StreamingInnerJoinTest. We will briefly walk through the most complex one – testJoinWithMultiValuesLeftAndRight – which tests the situation shown in *Figure 4.18*:

1. First, we need to create our input. We don't need to explicitly manipulate the watermark in this test, so instead of TestStream, we can use the Create transform, as follows:

```
PCollection<KV<String, String>> left =
  p.apply(
    Create.timestamped(
      TimestampedValue.of(KV.of("alice", "CA"), now),
      TimestampedValue.of(KV.of("bob", "CA"),
        now.plus(Duration.standardDays(1)))));
```

2. Now, we must create the right-hand side input in the same way:

```
PCollection<KV<String, String>> right =
  p.apply(
    Create.timestamped(
      TimestampedValue.of(
        KV.of("CA.1", "Los Angeles"), now),
      TimestampedValue.of(
        KV.of("CA.2", "San Francisco"),
        now.plus(Duration.standardDays(1))),
```

```
TimestampedValue.of(
    KV.of("CA.1", ""),
    now.plus(Duration.standardDays(2)))));
```

3. To apply our join, we need two tuple tags representing the left- and right-hand sides of the join and to create a `PCollectionTuple` from it:

```
TupleTag<KV<String, String>> leftTag = new TupleTag<>();
TupleTag<KV<String, String>> rightTag = new TupleTag<>();
PCollectionTuple joinInput = PCollectionTuple
  .of(leftTag, left)
  .and(rightTag, right);
```

4. The next step is to apply our transform:

```
joinInput
  .apply(
    new StreamingInnerJoin<>(
      leftTag,
      rightTag,
      KV::getKey,
      KV::getKey,
      KV::getValue,
      r -> r.getKey().substring(0, 2),
      StringUtf8Coder.of(),
      StringUtf8Coder.of()))
```

The most interesting part of the preceding code is how we extract our join key from the primary key on the right-hand side. The primary key is, for instance, `CA.1`, so we only need the first two characters from it.

5. Next, we will apply formatting – that is, converting the outputs into a string and adding a + or – sign based on whether it is an addition or retraction to easily `PAssert` the output – and add timestamps via `Reify.timestamps()`. The last step is to actually assert that we get the output shown in *Figure 4.18*:

```
PAssert.that(result)
  .containsInAnyOrder(
    TimestampedValue.of("+alice:CA:Los Angeles", now),
    TimestampedValue.of("+bob:CA:Los Angeles",
      now.plus(Duration.standardDays(1))),
```

```
TimestampedValue.of("+alice:CA:San Francisco",
    now.plus(Duration.standardDays(1))),
TimestampedValue.of("+bob:CA:San Francisco",
    now.plus(Duration.standardDays(1))),
TimestampedValue.of("-alice:CA:Los Angeles",
    now.plus(Duration.standardDays(2))),
TimestampedValue.of("-bob:CA:Los Angeles",
    now.plus(Duration.standardDays(2))),
TimestampedValue.of("+alice:CA:",
    now.plus(Duration.standardDays(2))),
TimestampedValue.of("+bob:CA:",
    now.plus(Duration.standardDays(2))));
```

6. As always, do not forget to run the pipeline; otherwise, the test will succeed, even if the code is not correct:

```
p.run();
```

The other tests are analogous to this one, so we'll skip them here. You can walk through these tests yourself to verify that they match the cases depicted in *Figure 4.15*, *Figure 4.16*, and *Figure 4.17*.

Deploying our solution

We have successfully implemented and tested a fully reusable generic transform, so to deploy it, we need a concrete instance. We will slightly modify our previous version of the SportTracker motivation solution in the `SportTrackerMotivation UsingJoinLibrary` class to create `SportTrackerMotivationUsingOwnJoin`. This change lies mostly in the way we apply the join, so instead of using the join library, we will use our implementation, as follows:

```
TupleTag<KV<String, Double>> longTag = new TupleTag<>();
TupleTag<KV<String, Double>> shortTag = new TupleTag<>();
PCollection<JoinResult<String, String, KV<String, Double>,
KV<String, Double>>> joined =
  PCollectionTuple.of(longTag, longAverage)
    .and(shortTag, shortAverage)
    .apply(
      "joinWithShort",
      new StreamingInnerJoin<>(
```

```
        longTag,
        shortTag,
        KV::getKey,
        KV::getKey,
        KV::getKey,
        KV::getKey,
        StringUtf8Coder.of(),
        StringUtf8Coder.of()));
```

Note that due to how we calculate our long- and short-term averages (within fixed windows), this approach will yield the same results as using the Join library but will cost more. This is because the full streaming join is more resource-intensive and has more strict requirements regarding droppable data. So, in practice, this approach would be discouraged – we have included it here to have a simple and provable `Pipeline` that can run our join.

In the last section of this chapter, we will explore the properties of tables that change over time and two types of streams.

Table-stream duality

We will conclude this chapter with something that should already feel natural but is worth noting explicitly – that is, **table-stream duality**. We will use this concept in the next chapter, but because we have already worked with primary keys, join keys, and values, the definition naturally fits into this chapter.

We have seen two types of streams supporting deletions – **upsert streams** and **retract streams**. The main difference is that the upsert stream has an explicit primary key, while the retract stream can contain exact duplicates. Let's define a specific reduction operation for each of these streams and see what would happen if we were to apply it to these particular streams:

- If the stream is a retract stream, then in addition, simply add the input element to a list and on retraction, find the matching element in the list and remove it.

- If the stream is an upsert stream, keep the data in a map with a key that's the primary key of each element. Then, replace the associated value on each upsert, or remove the key from the map if the value is `null`.

The first approach is illustrated in the following diagram:

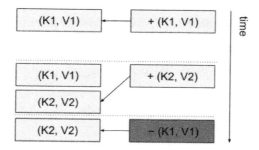

Figure 4.17 – A retract table stream reduction

We ended up with three versions of our list:

1. First, the list contained only the *[(K1, V1)]* element.

2. Next, the list contained two elements; that is, *[(K1, V1) and (K2, V2)]*.

3. Lastly, the list contained only one element; that is, *[(K2, V2)]*.

    But wait – does that mean we received three versions of a *table*? The answer is (without surprise) yes – what we have is a table that changes over time.

    Now, let's do the same for the upsert stream, as follows:

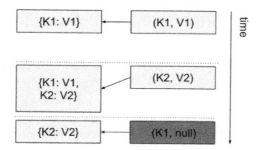

Figure 4.18 – An upsert table stream reduction

Again, we end up with three versions of our map – and again, a map can be viewed as a table, where each key value represents a single line.

In the same way that we can create a table from a stream, it is possible to create a stream from a table. Every time the table changes, we record the change as either an addition/retraction or a new key value for a primary key, depending on whether the table has a primary key. Because we can transform the table into a stream and back, we have what we call **table-stream duality**.

The last consequence of this is that – as mentioned at the beginning of the *Introducing the Join library DSL* section – a table is a relation. If a stream can be converted into a table that changes over time, this implies that it can be converted into a relation. A relation that changes over time is known as a **time-varying relation**. We use relational algebra to manipulate relational data – this algebra is used through a language called SQL. Can we use SQL to query streaming data? Yes. We'll learn about this in the next chapter!

Summary

In this chapter, we investigated various ways to effectively structure our code to enable better reusability. We learned how to write our own `PTransform` and how the `PTransform` **expansion** works. We saw different types of objects serving as `PInput` – input objects to `PTransform` – or `POutput` – the output objects of `PTransform`. We looked at the most common examples of these objects – `PCollection`, `PCollectionList`, and `PCollectionTuple`. We also looked at two special cases – `PBegin` and `PDone` – which serve as the root and leaf nodes in the computational DAG, respectively. We also learned about the `CoGroupByKey` composite transform, which can be used to perform **windowed joins**.

Then, we explored a DSL that offers a wrapper around `CoGroupByKey` – the **Join library**. This library offers all types of windowed joins – inner joins, one-sided outer joins, and full outer joins. We used this library to create an extension of our `SportTracker` application by enhancing it with runner motivation. We implemented several solutions for this problem based on `CoGroupByKey` and using side inputs.

The last part of this chapter was dedicated to understanding and implementing a full-flavored stream-to-stream inner join. We understood how **upsert streams** and **retract streams** work, what the expected streaming join semantics are, and how these semantics reduce to windowed (and classical batch global window) joins. We designed a `StreamingInnerJoin` transform from scratch to see how a fully generic DSL-type `PTransform` can be implemented.

We concluded this chapter by describing table-stream duality, a time-varying relation, and built a base for the start of the next chapter – *Chapter 5, Using SQL for Pipeline Implementation*. So, let's see how it works!

5
Using SQL for Pipeline Implementation

In the previous chapter, we explored how to view a stream as a changing table and vice versa. We also recalled that a table has a fancy name – a **relation** – and that a table that changes over time is called a **Time-Varying Relation (TVR)**. In this chapter, we will use this knowledge to make our lives easier when implementing real-life problems. Instead of writing a full-blown pipeline in the **Java SDK** – which can sometimes be a little lengthy – we will use a well-known language to express our data transforms. As the name of this chapter suggests, this language will be **Structured Query Language (SQL)**. The language itself needs some extensions to be able to manipulate the TVRs since the original version was not time-sensitive – the data was presumed to be static at the time of querying it.

Because SQL is a strongly typed language (a **Domain Specific Language (DSL)**, actually), we will need to have strong type information about our `PCollections`. We already know that **Apache Beam** has the concept of `Coder`; a `Coder` is an object that is responsible for serializing and deserializing Java objects present in a `PCollection` to and from a binary representation that can be transferred over the wire for distributed computation (among other things). This will not be enough for SQL. The type information that's brought by `Coder` is too weak for SQL to work, so we will need something new. This new concept is called a **schema**.

In this chapter, we will cover the following topics:

- Understanding schemas
- Implementing our first streaming pipeline using SQL
- Task 14 – Implementing SQLMaxWordLength
- Task 15 – Implementing SchemaSportTracker
- Task 16 – Implementing SQLSportTrackerMotivation
- Further development of Apache Beam SQL

As we can see, we will reuse a lot of tasks we have already solved using the Java SDK. The reason for this is that we can easily understand the benefits that SQL will bring us for solving some of the *simpler* tasks. Of course – as always with every tool – the SQL DSL is only suitable for solving some tasks. When dealing with low-level states and timers, which was the main subject of *Chapter 3, Implementing Pipelines Using Stateful Processing*, SQL probably won't help us. But even in these cases, we can use it to implement some parts of the pipeline, while others will need a more low-level approach.

Technical requirements

As always, please make sure that you have the current `main` branch cloned from this book's GitHub and that you have set up **minikube** based on the instructions provided in *Chapter 1, Introducing Data Processing with Apache Beam*. You will also need working knowledge of SQL as we will use it extensively in this chapter. Once all of this is ready, we can dive directly into schemas!

Understanding schemas

A **schema** is a way of describing a nested structure of a Java object. A typical Java object contains **fields** that have string names and data types.

Let's see the following Java class:

```
public class Position {
    double latitude;
    double longitude;
}
```

This class has two fields called `latitude` and `longitude`, respectively, both of which are of the `double` type. The matching `Schema` property of this class would be as follows:

```
Position: Row
    latitude: double
    longitude: double
```

This notation declared a `Position` type with a schema of the `Row` type containing two fields, `latitude` and `longitude`, both of the `double` type. A `Row` is one of Apache Beam's built-in schema types with a nested structure – the others are `Array`, `Iterable`, and `Map` with their usual definitions in computer science. The difference between `Array` and `Iterable` is that `Iterable` does not have a known size until it's iterated over. This is to allow large collections that might not fit into memory to be processed; for example, the result of `GroupByKey`.

Now, let's learn how to declare a schema on a `PCollection` and see what benefits this will bring us!

Attaching a schema to a PCollection

There are multiple ways of assigning a schema to a `PCollection` – the simplest one is to let `Schema` be *inferred* automatically. Sounds good, right? Well, almost. Let's learn how to do this for our `Position` class:

```
@DefaultSchema(JavaFieldSchema.class)
public class Position {
    double latitude;
    double longitude;
    @SchemaCreate
    public Position(double latitude, double longitude) { ... }
}
```

This declaration tells Apache Beam to use a `JavaFieldSchema` class, which is a built-in implementation of `SchemaProvider` for a class. The class then has to provide a constructor or a static method that will return an instance of the class whose *arguments names match the names of the corresponding fields*. That way, Apache Beam will be able to infer the data types and also know how to reconstruct the Java object from the fields.

Another possibility is to use a **Java bean**, another built-in `SchemaProvider` known as `JavaBeanSchema`:

```
@DefaultSchema(JavaBeanSchema.class)
public class Position {
    double latitude;
    double longitude;
    public Position() { }
    public double getLatitude() { ... }
    public double getLongitude() { ... }
    public void setLatitude(double latitude) { ... }
    public void setLongitude(double longitude) { ... }
}
```

Java Beans are classes that are most notably standardized in the way they modify and access their field types – they have standardized names for getter and setter methods, which are then used by Apache Beam to infer the corresponding `Schema`. This inference can be further affected using the `@SchemaFieldName` and `@SchemaIgnore` annotations:

```
@DefaultSchema(JavaFieldSchema.class)
public class Position {
    @SchemaFieldName("latitude")
    double _lat;
    @SchemaFieldName("longitude"
    double _lon;
    @SchemaIgnore
    String _provider;
    @SchemaCreate
    public Position(double latitude, double longitude) {
        ...
    }
}
```

> **Important note**
>
> Warning: To be able to use `Schema` inference using `JavaFieldSchema` and `SchemaProvider`, you must compile your sources using the `-parameters javac` command-line argument to preserve the names of method parameters in the compiled bytecode. Otherwise, the inference will fail and complain about a non-matching parameter name called `arg0`.

If we have a default `Schema` inference for a class, then the inferred schema will be attached to a `PCollection` every time we create a `PCollection` of the corresponding type. In the preceding case, this happens whenever we create a `PCollection<Position>`.

The other option is to attach a `Schema` to a `PCollection` manually. In that case, we need to create the actual `Schema` first, as follows:

```
Schema = new Builder()
  .addDoubleField("latitude")
  .addDoubleField("longitude")
  .addInt64Field("timestamp")
  .build();
```

This `Schema` can represent the `Position` object from `SportTracker` tasks. Then, we can apply this `Schema` to a `PCollection` analogously using `setCoder`, but in this case, we need to provide additional functions to convert a `Row` into our object and back:

```
result.setSchema(
  schema,
  TypeDescriptor.of(Position.class),
  pos ->
    Row.withSchema(schema)
      .withFieldValue("latitude", pos.getLatitude())
      .withFieldValue("longitude", pos.getLongitude())
      .withFieldValue("timestamp", pos.getTimestamp())
      .build(),
  r ->
    new Position(
      r.getDouble("latitude"),
      r.getDouble("longitude"),
      r.getInt64("timestamp")));
```

As we can see, the manual approach is more flexible but requires much more work.

Once we have a `PCollection` with a `Schema` attached (either inferred or manually assigned), we can apply a variety of new `PTransforms` to it or use a functionality previously not possible. One of these functionalities is a specific transform requiring a `Schema`, as we will see in the next section.

Transforms for PCollections with schemas

Once we have created a `PCollection` with a `Schema` attached, we can use several `PTransforms` that would not work without it.

Filter

The first example of such a transform would be a different (from what we saw earlier) version of the `Filter` transform that works on a specific field, as follows:

```
PCollection<AutoSchemaPosition> positions = ...;
positions
  .apply(
     Filter.<AutoSchemaPosition>create()
        .<Double>whereFieldName("latitude", f -> f > 0.0))
```

This code will filter only elements whose value in the `latitude` field is greater than zero.

Convert

One of the most useful transforms is converting into `Row`. We will work extensively with `Row` types of `PCollections` in the upcoming sections in this chapter, so let's learn how to create them:

```
PCollection<Row> rows = positions.apply(Convert.toRows());
```

This will work whenever we have a `Schema` available for the `PCollection` object we apply this transform to. What is notable about schemas is that different Java objects can have the same `Schema`. This follows the fact of how we can create a `PCollection` with a `Schema` by inferring from the fields of a class. This is a one-way process; converting a `Row` into an object requires a `Class` object to be able to recreate the instance. For instance, if we have a `Row` with a single field of the `int64` type, we can use the following code to convert the single field into a `Long`:

```
PCollection<Long> longs = rows.apply(Convert.to(Long.class));
```

This conversion generally requires registering the classes in `SchemaRegistry`. This is done the same way as we can use `setSchema` on a `PCollection` – we need to register `Class`, `Schema`, and the two conversion functions – one for converting `Row` into our `Object` and the other for converting it back.

Select

Besides `Convert`, we can use the `Select` transform to convert a `PCollection` with a `Schema` into a `PCollection<Row>`:

```
PCollection<Row> rows = positions.apply(Select.create());
```

The preceding code will select all the fields, but we can use a *projection* and select only a subset of the actual fields of the complete `Schema`:

```
PCollection<Row> rows = positions.apply(
    Select.fieldNames("latitude", "longitude"));
```

This will result in a `PCollection<Row>`, which will have only the selected subset of all the fields in the original `Schema`.

The `Select` transform has a mini DSL for selecting fields in various situations. Let's take a quick look at it:

1. For selecting a field from a nested `Row`, use the dot notation:

   ```
   Select.fieldNames("nested.field")
   ```

2. For selecting all the fields in a nested `Row`, use the wildcard notation:

   ```
   Select.fieldNames("nested.*")
   ```

3. For selecting a sub-array from an array of rows, use the following:

   ```
   Select.fieldNames("arrayOfRows[].field")
   ```

   This will result in an array that's the same type as the `field` property of the input `Row` array.

4. Lastly, for selecting a field with a given name from a map type, use the following:

   ```
   Select.fieldNames("mapType{}.field")
   ```

A `Schema` attached to a `PCollection` also impacts the functionality of existing `PTransforms` – for example, `ParDo`, which we will see in the following subsection.

Implications on ParDo

A PCollection with a Schema can be used just like any other PCollection with regard to ParDo transforms. The schema that's present in PCollection enables several new features:

1. An implicit type conversion between types with the same Schema:

```
positions.appy(ParDo.of(new DoFn<Position, Position>() {
  @ProcessElement
  public void processElement(
    @Element Row purchase,
    ...) { ... }
}))
```

2. The possibility to select only a projection of fields from the input Schema:

```
positions.appy(ParDo.of(new DoFn<Position, Position>() {
  @ProcessElement
  public void process(
    @FieldAccess("latitude") double latitude,
    @FieldAccess("longitude") double longitude,
    ...) { ... }}));
```

The syntax for the @FieldAccess selector is the same as for the Convert transform, which we mentioned earlier.

Group and Join

In *Task 15 – Implementing SchemaSportTracker*, we will learn how to apply a grouping operation on a PCollection with a schema to retrieve a Row, which we may then use to perform other queries using SqlTransform. The Group transform is currently a little more semantically expressive than its SQL variant, which we will see in the aforementioned task.

The Join transform can be used analogously to the Group transform, but we will prefer the SQL variant, which we will see in *Task 16 – Implementing SQLSportTrackerMotivation*. Please refer to the online documentation of Apache Beam for an explanation and examples of how to use the Join transform directly.

Now that we have walked through all the important properties of schemas, let's dive into some practical coding again!

Implementing our first streaming pipeline using SQL

We will follow the same path that we walked when we started playing with the Java SDK of Apache Beam. The very first pipeline we implemented, which was in *Chapter 1, Introducing Data Processing with Apache Beam*, was a pipeline that read input from a resource file named lorem.txt. Our goal was to process this file and output the number of occurrences of words within that file. So, let's see how our solution would differ if we used SQL to solve it!

We have implemented the equivalent of com.packtpub.beam.chapter1. FirstPipeline in com.packtpub.beam.chapter5.FirstSQLPipeline. The main differences are summarized here:

1. First, we need to create a Schema that will represent our input. The input is raw lines of text as String objects, so a possible Schema representing it is a single-field Schema defined as follows:

```
Schema lineSchema = Schema.of(
    Field.of("s", FieldType.STRING));
```

2. We then attach this schema to our input, which we materialize using the Create transform, as follows:

```
Create.of(lines)
  .withSchema(
    lineSchema,
     TypeDescriptors.strings(),
     s -> Row.withSchema(lineSchema).attachValues(s),
     r -> r.getString("s"))
```

3. Once we have a Schema defined for our PCollection, we can convert it into a PCollection<Row> using the following code:

```
PCollection<Row> rows = input.apply(Convert.toRows())
```

4. Once we have a PCollection of a Row, we can apply a SqlTransform, as follows:

```
PCollection<Row> resultRows = rows.apply(
  SqlTransform.query(
    "SELECT s as word, COUNT(*) as c FROM "
     + "PCOLLECTION GROUP BY s"))
```

5. The result of `SqlTransform` is `PCollection<Row>`; the schema is defined by the SQL query. In the preceding example, it would have two fields – one named `word` of the `String` type and another named `c` of the 64-bit integer (long) type. We can extract the result in a `KV<String, Long>` (which is the same as we had in our `FirstPipeline` example) and then map the Rows into KVs using the following transform:

```
MapElements
  .into(
    TypeDescriptors.kvs(TypeDescriptors.strings(),
    TypeDescriptors.longs()))
  .via(r -> KV.of(r.getString("word"), r.getInt64("c")))
```

6. We can run this *pipeline* the same way we did in *Chapter 1, Introducing Data Processing with Apache Beam*:

```
chapter5$ ../mvnw exec:java \
  -Dexec.mainClass=com.packtpub.beam.chapter5.
FirstSQLPipeline
```

Here, we can see that the output is the same as in the first chapter, with the same caveat; the order of the outputs (as opposed to the actual computed values) is not deterministically defined but can change with each run.

Let's see how our query changes when we create a `TestStream` with a schema to simulate a streaming source:

1. First, note that we need to pass a Schema to `TestStream.create`:

```
Schema lineSchema =   Schema.of(
    Field.of("word", FieldType.STRING),
    Field.of("ts", FieldType.DATETIME));

TestStream.Builder<Row> streamBuilder =
    TestStream.create(lineSchema);
```

2. Next, we must create `Row` objects for each word. We will need a field for the timestamp, which we will fill as follows:

```
Row.withSchema(lineSchema)
    .withFieldValue("word", w)
    .withFieldValue("ts", now.plus(i))
    .build()
```

3. Then, we must create `PCollection<Row>` directly by applying our `TestStream` to the pipeline:

```
PCollection<Row> input = pipeline.apply(
    streamBuilder.advanceWatermarkToInfinity());
```

4. The last required change is in the query itself. Since our input is now unbounded, we must provide a non-default `WindowFn`. We have several options here, with one possibility being specifying the window function in the query, as follows:

```
input
  .apply(
    SqlTransform.query(
        "SELECT word, COUNT(*) as c FROM PCOLLECTION "
            + "GROUP BY word, TUMBLE(ts, INTERVAL '1'
DAY)"))
```

5. The `GROUP BY TUMBLE(ts, INTERVAL '1' DAY)` statement says to use `SqlTransform` to use a fixed window for a duration of 1 day. SQL uses the `TUMBLE`, `HOP`, and `SESSION` functions, which correspond to fixed, sliding, and session windows, respectively. All these functions need a `TIMESTAMP` type field, which is used to assign the window. The function must then be called as part of the `GROUP BY` statement.

The `GROUP BY TUMBLE(ts, INTERVAL '1' DAY)` statement tells `SqlTransform` to use a fixed window of a duration of 1 day. SQL uses the `TUMBLE`, `HOP`, and `SESSION` functions, which correspond to fixed, sliding, and session windows, respectively. All these functions need a `TIMESTAMP` type field, which is used to assign the window. The function must then be called as part of the `GROUP BY` statement.

6. The complete code for our first streaming SQL pipeline can be found in the `com.packtpub.beam.chapter5.FirstStreamingSQLPipeline` class. We can run it by using the same command that we used previously:

```
chapter5$ ../mvnw exec:java \
    -Dexec.mainClass=\
com.packtpub.beam.chapter5.FirstStreamingSQLPipeline
```

In this section, we have seen very simplistic use of Apache Beam SQL. In the following sections, we will walk through more and more complex examples. By reimplementing already well-known tasks, we will see the simplifications we can gain in more complex cases.

Task 14 – Implementing SQLMaxWordLength

In *Chapter 2, Implementing, Testing, and Deploying Basic Pipelines*, we implemented a pipeline called `MaxWordLength`. In this task, we will reimplement it by using SQL and schemas. Note that although we already know how to structure code better and use `PTransforms` rather than using static methods to transform one `PCollection` into another, we will keep the approach from the original chapter so that we can easily spot the differences and compare both versions more easily.

For clarity, let's restate the problem.

Problem definition

Given a stream of text lines in Apache Kafka, create a stream consisting of the longest word seen in the stream from the beginning to the present. Use triggering to output the result as frequently as possible. Use Apache Beam SQL to implement the task whenever possible.

Problem decomposition discussion

The interesting parts will be centered around several problems that we need to solve:

1. How do we convert a line into a SQL result set containing words on each line?

2. How do we express the aggregation function that computes the longest word?

3. How do we specify our trigger (`AfterPane.elementCountAtLeast(1)`), which we need for the most frequent result emission?

Let's start with the last point. As we already know, DSLs (and SQL is a DSL) in Apache Beam are built as PTransforms –SqlTransform is not an exception. Each PTransform receives an input PCollection in its expand method. If PTransform (or any PTransform that it expands to) does not change its windowing strategy (including triggering), then the windowing strategy is preserved. And that is the answer to *question 3*; we need to specify the triggering before applying SqlTransform. The SQL syntax itself currently does not have a way to specify it.

The answers to *questions 1 and 2* share the same concept – **User-Defined Functions (UDFs)**. Apache Beam allows us to register a UDF for arbitrarily transforming data using SerializableFunction, which is a stateless transform – in our case, from String (representing line) to List<String> (representing words). Next, we need to transform the list of strings into a set of rows – which is what the UNNEST function is for.

Last, we will learn how to register a **User Defined Aggregate Function (UDAF)**, which we will use to aggregate (via a CombineFn) the longest word from a set of words. Now, that's enough theory, let's see how it works in code!

Solution implementation

As always, please see the full source code in the com.packtpub.beam.chapter5. SQLMaxWordLength class. As we mentioned previously, we have used the same structure of the source code as in the original com.packtpub.beam.chapter2. MaxWordLength so that we can highlight the differences. All the business logic is located in the computeLongestWord method. As usual, we will walk through the most relevant parts here:

1. First, we need to apply a Window transform to specify the trigger. As we mentioned previously, SQL currently has no way of expressing triggering but preserves it, if specified before SqlTransform:

```
lines
  .apply(
      Window.<String>into(new GlobalWindows()
        .triggering(
            Repeatedly.forever(
                AfterPane.elementCountAtLeast(1)))
        .withAllowedLateness(Duration.ZERO)
        .accumulatingFiredPanes())
```

2. The next step is to use a Schema and convert PCollection<String> into PCollection<Row>. We have created a (very simple) PTransform to add a Schema with a single String field called WithStringSchema. This class is located in the util package, so please feel free to investigate it yourself:

```
.apply(WithStringSchema.of("line"))
.apply(Convert.toRows())
```

3. Once we have a PCollection<Row>, we can apply SqlTransform. The syntax Apache Beam uses (by default) is the **Apache Calcite** SQL dialect. The complete syntax can be found online (see https://calcite.apache.org/docs/reference.html). Providing a complete walkthrough is outside the scope of this book, but we will highlight the most important parts here. The first one is the WITH keyword, which can be used to define a variable that is represented by some SELECT statement so that it can be used later as a (temporary) table. This is exactly what we do inside our SqlTransform on the first SQL line to define a *temporary table* called tokenized:

```
WITH tokenized AS (SELECT TOKENIZE(line) AS words
    FROM PCOLLECTION),
```

4. TOKENIZE is a UDF that we will define in a few moments. What we need to know now is that it takes String and returns List<String>, which represents tokenized words. The tokenized table contains a List<String> on each row. This is not what we need; we need a single word on each line, which is why we apply UNNEST to retrieve a temporary table called words:

```
words AS (SELECT EXPR$0 word
    FROM UNNEST(SELECT * FROM tokenized))
```

Note the EXPR$0 field –Apache Calcite's default name for fields without explicit naming.

5. Once we have the table containing words, we can aggregate the longest word by using LONGEST_WORD:

```
SELECT LONGEST_WORD(word) FROM words
```

6. We are missing the definitions of TOKENIZE and LONGEST_WORD. Let's begin with the first one. The method for registering a UDF is called SqlTransform. registerUdf. Note that due to some limitations of the Beam Calcite SQL dialect, we must provide a UDF called SerializableFunction using a fully declared class with a public default constructor (which means we cannot use Lambda functions):

```
.registerUdf("TOKENIZE", new TokenizeFn())
```

TokenizeFn is simply defined as a wrapper around Utils.toWords, which we used in the previous chapters as well:

```
public static class TokenizeFn
        implements SerializableFunction<String, List<String>>
    {
    @Override
    public List<String> apply(String input) {
        return Utils.toWords(input);
    }
}
```

7. Next is the LONGEST_WORD UDAF – an aggregation function takes a CombineFn and produces the result according to this function. Note that we need to be able to retrieve the output type of CombineFn at runtime, which should work for most CombineFns, but we might get into trouble when using a CombineFn that is generic (as in the case of MaxFn). Luckily, we can wrap the generic CombineFn into an anonymous class, which will make the generic arguments available at runtime, as follows:

```
.registerUdaf(
    "LONGEST_WORD",
    new TypedCombineFnDelegate<>(
        Max.of(
            (Comparator<String> & Serializable)
                (a, b) -> Integer.compare(
                    a.length(), b.length()))) {}))
```

8. Finally, we only convert the result from `PCollection<Row>` back into `PCollection<String>`:

```
.apply(
    MapElements
        .into(TypeDescriptors.strings())
        .via(r -> r.getString(0)));
```

And that is it – we have reimplemented `MaxWordLength` using SQL. As we can see, we did not gain too much from this. The reason for this is that the original problem was still quite simple and the benefits of SQL appear on more complex pipelines. We will see this in the following tasks. We will skip the testing and deployment part as that is the same as in the original `MaxWordLength` task in *Chapter 2, Implementing, Testing, and Deploying Basic Pipelines*. Instead, we will move on to the next task to get more from our `SqlTransform`!

Task 15 – Implementing SchemaSportTracker

In this section, we will reimplement a task from *Chapter 2, Implementing, Testing, and Deploying Basic Pipelines*. We have included this to learn how to overcome some limitations of SQL when using schemas – notably, the (current) inability to perform aggregation (UDAF) using multiple fields. In our computation, we need to aggregate a composite (a Row) that has three fields – `latitude`, `longitude`, and `timestamp`.

Again, for clarity, let's recap the definition of our problem.

Problem definition

Given a stream of GPS locations and timestamps for a workout of a specific user (a workout has an ID that is guaranteed to be unique among all users), compute the performance metrics for each workout. These metrics should contain the total duration and distance elapsed from the start of the workout to the present.

Problem decomposition discussion

The actual business logic of computing the distance from GPS location data was implemented in the `com.packtpub.beam.chapter2.SportTracker` class and we will simply reuse it here. The interesting part is how we would transform the grouped location data into the required metrics. And the answer is, again, a UDAF. If we had the option to register a UDAF for a composite type, our `SqlTransform` query would have looked something like this:

```
SELECT workoutId, TO_METRIC(position) FROM
    PCOLLECTION GROUP BY workoutId;
```

This query supposes that our `Schema` is defined as follows:

```
workoutId: string
position: Row
   latitude: double
   longitude: double
   timestamp: int64
```

Here, the task of the `TO_METRIC` UDAF would be to aggregate the `position` property of Row with the `latitude`, `longitude`, and `timestamp` fields to produce a final metric for a workout. Unfortunately, at the time of writing this book – at least up to Apache Beam version 2.31.0 – this is not possible. This is likely to change in future releases, but we have to work around this problem for now. We will use this as motivation to explore the `Group` transform for `PCollection` with a `Schema` (not limited to Row, as in the case of `SqlTransform`) and see how we can use its built-in ability to aggregate over multiple fields.

Solution implementation

The complete implementation is, again, at your disposal in the `com.packtpub.beam.chapter5.SchemaSportTracker` class. Let's take a closer look:

1. First, we must mention that we take for granted that we already have methods for computing the distance between two GPS locations. We will also not discuss how we read and store input as that has not changed from the original version. So, we will only focus on the logic in the `computeTrackerMetrics` method here.

2. Next, as we did in the previous task, we need to apply a `Window` transform to specify allowed lateness and triggering. As we already know, these properties are preserved.

3. After the `window` function, we need to specify a schema for `PCollection`. This schema is not defined by the source, so we must add it manually. Although the *real* schema is a nested `Row`, for the sake of this task, we can flatten it into the following:

```
private static Schema rowSchema =
    Schema.of(
        Field.of("workoutId", FieldType.STRING),
        Field.of("latitude", FieldType.DOUBLE),
        Field.of("longitude", FieldType.DOUBLE),
        Field.of("ts", FieldType.INT64));
```

4. Our `PCollection` is of the `KV<String, Position>` type, but we can easily apply the preceding `Schema` to it:

```
.setSchema(
  rowSchema,
  TypeDescriptors.kvs(
    TypeDescriptors.strings(),
    TypeDescriptor.of(Position.class)),
  kv ->
    Row.withSchema(rowSchema)
      .attachValues(
        kv.getKey(),
        kv.getValue().getLatitude(),
        kv.getValue().getLongitude(),
        kv.getValue().getTimestamp()),
  r -> KV.of(
    r.getString(0),
    new Position(
      r.getDouble(1), r.getDouble(2), r.getInt64(3))))
```

The interesting part here is how we transform the data from `KV<String, Position>` into `Row` and back. Note that we can use numerical indices of fields, which has a little better performance than accessing fields by name. On the other hand, the index is sensitive to field permutations within `Schema`, while names are not. The index of a field is defined by the order it appears in `Schema`. The same is true for the `attachValues` method, which adds all the fields to a `Row` in one call, but the order of the fields must match the schema.

5. Once we have a `Schema` on our `PCollection` (still of the `KV<String, Position>` type), we can apply the `Group` transforms:

```
.apply(
  Group.<KV<String, Position>>byFieldIds(0)
   .aggregateFields(
     Arrays.asList("latitude", "longitude", "ts"),
     new MetricUdaf(),
     Field.of("metric", FieldType.row(METRIC_SCHEMA))));
```

The previous code tells Apache Beam to extract the first field as a key and three fields called `latitude`, `longitude`, and `ts`, group the elements by the first, and then apply a `CombineFn` called `MetricUdaf`. The input type of `CombineFn` has to be `Row` because that is what Apache Beam converts the `latitude`, `longitude`, and `ts` fields into. The output of the `Group` transform is a `PCollection<Row>`, with `Schema` having two fields called `key` and `value`, where `key` has a single field called `workoutId` (which was our aggregation field, we can specify multiple aggregation fields) and `value` has a schema specified in the `aggregateFields` method – in our case, `METRIC_SCHEMA` (see sources). Note that when in doubt, you can extract a schema from a `PCollection` (using `PCollection.getSchema()`) and print it to help with debugging or its implementation. If we print `Schema` of the resulting grouped `PCollection`, we will get something like this:

```
Fields:
Field{name=key, description=, type=ROW<workoutId STRING
NOT NULL> NOT NULL, options={{}}}
Field{name=value, description=, type=ROW<metric
ROW<distance DOUBLE NOT NULL, duration INT64 NOT NULL>
NOT NULL> NOT NULL, options={{}}}
Encoding positions:
{value=1, key=0}
Options:{{}}UUID: 199743aa-5c2e-48f6-b4af-eb1b3c8c153a
```

6. We will leave walking through the code of `MetricUdaf` on you as it is only a list aggregation that sorts by timestamp and outputs the resulting distance and duration.

The test and deployment stages are the same as in the corresponding `SportTracker` task, so we will skip this here. Instead, we will demonstrate how SQL (and schemas) can help us when we are dealing with joins – which is what we did when we were implementing our `SportTrackerMovation` example. So, let's reimplement that as well!

Task 16 – Implementing SQLSportTrackerMotivation

In this task, we will explore the benefits that SQL DSL brings us when it comes to more complex pipelines that are composed of several aggregations, joins, and so on. Again, as a recap, let's restate the problem definition.

Problem definition

Given a GPS location stream per workout (the same as in the previous task), create another stream that would contain information if the runner increased or decreased pace in the past minute by more than 10% compared to the average pace over the last 5 minutes. Again, use SQL DSL as much as possible.

The test and deployment are the same as in the corresponding `SportTracker` task, so we will skip this here. Instead, we will demonstrate how SQL (and schemas) can help us when we are dealing with joins – which is what we did when we were implementing our `SportTrackerMovation` example. So, let's reimplement that as well!

Problem decomposition discussion

In the original `SportTrackerMotivation` task, as defined in *Chapter 4*, *Structuring Code for Reusability*, we introduced a user-defined `PTransform` to reuse the computation of the average pace over a certain time interval (5 minutes in a sliding window or a 1-minute fixed window). The SQL approach is simpler in that expressing the logic (computing the average pace) is simple enough that we don't have to bother creating a reusable transform and can simply redeclare the computation using two SQL statements. This is because it should not significantly increase the maintenance burden.

When we solved this task for the first time, we spent some time figuring out how to get the correct alignment regarding the pace metrics within the fixed and sliding windows – we will reuse the `ToMetric` transform in this task as well. As we've already mentioned several times, SQL is a DSL and, as such, should be used in cases where it can save implementation time or improve the future maintainability of the code. Low-level stateful transforms – as is the case of the `ToMetric` transform – are better written in the SDK itself.

Solution implementation

The complete implementation for this task can be found in the com.packtpub.beam. chapter5.SQLSportTrackerMotivation class. We have kept the structure the same as it was in the previous cases where we were dealing with this problem, so the main focus will be on the modified expand method of PTransform. Let's get started:

1. We will need to set Schema to our PCollection to be able to use it via SQL. Because of the current way SQL windowing works, we need a TIMESTAMP field, although it is already part of the Apache Beam model and thus present in every row. This is the reason the schema of the rows contains the output of the ToMetric transform:

```
private static final Schema METRIC_SCHEMA =
  Schema.of(
    Field.of("workoutId", FieldType.STRING),
    Field.of("length", FieldType.DOUBLE),
    Field.of("duration", FieldType.INT64),
    Field.of("ts", FieldType.DATETIME));
```

2. The input PCollection is of the PCollection<KV<String, Position>> type, which is also the same as in the previous cases, so we must apply the ToMetric transform to it and add our Schema:

```
input
  .apply("computeMetrics", new ToMetric())
  .apply(Reify.timestamps())
  .setSchema(
    METRIC_SCHEMA,
    (TypeDescriptor) TypeDescriptor.of(
      TimestampedValue.class),
    kv ->
      Row.withSchema(METRIC_SCHEMA)
        .attachValues(
          kv.getValue().getKey(),
          kv.getValue().getValue().getLength(),
          kv.getValue().getValue().getDuration(),
          kv.getTimestamp()),
    r ->
```

```
TimestampedValue.of(
    KV.of(
        r.getString(0),
        new Metric(r.getDouble(1), r.getInt64(2))),
        r.getDateTime(3).toInstant()));
```

Here, we can see that we need to extract the timestamp of the records and push them into `Schema` via `Reify.timestamps()`. As we've already mentioned, this is necessary for SQL window assignment functions to work.

> **Important note**
>
> The requirement of the `TIMESTAMP` field being an argument of the `TUMBLE`, `HOP`, and `SESSION` functions, which are the SQL definitions of Windows, comes from the current requirements of Calcite. These requirements may be relaxed in future versions so that the timestamp doesn't have to be brought up to the schema manually.

3. Once we have a `PCollection` with a `Schema` assigned, we convert it into `PCollection<Row>` as usual. Then, we have to calculate the two averages – one in a window whose duration is 5 minutes, sliding every minute, and the other with a 1-minute fixed window. We can compute the sliding window long-term average using the following SQL:

```
SELECT workoutId, SUM(length) / SUM(duration) longPace
    FROM PCOLLECTION GROUP BY workoutId,
    HOP(ts, INTERVAL '1' MINUTE, INTERVAL '5' MINUTE)
```

4. The short-term average will be analogous, with the difference that the `HOP` function will be replaced with `TUMBLE`:

```
SELECT workoutId, SUM(length) / SUM(duration) shortPace
    FROM PCOLLECTION GROUP BY workoutId,
    TUMBLE(ts, INTERVAL '1' MINUTE)
```

5. Now, we have both sides with different windows, and because of the currently supported type of `JOIN` operation that the Apache Beam SQL has is **windowed join**, we need the `Window` functions to be the same on both sides. We will do this by manually applying the window to the output of the `longAverage` query:

```
.apply(Window.into(FixedWindows.of(
    Duration.standardMinutes(1))));
```

6. There are several ways to apply a JOIN – for example, by using the WITH statement to declare the two sides, or by using PCollectionTuple, which can be used as a container for multiple PCollections representing the left-hand and right-hand sides of JOIN. We will use the PCollectionTuple approach here. First, we must create it:

```
PCollectionTuple.of("longAverage", longAverage)
    .and("shortAverage", shortAverage)
```

7. Then, we must apply SqlTransform with the following query to it:

```
SELECT longAverage.workoutId workoutId, longPace,
shortPace
    FROM longAverage NATURAL JOIN shortAverage
```

Because our join field has the same name on both sides, we can use NATURAL JOIN, which makes the code even shorter.

8. The last part is to convert the joined long-term and short-term averages into a Boolean value that will tell us what kind of notification we want to send to our user:

```
WITH ratios AS (
    SELECT workoutId, shortPace / longPace AS ratio
        FROM PCOLLECTION)
    SELECT workoutId, ratio > 1 FROM ratios
        WHERE ratio < 0.9 OR ratio > 1.1"));
```

9. Finally, we only convert Row back into KV<String, Boolean> to have the same output we had in all the previous implementations of this task. With that, we are done.

As in the previous tasks that we implemented using SQL, we will skip the usual deployment and testing parts as these are still the same as they were previously. We will conclude this chapter by providing a brief discussion of open and yet-to-be-implemented parts of Apache Beam SQL.

Further development of Apache Beam SQL

In this section, we will sum up the possible further development of Apache Beam SQL and what parts are currently expected to be missing or somewhat incomplete.

At the end of the previous chapter, we described the **retract** and **upsert** streams and defined **time-varying relations** on top of these streams. Although Apache Beam does contain generic retractions as part of its model, they are not implemented at the moment. The same is true for SQL. Among other things, it implies that Apache Beam SQL currently does not support full stream-to-stream joins, only windowed joins.

A windowed join, by itself, does not guarantee that retractions will not be needed, but when using a default trigger without allowed lateness – or a trigger that fires past the end of the window, plus allowed lateness only –no retractions are needed. The reason for this is that all the data is projected onto the timestamp at the end of the window, and the window ends (and the state is therefore cleared) immediately after that. This makes it impossible to observe a chance in the join key, which can result in the necessity to retract in downstream processing.

The full implementation of retractions in the Apache Beam SDK is tricky and is likely to still take some time. The retractions within SQL DSL are somewhat easier because they can focus on the primitives allowed in SQL, so it can be expected that SQL will be the first place to support retractions in Apache Beam. It is still true that retractions will be needed in the SDK as well – this is implied by the fact that the `PCollection` output that comes from `SqlTransform` can be transformed and consumed by any other logic written in any other DSL or the SDK itself.

Another interesting piece of Apache Beam SQL is the **Apache Beam SQL shell**. This shell makes it possible to interactively query (both batch and streaming) data and retrieve the results interactively. This is handy for speeding up development by visualizing the output schema of the query or samples of data in real time. The shell can be started by following the instructions at `https://beam.apache.org/documentation/dsls/sql/shell/`. After running the shell, we can use the full set of Apache Beam SQL queries. What we need is a table to be able to query the data. The shell uses the `CREATE EXTERNAL TABLE` statement (the DDL part of SQL). The syntax and various sources that this statement supports can be also found online at `https://beam.apache.org/documentation/dsls/sql/extensions/create-external-table/`. Currently, the list of supported sources is somewhat limited; it includes sources from Google Cloud Platform (**BigQuery**, **BigTable**, and **PubSub**) and three open source alternatives – text CSV files, **Apache Kafka,** and **MongoDB**. The list of sources is not exhaustive and it may grow in time to include more data sources that can be queried using the shell, which is then likely to make the shell even more interesting for real-time data querying. Currently, the shell is mostly handy when using Apache Beam within Google Cloud Platform.

Summary

In this chapter, we learned how unbounded streams of data can be viewed as **time-varying relations** and, as such, are suitable to be *queried* using SQL. We saw how standard SQL needs to be adjusted to fit streaming needs – we introduced three special functions called TUMBLE, HOP, and SESSION to be used in the GROUP BY clauses of SQL to apply a windowing strategy within SQL statements.

We explored that the prerequisite of applying Apache Beam SQL to PCollection is to create a PCollection<Row>, where Row represents the relational view of a stream, broken down to a structure with a given Schema, which represents the individual (possibly nested) fields of data elements inside PCollection. We also learned how to either automatically infer a schema from the given type using the @DefaultSchema annotation with a SchemaProvider such as JavaFieldSchema or JavaBeanSchema. When we cannot (or do not want to) use a @DefaultSchema, we can set the schema to a PCollection manually using the setSchema method.

We then saw which additional transforms can be applied to a PCollection with a Schema attached, and how automatic conversions between schema-compatible types work. One of the objects that can have an arbitrary Schema is Row – each object with a Schema can therefore be converted into a Row object with a matching Schema using the Convert.toRows() transform.

Once we have a PCollection<Row>, we can apply SqlTransform, which can make certain tasks much easier than the standard Apache Beam Java SDK. A typical pipeline that can benefit greatly from Apache Beam SQL does a lot of joins, which can easily be expressed using SQL compared to using other options. The downside to this is that the currently supported joins are windowed joins – where we must first apply compatible window functions on both sides and only after that can we perform the join operation. This is because, for generic join types, we need support for retractions, which are currently unsupported in Apache Beam. There is an ongoing effort to make them supported, ideally in a fully generic way. In the first iteration, retractions will likely be only supported in SQL.

We also reimplemented three interesting problems from earlier in this book to see how we can work with SQL in practice and how it can save us some boilerplate code.

In the next chapter, we'll learn how to implement our pipelines using a different programming language and how the Apache Beam portability layer works by diving into the **Apache Beam Python SDK**!

6
Using Your Preferred Language with Portability

In the previous chapters, we focused on the **Java SDK** – or various Java SDK-based DSLs – but what if we want to implement our data transformation logic in a completely different language, such as **Python** or **Go**? One of the main goals of **Apache Beam** is *portability*. We have already seen the portability of pipelines between different Runners and between batch and streaming semantics. In this chapter, we will explore the last aspect of portability – portability between SDKs.

We will outline how the portability layer works (Apache Beam often calls it the **Fn API** – pronounced *Fun API*) so that the result is portable. The desired goal is to enable Runners so that they don't have to understand the SDK (the language we want to use to implement our pipeline), yet can still execute it successfully. That way, new SDKs can be created *without us needing to make modifications to the currently existing Runners*.

After covering this theory, we will explore a completely new SDK – the **Python SDK**. As in the previous chapter, we will use tasks we have already solved in the Java SDK to speed up the learning curve. We will highlight all the differences between the Java and Python SDKs. The most important thing is that – conceptually – the SDKs should be equivalent. This means that concepts such as windows, triggers, watermark, timers, state, transforms, and more should have equivalent definitions in all SDKs.

In the last section, we will uncover the way Apache Beam implements language portability – through *cross-language pipelines*. This is a feature that is still undergoing development and should be considered experimental, but we have included it because of its practical applications – mostly when it comes to I/O modules.

In this chapter, we will cover the following topics:

- Introducing the portability layer
- Implementing our first pipelines in the Python SDK
- Task 17 – Implementing MaxWordLength in the Python SDK
- Python SDK type hints and coders
- Task 18 – Implementing SportTracker in the Python SDK
- Task 19 – Implementing RPCParDo in the Python SDK
- Task 20 – Implementing SportTrackerMotivation in the Python SDK
- Using the DataFrame API
- Interactive programming using InteractiveRunner
- Introducing and using cross-language pipelines

Technical requirements

The toolset we are using will only change slightly in this chapter. Besides the classical **Docker** and **minikube**, we will need to install **Python3**. Let's take a look:

1. Python can be installed by following the instructions at `https://realpython.com/installing-python/`.

2. We will also need to install the `apache_beam` package using `pip`:

```
$ python3 =m pip install apache_beam
```

If something goes wrong, make sure you have the latest version of `pip` by using the following command:

```
$ python3 =m pip install --upgrade pip
```

3. The highest fully Apache Beam-supported version of Python is 3.7. If you have a higher version installed and do not want to downgrade, you can use the `pack-beam` pod in minikube, which has the correct Python version bundled with it. All the examples in this chapter can be run using the following command:

```
$ kubectl exec -t packt-beam -- \
    /usr/local/bin/<name_of_script.py>
```

You will also need to have a basic understanding of the Python language as we will be using it to code our pipelines throughout this chapter.

Introducing the portability layer

In this section, we will walk through the design of the **portability layer** – the FnAPI – to understand which components are orchestrated together to allow pipelines to be executed from different SDKs on the same Runner.

First, let's see how the whole portability layer works. This concept is illustrated in the following (somewhat simplified) diagram:

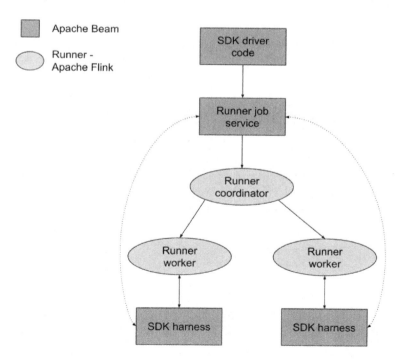

Figure 6.1 – The portability layer architecture

As we can see, the architecture consists of two types of components – *Apache Beam components* and *Runner components*. In this case, a Runner is a piece of technology that performs the actual execution – it may be **Apache Flink**, **Apache Spark**, **Google Cloud Dataflow**, or any other supported Runner. Each of these Runners typically has a coordinator that needs to receive a job submission and use this submission to create work for worker nodes. By doing this, it can orchestrate its execution. This coordinator typically uses a language-dependent API, depending on which technology the Runner is based on. The majority of open source Runners use Java, as is the case for Apache Flink. The Flink coordinator is called **JobManager** and expects to receive a Java JAR file for execution. When it receives the JAR, it sends it to the workers, along with the graph of transforms that represent its computation. This graph contains transforms, which, in turn, contain **User-Defined Functions** (**UDFs**), which is user code that needs to be executed (for instance, a mapping function that converts lines of text into words).

So, we have two problems to solve:

1. How will the non-native SDK (let's say, the Python SDK for Java Runner) convert the Beam Python pipeline into a Java JAR that is understood by the Runner?

2. How will the Runner worker nodes execute in Java non-native (again, Python) user code?

To solve both these problems, Apache Beam has created services that fill the gaps where needed. These components are called *portable pipeline representation*, *Job Service*, and *SDK harness*, all of which we will cover in the upcoming subsections.

Portable representation of the pipeline

When we submit a job from a particular SDK (Python), it is the responsibility of the SDK to convert our pipeline into a portable representation. This representation includes the **Directed Acyclic Graph** (**DAG**) of transforms, serialized user code (Python script, the name of a function, and so on), and everything that can be expressed using a particular SDK. This representation uses **protocol buffers** for the wide variety of languages that support them. Once the portable pipeline representation has been created, it is submitted to Job Service.

Job Service

The main task of **Job Service** is to receive the portable representation of the pipeline and convert it into the format that is understood by a particular Runner. This means that each supported Runner (Apache Flink, Apache Spark, Google Cloud Dataflow, and so on) has to have its own Job Service. This Job Service must create the submitted job in such a way that it replaces calls to UDFs with calls to the SDK harness process. It must also instruct the Runner coordinator to create an SDK harness process for each worker.

SDK harness

The **SDK harness** is the last missing piece of the puzzle – once the code that's executing on the Runner worker needs to call the UDFs, it delegates the call to the harness using **gRPC** – an HTTP/2 based protocol that relies on protocol buffers as its serialization mechanism. The harness is specific to each SDK, which means that every new SDK must provide a harness that will execute UDFs for the Runner. The harness will obtain the necessary data from Job Service (strictly speaking, Artifact Service, but that is a technical detail) – for example, the Python script that was used to run the job.

This completes the cycle. To support the new SDK, we have to do the following:

1. Provide a way to create a portable pipeline representation from the SDK-dependent pipeline description.

2. Provide an SDK harness that accepts a portable description of the UDF and executes it.

3. On the other hand, when creating a new Runner, all we have to care about is converting the portable pipeline representation into the Runner's API. Therefore, the Runner does not have to know anything about the Apache Beam SDKs and, at the same time, the SDKs do not have to know anything about the existing Runners. All these parts are completely separated, which is what makes the approach truly portable.

Now that we have a brief understanding of what the portability layer is about, let's use it to create our first Python pipeline!

Implementing our first pipelines in the Python SDK

In this section, we will learn the basics of the Python SDK. Namely, we will learn how to create the pipeline, how to run it using `DirectRunner`, and how to test our pipelines. Again, our very first pipeline will take our well-known input file, called `lorem.txt`, which we used in *Chapter 1*, *Introducing Data Processing with Apache Beam*, and output the number of occurrences of each word present in the file. So, let's dive into the Python SDK.

Implementing our first Python pipeline

The source code can be found in the `first_pipeline.py` script, which is located in `chapter6/src/main/python/`. Let's get started:

1. The script uses the name of its file as an argument, so we can run it locally using the following command:

```
$ chapter6/src/main/python/first_pipeline.py \
    chapter1/src/main/resources/lorem.txt
```

2. After running the preceding command, we will see the usual output, which consists of a word and the number of occurrences of this word. So, let's see what is inside the script!

3. First, we need to import some dependencies. We will use the `re` module for regular expressions, `sys` for retrieving command-line arguments, and then we need two dependencies coming from Apache Beam:

```
import re
import sys
import apache_beam as beam
from apache_beam.options.pipeline_options \
    import PipelineOptions
```

We have imported `PipelineOptions` to make the code more concise.

4. Next, we must read the name of the input file from the command line:

```
def usage():
  sys.stderr.write(
      "Usage: %s <input_file>\n" % (sys.argv[0], ))
  sys.exit(1)
```

```
if len(sys.argv) < 2:
    usage()
input_file = sys.argv[1]
```

5. The last part is the actual logic. First, we need to create a pipeline and wrap it into a `with` statement. When we leave the scope of the statement, the pipeline gets executed:

```
with beam.Pipeline(options=PipelineOptions()) as p:
```

We create the pipeline with empty `PipelineOptions`, which means it gets filled with defaults. The default is (among other things) that the pipeline will execute using `DirectRunner`.

6. A transform is applied on a pipeline or a `PCollection` with the pipe (`|`) operator. To read a text file, we can use Beam's `ReadFromText` transform from the `io` package:

```
p | beam.io.ReadFromText(input_file)
```

7. The result of this operation is an object of the `Pcollection` type. We can apply a transform to this `PCollection` by using another pipe operator. Since Python uses the newline character to terminate commands, we would have to terminate each line with a backslash (`\`). To overcome this, we can wrap a set of transforms that will be applied to a row in parenthesis, as follows:

```
(p | beam.io.ReadFromText(input_file)
   | beam.FlatMap(...)
   | ...)
```

8. When we have the input file as `PCollection`, we must tokenize the lines as usual:

```
| "Tokenize" >> beam.FlatMap(
    lambda line: re.findall(r'[A-Za-z\']+', line))
```

Notice the `"Tokenize"` string and the `>>` operator. This is the Python SDK equivalent of the Java SDKs:

```
input.apply("Tokenize", MapElements.into(...).via(...))
```

The `FlatMap` transform is well-known – it returns an `Iterable` of elements, each of which is then converted into a separate downstream element.

9. Next, we need to apply the `Count` transform, which is simple, as follows:

```
| "CountWords" >> beam.combiners.Count.PerElement()
```

10. The last part is to print the data on standard output using the following command:

```
| "PrintOutput" >> beam.ParDo(lambda c: print(c))
```

As we can see, we can create a `DoFn` using a `lambda` expression in the Python SDK. And that's it. We have just created our very first Python SDK pipeline!

Implementing our first streaming Python pipeline

In our first streaming Java pipeline, we were using `TestStream` to build a streaming source from the input text file. The Python SDK very much mirrors the Java one, so the same object or utilities have the same (or similar) name in both SDKs. Therefore, the Python SDK also has a `TestStream`, which is located in the `apache_beam.testing.test_stream` module.

The source code for our streaming pipeline is in `first_streaming_pipeline.py` in the Python source code of this chapter. Let's quickly walk through the important differences from the previous batch:

1. First, we need to create `TestStream` from the input file, which we can do as follows:

```
def readToStream(filename):
  lines = map(
      lambda line: line.strip(),
      open(filename, "r").read().split("\n"))
  return TestStream() \
      .add_elements(lines) \
      .advance_watermark_to_infinity()
```

2. Now, we must apply `TestStream` to the pipeline analogously, similar to how we would in the Java SDK:

```
p | readToStream(input_file)
```

3. Next, we need to ensure that our pipeline will run as a *streaming* pipeline. Otherwise, the pipeline would run as a batch, which would result in reading the streaming source until the watermark reaches the maximal value and executes the rest of the pipeline. So, we need to switch to the streaming mode by passing the `--streaming` argument to `PipelineOptions`, as follows:

```
beam.Pipeline(options=PipelineOptions(["--streaming"]))
```

4. The last change is – as in the Java case – that we must apply a `Window` transform to specify either a non-global window or a non-default trigger. We will use `AfterWatermark` here, which is analogous to `AfterWatermark.pastEndOfWindow()` from the Java SDK:

```
beam.WindowInto(
    window.GlobalWindows(),
    trigger=trigger.AfterWatermark(),
    accumulation_mode=
        trigger.AccumulationMode.DISCARDING,
    allowed_lateness=window.Duration.of(0))
```

Looks familiar, right? Let's learn how to reimplement our well-known `MaxWordLength` task into Python, how to test it, and how to deploy it to run on Flink!

Task 17 – Implementing MaxWordLength in the Python SDK

We will use the well-known examples, which have mostly been implemented using the Java SDK, from *Chapter 2, Implementing, Testing, and Deploying Basic Pipelines*, and *Chapter 3, Implementing Pipelines Using Stateful Processing*. We will also build on our knowledge from *Chapter 4, Structuring Code for Reusability*, regarding using user-defined PTransforms for better reusability and testing.

Our first complete task will be the task we implemented as *Task 2* in *Chapter 2, Implementing, Testing, and Deploying Basic Pipelines*, but as always, for clarity, we will restate the problem here.

Problem definition

Given an input data stream of lines of text, calculate the longest word found in this stream. Start with an empty word; once a longer word is seen, output the newly found candidate.

Problem decomposition discussion

From a logical perspective, this problem is the same as in the case of *Task 2*. So, let's focus this discussion on specific aspects of the Python SDK and/or the portability layer in general.

The `MaxWordLength` task requires us to define the following:

- A trigger on `GlobalWindow` that triggers as often as possible
- A combine aggregation that will find the word with the maximal length

In the Java SDK, we used a transform called `Max`. The Python SDK does not (out of the box) define such a transform; instead, it defines a closely related transform called `Top(n)`, which can be used to derive the same functionality with `n=1`.

We have already seen how to use the `WindowInto` transform in the Python SDK, so we need to learn how to use a trigger similar to `Repeatedly.forever(AfterPane.elementCountAtLeast(1))`, which we know from the Java SDK. We will see this in the next sub-section, where we will walk through the complete implementation.

Solution implementation

As always, you can find the complete source code in the cloned GitHub repository for this book, in the `chapter6` directory. The complete path to the source file is `chapter6/src/main/python/max_word_length.py`. Let's get started:

1. First, we must define and implement a `PTransform` that will compute our longest word from a stream of text lines. The Apache Beam Python SDK has two ways to do that – either by creating a class that extends the `PTransform` base class or via a `@ptransform_fn` decorator that can be placed on a method that will, in turn, define the transform's `expand` method. We have chosen the latter method because it makes the code more concise:

```
@beam.ptransform_fn
def ComputeLongestWord(input):
```

2. With this definition, we can immediately use this function in place of a transform. So, for example, the following statement would produce a `PCollection` of the longest words from a `PCollection` of lines:

```
lines | "ComputeLongestWord" >> ComputeLongestWord()
```

3. Let's see the expansion of the `ComputeLongestWord` transform. First, we must transform the lines into words using the `FlatMap` transform and Python's standard library module to process regular expressions called `re`:

```
return (input
    | "Tokenize" >> beam.FlatMap(
        lambda line: re.findall(r'[A-Za-z\']+', line))
```

4. Next, we must assign our words to `GlobalWindow` with the appropriate trigger, as follows:

```
| beam.WindowInto(
    window.GlobalWindows(),
    trigger=trigger.Repeatedly(trigger.AfterCount(1)),
    accumulation_mode=trigger.AccumulationMode.
ACCUMULATING,
    allowed_lateness=window.Duration.of(0))
```

5. Once we have defined the window and trigger, we are left with applying the `Top` transform. We need to specify a `key` function that will be used for comparing elements to find out which element is greater than the other. In our case, it is the predefined `len` function, which returns the length of a string:

```
| "MaxLength" >> beam.combiners.Top.Of(1, key=len)
```

6. As we can see, the `Top` transform takes the number of elements it should find. We are only interested in a single element here, but given that the transform can return multiple elements, it has to return a list of elements in its output. Therefore, we must apply a `FlatMap` transform, which will convert a single-element-sized list into the element itself:

```
| "Flatten" >> beam.FlatMap(lambda x: x)
```

7. The interesting part is the way we read data from **Kafka** and write the data back.
    Apache Beam's Python SDK offers a transform for reading data from Kafka and
    writing it back with the `ReadFromKafka` and `WriteToKafka` transforms,
    respectively. Both these transforms take a to-be-expected set of parameters –
    bootstrap servers and topics to read or write. Besides that, it takes an (optional)
    argument called `expansion_service`. We will see the purpose of this at the end
    of this chapter. For now, we can take for granted that reading from Kafka can be
    done with the following code:

```python
p | ReadFromKafka(
    consumer_config={'bootstrap.servers':
bootstrapServer},
    topics=[inputTopic],
    expansion_service=get_expansion_service())
```

With that, we have walked through the most important parts of the implementation. As
always, we will now learn how to verify that our implementation does what we want it to
do – let's write our very first pipeline test with the Apache Beam Python SDK!

Testing our solution

We will use Python's standard `unittest` module to test our pipelines. The tests have
a common structure – each test case is a class extending `unittest.TestCase`.
All the tests in a module are run using the `unittest.main()` method. This call will
(by default) execute all the methods whose names begin with `test`.

Another convention is that tests for Python modules are placed in the same directory as
the module and typically start with `test_`.

With the theory out of the way, let's look at the test for our `ComputeLongestWord`
transform. This test is located in `test_max_word_length.py`:

1. First, we must define our test case, as follows:

```python
class TestMaxWordLength(unittest.TestCase):
```

2. Inside, we have a single test, which is declared as follows:

```python
def test_pipeline(self):
```

3. Next, we must define a list of inputs that we will feed into our transform. Note that
    the inputs represent lines of text and can therefore contain multiple words:

```python
input = ["a bb ccc", "longer", "longest short"]
```

4. We must declare our pipeline using `TestPipeline` using the `with` keyword:

```
with TestPipeline() as p:
```

5. Next, we must add a source with our defined inputs using the `Create` transform, which we already are familiar with from the Java SDK, and apply our `ComputeLongestWord` transform:

```
res = (p
    | beam.Create(input)
    | ComputeLongestWord())
```

6. The last part is to assert the output. This is similar to how `PAssert.that(...).containsInAnyOrder(...)`, from the Java SDK, works:

```
assert_that(res, equal_to(["longest"]))
```

The pipeline will be automatically run once we leave the `with` statement so that we don't have to run it manually.

7. We can run the test with the following command:

```
chapter6/src/main/python$ python3 -m unittest \
    test_max_word_length.py
```

Now that we have implemented and tested our solution, let's deploy it to our Flink cluster and feed it some real data through Kafka!

Deploying our solution

We will deploy the Python SDK pipeline similar to how we deployed our Java SDK pipelines. Instead of running a Java application, we will run the Python script instead. Besides specifying the Runner and address of Flink's JobManager, we need to specify other parameters that are specific to the portability layer.

The most important option is `environment_type`. This defines how the Runner (Flink, in our case) is supposed to run the SDK harness (a **gRPC** server that will be responsible for executing user code; please refer to *Figure 6.1*). The default option is `DOCKER`, which is the best option in environments where Docker is available. The Runner then launches the SDK harness as a Docker application and manages its life cycle.

Unfortunately, we are using minikube as our execution environment, and that is already running inside Docker. Although running Docker inside Docker is somewhat possible, it has its caveats. So, we will choose a different option – as part of the deployment, we created a sidecar container for each instance of Flink's TaskManager that runs the Python SDK harness worker. This worker listens to the `localhost:50000` address (from the perspective of each TaskManager), so we only need to pass this address to the Runner so that it can establish the connection. We can do that by specifying the address in the `environment_config` parameter. We also have to set the value of `environment_type` to `EXTERNAL` so that the Runner knows how to connect to the worker.

For details on deploying the SDK worker as part of TaskManager, please refer to the manifest located at `env/manifests/flink.yaml` in your cloned version of this book's GitHub repository.

Another portability-related option is `flink_submit_uber_jar`, which tells the submitting SDK to package all the dependencies into a single Java JAR, which will then be submitted to Flink so that it has all the dependencies right away.

Now, let's run our pipeline:

1. First, we must run our pipeline. As always, remember to replace `packt-beam` with the actual name of your pod:

```
$ kubectl exec -it packt-beam -- \
  /usr/local/bin/max_word_length.py kafka:9093 \
    input_topic output_topic \
    --runner=flink --flink_master=flink-jobmanager:8081 \
    --flink_submit_uber_jar --environment_type=EXTERNAL \
    --environment_config=localhost:50000 \
    --checkpointing_interval=2000
```

2. Then, we must wait until the application appears in Flink's UI, which we can access by running and then pointing our browser to `http://localhost:8001/api/v1/namespaces/default/services/flink-jobmanager:ui/proxy/#/overview`:

```
$ kubectl proxy
```

3. Please note that it might take a while before the application is run – at least when running for the first time – because the SDK has to build a JAR for FlinkRunner from its sources. Once the application is running, we can run a consumer message that will arrive at our `output_topic`:

```
$ ./env/kafka-consumer.sh --topic output_topic \
    --bootstrap-server kafka:9093
```

4. Once our consumer is running, we can use the same input file that we used when we were solving this in *Task 2*. There is a slight difference in that we need to add a key separator to each line so that we publish an empty key (" ") into Kafka; otherwise, the publisher would publish the key as null, which is currently unsupported by the Beam Python Kafka I/O. Hopefully, this will be addressed soon:

```
$ IFS=$'\n'; \
    for line in $(cat ./LICENSE); do echo ";$line"; done \
    | ./env/delay_input.sh 0.2 \
    | ./env/kafka-producer.sh --topic input_topic \
    --bootstrap-server=kafka:9093\
      --property parse.key=true --property 'key.
separator=;'
```

Once we start publishing data to our `input_topic`, we will see that `output_topic` starts to fill with longer and longer words as the input streams through the pipeline.

One notable thing is that – as opposed to the Java SDK – while solving this task, we didn't have to deal with **coders** and **types** in general. This is because Python can use a default serialization mechanism using the `pickle` module. This module can serialize essentially any Python object for sending it over the wire. This works somewhat fine (with maybe some questions about performance, but at least for some applications, this might be good enough), but it has the drawback that the pickle protocol is defined only for Python. Having said that, whatever is serialized by Python's pickle can be (safely) deserialized only by Python. That is not very useful when it comes to writing data to output storage (such as Kafka), where we would like to use wire formats that can be serialized and deserialized in a language-agnostic way.

This is where we will want to make use of *type hints*, user-defined coders, or both.

Python SDK type hints and coders

Python3 can provide **type hints** on functions, as shown in the following code:

```python
def toKv(s: str) -> beam.typehints.KV[bytes, bytes]:
    return ("".encode("utf-8"), s.encode("utf-8"))
```

The previous code defines a method called `toKv` that takes a string (`str`) as input and outputs an object that's compatible with `beam.typehints.KV[bytes, bytes]`. When we use such a function in a simple transform such as `beam.Map(toKv)`, Beam can infer the type of the resulting `PCollection` and can automatically use a special-purpose coder instead of pickle. In the case of bytes, this would be `ByteArrayCoder`.

Besides declaring type hints to mapping functions, we can use a decorator for `DoFns`, which will declare the (input or output) type hint explicitly for the whole transform:

```python
@beam.typehints.with_input_types(
    beam.typehints.Tuple[
        str, beam.typehints.Tuple[float, float, float]])
class MyDoFn(DoFn):
```

The preceding declaration tells Beam that `MyDoFn` is going to return a tuple of a string and another tuple of three floats.

Once the type of `PCollection` is known to Beam, it will use the most appropriate `Coder`, if a `Coder` for the specific type is known.

If a `Coder` is not known, the user can implement their own `Coder` by extending the `beam.coders.Coder` class:

```python
class MyFancyCoder(beam.coders.Coder):
    def encode(self, my_object):
        # return byte representation of my_object
        return ...
    def decode(self, s):
        # decode my_object from bytes
        return ...
    def is_deterministic(self):
        # if the byte representation can be used for comparison
        return True
```

The last step is registering this coder in Beam's `Coder` registry:

```
beam.coders.registry.register_coder(MyFancyObject,
MyFancyCoder)
```

As we can see, these concepts closely mirror those of the Java SDK. On the other hand, we will not have to implement our own coders. Defining type hints is handy in most situations because the resulting coders should be more efficient and – more notably – portable between different languages, which is an aspect that we will investigate at the end of this chapter.

Now, let's continue with our practical Python SDK examples with the next task – `SportTracker`.

Task 18 – Implementing SportTracker in the Python SDK

This task will be a reimplementation of *Task 5* from *Chapter 2, Implementing, Testing, and Deploying Basic Pipelines*. Again, for clarity, let's restate the problem definition.

Problem definition

Given an input data stream of quadruples (workoutId, gpsLatitude, gpsLongitude, and timestamp), calculate the current speed and total tracked distance. The data comes from a GPS tracker that sends data only when the user starts a sports activity. We can assume that workoutId is unique and contains userId in it.

The caveats of the implementation are the same as what we discussed in the original *Task 5*, so we'll skip to its Python SDK implementation right away.

Solution implementation

The complete implementation can be found in the source code for of this chapter, in `chapter6/src/main/python/sport_tracker.py`. The logic is concentrated in two functions – `SportTrackerCalc` and `computeMetrics`:

1. The first one is a `PTransform` function declared as before:

```
@beam.ptransform_fn
def SportTrackerCalc(input):
```

2. Inside the function, we apply a `Window` function. Please see the discussion in *Task 5* about why this window function, trigger, and timestamp combiner satisfies our needs. This is mostly based on part of the Beam model that we've already discussed, so we will focus on the Python API here:

```
beam.WindowInto(
    window.GlobalWindows(),
    trigger=trigger.AfterWatermark(
        early=trigger.AfterProcessingTime(10)),
    timestamp_combiner=
        window.TimestampCombiner.OUTPUT_AT_LATEST,
    accumulation_mode=
        trigger.AccumulationMode.ACCUMULATING,
    allowed_lateness=window.Duration.of(0))
```

3. Once we have the correct window function and trigger, we can apply `GroupByKey` and map the resulting pair of `workoutId` and `Iterable` GPS data points via the `computeMetrics` function:

```
| "GroupByWorkout" >> beam.GroupByKey()
| "ComputeMetrics" >> beam.Map(lambda x:
computeMetrics(*x))
```

The asterisk operator (`*`) unpacks the tuple from `GroupByKey` into the arguments of the `computeMetrics` function.

4. `computeMetrics` is a plain Python function that sorts the input GPS coordinates, computes the total distance and time spent, and returns this as a tuple.

5. Besides these two methods, there are two more notable parts – as in the previous case, we must convert the computed tuple into something we can store in Kafka. Once again, we need to use type hints for this:

```
def toKv(t: beam.typehints.Tuple[str, float, float]) \
    -> beam.typehints.KV[str, str]:
    return ("", "%s\t%f\t%f" % t)
```

6. We will apply this method to elements of our `PCollection` of tuples via a simple `Map`:

```
| "ToKv" >> beam.Map(toKv)
```

The previous code will yield the result we need to be able to apply a `WriteToKafka` transform to it, with one important detail. Because we produce the outputs as strings, we must tell this to the output transform through the `key_serializer` and `value_serializer` parameters, both of which must be set to `org.apache.kafka.common.serialization.StringSerializer`. Note that this is the Java class that we reference from Python code. Both reading and writing to Kafka from Python is implemented as a *cross-language transform*. We will explain what this means at the end of this chapter.

7. Because we want to be able to replay data from the past to be able to get outputs from the pipeline in an accelerated time frame, we must provide a timestamp policy to the `ReadFromKafka` transform. When we implemented this in the Java SDK, we implemented a custom `TimestampPolicyFactory` that we passed to the `KafkaIO` transform, since our timestamps were present in the data. Unfortunately – due to reasons we will describe at the end of this chapter – the Python SDK's `ReadFromKafka` transform supports only three predefined timestamp policies – `processing_time_policy`, `log_append_policy`, and `create_time_policy`. These three assign event timestamps to records based on their current processing time, the timestamp of the Kafka partition, or the timestamp provided explicitly to Kafka when writing the record, respectively. Because we want to be able to shift in time, we cannot use either processing time or log-append time. Therefore, we must specify `create_time_policy` using the following code:

```
(p | ReadFromKafka(
    consumer_config={'bootstrap.servers':
bootstrapServer},
    topics=[inputTopic],
    timestamp_policy=ReadFromKafka.create_time_policy,
    expansion_service=get_expansion_service())
```

Specifying this will mean we must write the data to Kafka with the timestamp set appropriately.

Testing our solution

As always, we need to make sure that our implementation is working as expected. We took the same set of data points we were using to test *Task 5* and reimplemented the same test in the Python SDK to see the differences. The complete test can be found in `test_sport_tracker.py`. Let's get started:

1. First, we must specify the data points for two workouts in `TestSportTracker.data`.

2. Next, we must use `TestStream` – an already well-known testing facility – to produce the data:

```
res = (p
    | TestStream()
        .add_elements(TestSportTracker.data)
        .advance_watermark_to_infinity()
```

Although we could have used the `Create` transform for this test, as well as the one in *Task 17* – we have included `TestStream` to emphasize that we have the same set of testing tools as in the Java SDK.

3. Once we have a `PCollection` with our input data, we can apply the transform we want to test:

```
    | SportTrackerCalc()
```

4. As in the case of when we tested *Task 5*, we need to make sure that the floating-point arithmetic that's used to compute the distance along the track is stable. So, we must apply a formatting transform, as follows:

```
    | beam.Map(
        lambda x: "%s:%d,%d" % (x[0], round(x[2]),
round(x[1]))))
```

5. The last step is to assert that the computation yields the same result as what was asserted in the test for *Task 5*:

```
assert_that(res, equal_to([
    "track1:614,257", "track2:5641,1262"]))
```

Now that we've tested our solution, we will deploy it to see how it runs!

Deploying our solution

We will deploy the `sport_tracker.py` script to our Flink Runner using the following commands:

1. First, we must start the application:

```
$ kubectl exec -it packt-beam -- \
    /usr/local/bin/sport_tracker.py \
    kafka:9093 input_topic output_topic \
    --runner=flink --flink_master=flink-jobmanager:8081 \
    --checkpointing_interval=2000 --flink_submit_uber_jar \
    --environment_type=EXTERNAL \
    --environment_config=localhost:50000
```

2. Next, we must start consuming `output_topic`:

```
$ ./env/kafka-consumer.sh --bootstrap-server kafka:9093 \
    --topic output_topic
```

3. Finally, we need to produce data for `input_topic`. Recall that we need to write messages, including the correctly specified `timestamp` field of `KafkaRecord`. For this, we have created a (Java) tool called `WritePositionsToKafka` that parses standard input and writes the results to Kafka with the timestamp filled. So, we will take the data we used for this task in *Chapter 2, Implementing, Testing, and Deploying Basic Pipelines*, and pass it through this tool using the following command:

```
$ cat chapter2/src/test/resources/test-tracker-data-200.txt \
  | ./env/delay_input.sh 0.05 \
  | kubectl exec packt-beam -i -- run-class.sh \
    com.packtpub.beam.util.WritePositionsToKafka kafka:9093 \
    input_topic
```

Now, we can watch Flink's web UI process the various elements. Our `output_topic` will start to fill with information about the lengths of the individual tracks.

> **Important note**
>
> To simplify running the pipeline, we have included all the dependencies in a single file. If we wanted to split the logic into multiple packages, we would have to use `setuptools`, `setup.py`, and `requirements.txt` to specify how our module is built. We would then pass these files to the Runner via the `setup_file` and `requirements_file` command-line arguments.

Now, let's learn how to implement something more low-level using stateful DoFns in the Python SDK.

Task 19 – Implementing RPCParDo in the Python SDK

This task will be a reimplementation of *Task 8* from *Chapter 3*, *Implementing Pipelines using Stateful Processing*. We will use a stateful `DoFn` to batch the elements for a defined maximal amount of time. As always, we will restate the problem again for clarity.

Problem definition

Use a given RPC service to augment data in the input stream using batched RPCs with batches whose size are about K elements. Also, resolve the batch after, at most, time T to avoid (possibly) an infinitely long waiting time for elements in small batches.

As in the previous task, we will skip the discussion of the problem's decomposition as we discussed that when we implemented *Task 8*. Instead, we will jump directly into its implementation using the Python SDK.

Solution implementation

The implementation can be found in `chapter6/src/main/python/rpc_par_do.py`. It can be broken down into the `RPCParDoStateful` transform, which is declared using `@beam.ptransform_fn`:

1. Expanding `RPCParDoStateful` is straightforward; we can do this by applying a stateful `ParDo`:

    ```
    @beam.ptransform_fn
    def RPCParDoStateful(
    ```

```
        input,
        address="localhost:1234",
        batchSize=10,
        maxWaitTime=None):
    return (input
        | beam.Map(toBuckets)
        | beam.ParDo(RPCDoFn(address, batchSize,
maxWaitTime)))
```

2. We need to assign a key to each element. Although we could use Python's built-in `hash` function, the hashing would not be stable between different Python processes. We want to take advantage of the possible optimization of avoiding calling the RPC service multiple times for the same word in the same batch. So, we need the hashing function to be deterministic and stable between different processes, which is why we have chosen a very simplistic bucketing function that splits words based on the first character only. We need to add type hints so that Beam can use the correct coder for the stateful `ParDo` transform. We can do this using a named function, rather than a lambda:

```
def toBuckets(x: str) -> beam.typehints.KV[int, str]:
    return (ord(x[0]) % 10, x)
```

3. The stateful `DoFn` first declares the states and timers we will need. The set of required states and timers is exactly the same as in *Task 8*, so please refer to that for an explanation on what these will be used for:

```
BATCH_SIZE = ReadModifyWriteStateSpec(
    "batchSize", beam.coders.VarIntCoder())
BATCH = BagStateSpec("batch", beam.coders.StrUtf8Coder())
FLUSH_TIMER = TimerSpec("flushTimer", TimeDomain.REAL_
TIME)
EOW_TIMER = TimerSpec("endOfTime", TimeDomain.WATERMARK)
```

4. The complete logic is implemented in RPCDoFn. The Beam model is language-agnostic, so it applies to both the Java SDK and Python (or any other possible language). Because of this, we can define the setup and teardown methods, which are bound to the appropriate DoFn life cycle phase. In setup, we create a (gRPC) channel to our RPC backend, and we close it in teardown, respectively:

```
def setup(self):
  self.channel = grpc.insecure_channel(self.address)
  self.stub = service_pb2_grpc.RpcServiceStub(self.
channel)


def teardown(self):
  self.channel.close()
```

5. In the process method, we will need to access the state and timers, which we can declare as follows:

```
def process(
    self,
    element,
    batch=DoFn.StateParam(BATCH),
    batchSize=DoFn.StateParam(BATCH_SIZE),
    flushTimer=DoFn.TimerParam(FLUSH_TIMER),
    endOfTime=DoFn.TimerParam(EOW_TIMER)):
```

6. The rest of the process method should be self-explanatory. First, we must initialize or update the batchSize state and timers:

```
currentSize = batchSize.read()
if not currentSize:
  currentSize = 1
  flushTimer.set(Timestamp.now()
      + Duration(micros=self.maxWaitTime * 1000))
  endOfTime.set(GlobalWindow().max_timestamp())
else:
  currentSize += 1
```

7. Then, we must add the element to the current batch and optionally flush it. Note that the element contains the complete KV; that is, `element[0]` refers to the key, while `element[1]` refers to the value:

```
batchSize.write(currentSize)
batch.add(element[1])
if currentSize >= self.batchSize:
    return self.flush(batch, batchSize)
```

8. Next, we need to define a callback to be called when `flushTimer` fires:

```
@on_timer(FLUSH_TIMER)
def onFlushTimer(
    self,
    batch = DoFn.StateParam(BATCH),
    batchSize = DoFn.StateParam(BATCH_SIZE)):

    return self.flush(batch, batchSize)
```

9. Note that this is the same as the `endOfTime` timer:

```
@on_timer(EOW_TIMER)
def onEndOfTime(
    self,
    batch = DoFn.StateParam(BATCH),
    batchSize = DoFn.StateParam(BATCH_SIZE)):

    return self.flush(batch, batchSize)
```

10. The rest of the logic is left to the `flush()` method, which does all the business logic – it creates `RequestList`, performs an RPC query, and outputs the results:

```
def flush(self, batch, batchSize):
    batchSize.clear()
    req = service_pb2.RequestList()
    inputs = batch.read()
    req.request.extend([service_pb2.Request(input=item)
        for item in set(inputs)])
    batch.clear()
```

```
res = self.stub.resolveBatch(req)
resolved = {req.request[i].input: res.response[i].
output
    for i in range(0, len(req.request))}
return [(elem, resolved[elem]) for elem in inputs]
```

Now that we have walked through the `rpc_par_do.py` script, let's see if it works as expected.

Testing our solution

The tests are located in the `test_rpc_par_do.py` script. The first test – the `test_server` method – tests that our gRPC server implementation works as expected. This is not related to Beam, so we will skip it and walk through the `test_computation` method instead:

1. First, we must define a set of inputs:

    ```
    inputs = ["a", "bb", "ccc", "aa", "c", "bbb", "aa"]
    ```

2. Next, we must start our RPC server instance and create a pipeline:

    ```
    with RPCServer(1234), beam.Pipeline(
        options=PipelineOptions(
            ["--streaming", "--runner=flink"])) as p:
    ```

    We use a Flink Runner for this test because there is some deficiency in Python's DirectRunner (the default) that, in the current release (Beam 2.33.0), causes this test to fail. This is likely to be fixed in an upcoming release.

3. Next, we must add our inputs and apply the tested transform:

    ```
    res = (p | beam.Create(inputs)
        | RPCParDoStateful("localhost:1234", 4, 500))
    ```

4. Finally, we must make an assertion about the outputs:

    ```
    assert_that(res, equal_to([(x, len(x)) for x in inputs]))
    ```

Now that we have tested the implementation, we can deploy the solution to our Flink cluster.

Deploying our solution

Deploying and running the pipeline is similar to the previous cases:

1. Note that because our pipeline depends on two other modules (`service_pb2` and `service_pb2_grpc`), we need to create a `setup.py` file, which will package these dependencies using `setuptools`, as follows:

```
from setuptools import setup
setup(name='packt_beam_chapter6',
    version='1.0',
    description='...',
    py_modules=['service_pb2', 'service_pb2_grpc'])
```

2. Then, we must run the pipeline with the following command. Note the `setup_file` argument, where we pass our `setup.py` to the pipeline:

```
$ kubectl exec -it packt-beam -- \
    /usr/local/bin/rpc_par_do.py  kafka:9093 input_topic \
    output_topic 10 100 --runner=flink \
    --flink_master=flink-jobmanager:8081 \
    --checkpointing_interval=2000 --flink_submit_uber_jar \
    --environment_type=EXTERNAL  \
    --environment_config=localhost:50000 \
    --setup_file=/usr/local/bin/setup.py
```

3. The rest is similar to what usually happens – run `kafka-consumer.sh` to consume from `output_topic` and run `kafka-producer.sh` to publish data to `input_topic`. Do not forget to add the key:

```
$ ./env/kafka-producer.sh --bootstrap-server kafka:9093 \
    --topic input_topic --property parse.key=true \
    --property 'key.separator=;'
```

With that, we have learned how to use a stateful `DoFn` in the Python SDK. We saw that the main concepts are the same as with the Java SDK, which is the case for the next task as well. In the next task, we will learn how to write more complex pipelines and how to use the `CoGroupByKey` transform.

Task 20 – Implementing SportTrackerMotivation in the Python SDK

The last task we will implement in this chapter is a well-known task that we have used multiple times in *Chapter 4, Structuring Code for Reusability* – for example, in *Task 11*. First, let's restate the problem definition.

Problem definition

Calculate two per-user running averages over the stream of artificial GPS coordinates that were generated for Task 5. One computation will be the average pace over a longer (5-minute) interval, while the other will be over a shorter (1-minute) interval. Every minute, for each user, output information will be provided about whether the user's current 1-minute pace is over or under the longer average if the short average differs by more than 10%.

We implemented this task in several versions while using a playground to demonstrate various aspects of the Java SDK. In this case, we will implement only one version and use the CoGroupByKey transform to join two streams. We leave this an exercise to you to find and implement the other cases – the side input and the full-streaming join.

As in the previous three cases in this chapter, we will skip the decomposition discussion as it remains the same as in the previous implementations. So, let's jump straight into the implementation.

Solution implementation

The solution can be found in chapter6/src/main/python/sport_tracker_motivation.py. As always, we will only highlight the most relevant parts here. We will split it into several pieces for clarity. The first one is the SportTrackerMotivation transform expansion itself:

1. First, we need to transform the raw GPS coordinates into distance and time at specific discrete time intervals – on the borders of the short (1-minute) interval. We can do this by implementing the ComputeBoxedMetrics transform (which we will walk through in a few moments) and then simply apply this transform to our input:

```
boxed = input | "ComputeMetrics" \
    >> ComputeBoxedMetrics(shortDuration)
```

2. After that, we must compute two averages using another custom transform – `CalculateAveragePace`. First, let's compute the short-time average:

```
shortAverage = (boxed
    | "shortWindow" >> \
        beam.WindowInto(window.
FixedWindows(shortDuration))
    | "shortAverage" >> CalculateAveragePace())
```

3. Now, let's compute the long-time average. Note that we must re-window the long average to a fixed window so that we can retrieve the same windowing as in *Step 2*:

```
longAverage = (boxed
    | "longWindow" >> beam.WindowInto(
        window.SlidingWindows(longDuration,
shortDuration))
    | "longAverage" >> CalculateAveragePace()
    | "longIntoFixed" >> beam.WindowInto(
        window.FixedWindows(shortDuration)))
```

4. The last part of expanding `SportTrackerMotivation` is applying `CoGroupByKey` and producing the final motivation for each Runner:

```
return ((shortAverage, longAverage)
    | beam.CoGroupByKey()
    | beam.FlatMap(asMotivation))
```

5. The `asMotivation` function could have been inlined into `lambda`, but for readability, is has been separated. The input is an array of `[Key, Result]`, where the result is another array of two arrays – each of the two arrays contains elements from left and right co-grouped PCollections, respectively. So, we have `[key, [[left1, left2, ..], [right1, right2, ...]]]` here. We know that we can co-group a single value per window on both sides, so we only take the first element in the array into account. Note that if we wanted to handle late data, this presumption would not hold anymore, and we would have to pick the correct value based on `PaneInfo`:

```
def asMotivation(x):
    if not x[1][0] or not x[1][1] or \
        0.9 < x[1][0][0] / x[1][1][0] < 1.1:
        return []
    return [(x[0], x[1][0][0] > x[1][1][0])]
```

6. The next part is the `ComputeBoxedMetrics` transform, which is more involved. It is built around a stateful `ParDo` transform.

7. The expansion uses `@beam.ptransform_fn`, as we are already used to. Note that besides the `input` parameter, we also pass the `duration` parameter, which is the parameter of the transform:

```
@apache_beam.ptransform_fn
def ComputeBoxedMetrics(input, duration):
 return (input
   | beam.WindowInto(window.GlobalWindows())
   | beam.ParDo(ToMetricFn(duration)))
```

8. `ToMetricFn` is the actual stateful `DoFn`. We will need two states and a timer here. Note that we need to specify coders. We will represent our data points as a triple, `(latitude, longitude, timestamp)`, so we need to pass three sub-coders to `TupleCoder`:

```
BUFFER = BagStateSpec(
    "buffer",
    beam.coders.TupleCoder([
        beam.coders.FloatCoder(),
        beam.coders.FloatCoder(),
        beam.coders.FloatCoder()]))
MIN_STAMP = ReadModifyWriteStateSpec(
    "minStamp", beam.coders.FloatCoder())
FLUSH_TIMER = TimerSpec("flush", TimeDomain.WATERMARK)
```

9. The `process` method is straightforward; it stores `element` in `buffer`, and if needed, it updates the minimal stamp and sets a new timer, depending on the new minimum:

```
def process(
    self,
    element,
    stamp=DoFn.TimestampParam,
    buffer=DoFn.StateParam(BUFFER),
    minStamp=DoFn.StateParam(MIN_STAMP),
```

```
      flushTimer=DoFn.TimerParam(FLUSH_TIMER)):

    currentMinStamp = minStamp.read() or stamp
    if currentMinStamp == stamp:
      minStamp.write(stamp)
      flushTimer.set(currentMinStamp)
    buffer.add(element[1])
```

10. Once the watermark passes the timestamp of the minimal timestamp from the buffer, we must extract all the elements whose timestamp is lower than or equal to the firing timestamp and output the metrics. This is copied logic from our previous implementations, only rewritten from Java to Python, so we will skip the details here, but please have a look at `ToMetricFn.flush` and `ToMetricFn.flushMetrics` methods yourself.

    Once we have computed the metrics on the boundaries of the 1-minute intervals, we only need to average them out. We cannot use the built-in `Mean` combiner directly because we need a weighted average. Due to this, we implemented a custom `CombineFn` to demonstrate how is that done in the Python SDK.

11. As we already know from *Chapter 2, Implementing, Testing, and Deploying Basic Pipelines*, a `CombineFn` needs four methods, the same as in the Python SDK. We can use a tuple of (`totalDistance, totalTime`) as an accumulator, which makes everything else straightforward:

```
class MeanPaceCombineFn(beam.core.CombineFn):

  def create_accumulator(self):
    return (0, 0)

  def add_input(self, acc, element):

    return tuple(map(sum, zip(acc, element)))

  def merge_accumulators(self, accumulators):
    return tuple(map(sum, zip(*accumulators)))
```

```
def extract_output(self, acc):
    (distance, time) = acc
    if time == 0:
        return float('NaN')
    return distance / float(time)
```

With that, we have walked through (rather quickly, but we are already pretty familiar with the details of this task) our last Python example for this chapter. So, let's finish it by deploying it to see how it works!

Deploying our solution

Let's deploy our solution by following these steps:

1. First, we must run the pipeline:

```
$ kubectl exec -it packt-beam -- \
  /usr/local/bin/sport_tracker_motivation.py \
  kafka:9093 input_topic output_topic \
  --runner=flink --flink_master=flink-jobmanager:8081 \
  --checkpointing_interval=2000 --flink_submit_uber_jar \
  --environment_type=EXTERNAL \
  --save_main_session \
  --environment_config=localhost:50000
```

2. Next, we must start consuming output_topic:

```
$ ./env/kafka-consumer.sh --bootstrap-server kafka:9093 \
    --topic output_topic
```

3. We need to produce data for input_topic in the same way that we did in *Task 8*. We will use the same script – emit_tracks.py. We also need to add a timestamp to the Kafka records we publish. Once again, we can use the WritePositionsToKafka tool for this:

```
$ ./chapter4/bin/emit_tracks.py 20 \
  | kubectl exec -i packt-beam -- \
  run-class.sh com.packtpub.beam.util.
WritePositionsToKafka \
  kafka:9093 input_topic
```

This example used more involved Apache Beam concepts. We will conclude this chapter on the Apache Beam Python SDK with a more lightweight way of expressing data transformations using the DataFrame API.

Using the DataFrame API

For those who are familiar with Python's pandas package, it might be interesting to know that Apache Beam has a pandas-compatible API. It is called the *DataFrame API*, and we will briefly introduce it here. We will not walk through the details of the pandas API itself; it can easily be found online. Instead, we will explain how to use it and how to switch between the *DataFrame API* and the classical *PCollection API*.

The basic idea behind a DataFrame (both in Beam and in pandas) is that a data point can be viewed as a row in a table, where each row can have multiple *fields* (columns). Each field has an associated name and data type. Not every row (data point) has to have the same set of fields.

We can either use the DataFrame API directly from the beginning or swap between the classical API and the DataFrame API, depending on the situation and which API gives more readable code.

We'll start by introducing the first option – creating a DataFrame directly:

```
import apache_beam as beam
from apache_beam.dataframe.io import read_csv
input_path = ....
output_path = ...
with beam.Pipeline() as p:
  df = p | read_csv(input_path)
  agg = df[['field1', 'field2']].groupby('field3').sum()
  agg.to_csv(output_path)
```

As we can see, we can create a DataFrame object by applying (|), a DataFrame I/O operation, directly on the pipeline. We can then use the DataFrame as we would in pandas and store the output somewhere.

The alternative approach is to use the standard Python SDK and switch between the DataFrame API when it is convenient:

```
import apache_beam as beam
from apache_beam.dataframe.convert import to_dataframe
from apache_beam.dataframe.convert import to_pcollection
with beam.Pipeline() as p:
  records = p | "ReadFromKafka" >> ReadFromKafka(...)
  # convert to Rows with schema for conversion to DataFrame
  rows = records | "ToRows" >> beam.Map(
      lambda record: beam.Row(key=record[0], value=record[1]))
  df = to_dataframe(rows)
  # use DataFrame API
  ...
  # convert back to PCollection with schema
  pc = to_pcollection(df, include_indexes=True)
```

Here, we can see that we can use the `to_dataframe` and `to_pcollection` methods to convert from one API into the other. One important requirement is that we must associate a schema with `PCollection` before applying `to_dataframe`. We can use the `Row` object for this.

Now, let's briefly introduce the possibilities of analyzing (streaming) data using a REPL shell.

Interactive programming using InteractiveRunner

The Python SDK lets us develop pipelines in **Read-Evaluate-Print-Loop** (**REPL**) fashion. This is especially useful for various data science tools, such as Python notebooks. This book focuses on the data engineering part, so we will not install the complete notebook. Instead, will use a command-line utility. This should be able to demonstrate the benefits of interactive programming.

We will run IPython for a better user experience by using the following command:

```
$ kubectl exec -it packt-beam-5686785d65-2ww5m -- /bin/bash -c
"python3 \'which ipython3\'"
```

This will create an **IPython** console whose prompt looks like this:

```
Python 3.7.12 (default, Sep  8 2021, 01:20:16)
Type 'copyright', 'credits' or 'license' for more information
IPython 7.27.0 -- An enhanced Interactive Python. Type '?' for
help.


In [1]:
```

Now, we can start REPL coding. We have included a sample text file in /usr/
share/lorem.txt in the Docker image so that we can try to parse it using
InteractiveRunner. Let's get started:

1. First, we will need the following imports:

    ```
    import re
    import apache_beam as beam
    from apache_beam.io import textio
    from apache_beam.runners.interactive.interactive_runner
    import InteractiveRunner
    import apache_beam.runners.interactive.interactive_beam
    as ib
    ```

2. Next, we must read from our text file using the following code:

    ```
    with beam.Pipeline(
        InteractiveRunner(),
        options=beam.pipeline.PipelineOptions([
            "--streaming"])) as p:
      text = p | textio.ReadFromText("/usr/share/lorem.txt")
      words = text | beam.FlatMap(lambda line: re.findall(
          r'[A-Za-z\']+', line))
      counted = words | beam.combiners.Count.PerElement()
      print(ib.collect(counted))
    ```

3. When we execute the preceding code (hitting *Enter* twice to terminate the with
    statement) we receive a pandas DataFrame, partly printed on the screen. We can
    use the pandas API to manipulate it further.

4. Note that, as we mentioned previously, we don't have a notebook frontend, so Beam prints a warning about that. We will leave installing a full Beam notebook as an exercise to you, as that is outside the scope of this book.

We leave exploring Beam to you; the relevant resources can easily be found online. You can search for *Apache beam interactive runner* or similar.

Now, let's conclude this chapter with something we have touched on several times during this chapter – cross-language pipelines.

Introducing and using cross-language pipelines

Cross-language pipelines are a natural concept that comes with Beam's portability. Every executed PTransform in a pipeline has an associated environment. This environment describes *how* (DOCKER, EXTERNAL, PROCESS) and *what* (the Python SDK, Java SDK, Go SDK, and so on) should be executed by the Runner so that the pipeline behaves as intended by the pipeline author. Most of the time, all PTransforms in a single pipeline share the same SDK and the same environment. This doesn't necessarily have to be a rule and – when we view this via the optics of the Runner only, the Runner does not care if it executes a Python transform or a Java transform. The Runner code is already written in an (SDK) language-agnostic way, so it should not make any difference.

The first thing we must understand is how is the portable pipeline is represented. When an SDK builds and starts to execute a pipeline, it first compiles it into a *portable representation*. Essentially, this is the complete DAG of the pipeline transforms (and all the other components) serialized in a language-agnostic way. A perfect fit for this task is a technology called *protocol buffers*. Inside the serialized representation, each transform has an associated environment and an *SDK-dependent payload*, which will be used by the SDK harness to run the transform. In the most common case, both the SDK that builds the pipeline and the SDK that runs a particular transform are the same. For example, the Python SDK serializes the name of the function that should be executed inside beam.Map.

This situation changes when we want to mix transforms from different SDKs inside a single pipeline. How would the Python SDK know and understand how to serialize data for a Java SDK harness? The answer is – it does not. It needs a Java process that will do the expansion for it. This is called the *expansion service* and the complete process is illustrated in the following diagram:

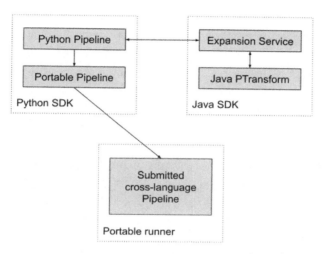

Figure 6.2 – Cross-language pipeline

The process works as follows:

1. A thin wrapper is (typically) defined in the SDK that wants to make use of the transform that's been defined in some other SDK.

2. The purpose of this wrapper is to create an *expansion request*, which contains the **Uniform Resource Name (URN)** of the requested transform and a set of transform-dependent parameters.

3. When the source SDK (Python) wants to submit the pipeline to the Runner, it needs to create the portable (proto) representation. During this process, it sees the external (cross-language) transform, so it sends a request to the expansion service, asking it to expand the transform into a portable representation.

4. The expansion service creates the portable representation in the same way it would do so if it were submitting any other transform written in its native SDK. Then, it returns the resulting portable representation.

5. This subgraph is then inserted into the complete pipeline proto and submitted to any portable Runner.

This is how the Python SDK `ReadFromKafka` and `WriteToKafka` transforms work. The good thing is that the expansion service is started by the Python SDK automatically, so you, as a user, don't have to (generally) worry about it – unless you need to customize the expansion service itself, such as by passing it some specific arguments. This is why we created the function in `utils.get_expansion_service`. It uses Beam's built-in object to run the Java-based expansion service, as follows:

```
def get_expansion_service(
    jar="/usr/local/lib/beam-chapter6-1.0-SNAPSHOT.jar",
    args=None):
  if args == None:
    args = [
        "--defaultEnvironmentType=PROCESS",
        "--defaultEnvironmentConfig={"
            + \"command\": \"/opt/apache/beam/boot\"}",
        "--experiments=use_deprecated_read"]
    return JavaJarExpansionService(jar, ['{{PORT}}'] + args)
```

The `{{PORT}}` argument is automatically filled with the required port, where the expansion service should start. As we can see, we pass the required `defaultEnvironmentType` and `defaultEnvironmentConfig` to the expansion service. This is because the environment is part of the expanded portable representation of the transform. So, this is our only chance to override the (global) default, which is DOCKER.

The last part is setting the `use_deprecated_read` experiment, which relates to the current (as of Beam 2.33.0) deficiency of the Flink Runner, which has issues with running the splittable `DoFn` version of `KafkaIO`. This will hopefully be fixed in a future release.

There is one very important detail regarding cross-language pipelines we have not talked about yet. Ordinary (single-SDK) pipelines all encode and decode data between transforms *using the same SDK*. This guarantees that both the side that produces the data and the side that consumes it will have the same set of coders available. This is not the case for cross-language transforms. If we were to produce data in a Java transform using a Java coder, we could not decode this data in a Python SDK harness, because we cannot instantiate the Java coder in Python. How do we solve this issue?

Apache Beam solves this by introducing a set of well-known coders. These coders are defined in a language-agnostic way so that all the SDKs can implement the encode/decode methods for these coders themselves. The implication is that once we use cross-language pipelines, the type of data that's produced by the producing transform must be among the types encoded by the well-known coders. This is why we must take special care of data types when writing data to Kafka using the `WriteToKafka` transform. If we don't use the correct type hints so that the coder is deduced correctly (for instance, a `ByteArrayCoder`), the Python SDK might use the pickle module to serialize the data. The result would be an exception that looks like this:

```
java.lang.IllegalArgumentException: Unknown Coder URN
beam:coder:pickled_python:v1.
```

This tells us exactly what to do – we need to use (and specify using type hints) a type that is among the set of standard types (`string`, `int`, `float`, `KV`, and so on). Generally, objects, which can be expected to have equivalents in all languages, are likely to be among the standard types.

Summary

In this chapter, we looked at the general design of Apache Beam's *portability layer*. We understood how this layer is designed so that both Runners and various SDKs can be developed independently so that once a portable Runner is implemented, it should be capable of running any SDK, even if the SDK did not exist at the time the Runner was implemented.

We then had a deep dive into the Python SDK, which builds heavily on the portability layer. We saw that the core Apache Beam model concepts are mirrored by all SDKs. Not all SDKs have the same set of features at the moment, but the set of supported features should converge over time.

We reimplemented some of our well-known examples from the Java SDK into the Python SDK to learn how to write and submit pipelines to a portable Runner – we used `FlinkRunner` for this, and we will continue to do so for the rest of this book. Next, we explored interactive programming using `InteractiveRunner` and Python notebooks. We saw what benefits this style of programming can bring.

We concluded this chapter with a deep dive into cross-language pipelines, which are handy for I/O transforms or when there is a lack of support for a transform in a particular SDK.

In the next chapter, we will learn how to write our own I/O transforms for both reading and writing to extend the I/O capabilities of Apache Beam!

Section 3
Apache Beam: Advanced Concepts

In this section, you will cover more advanced concepts and see how splittable DoFn closes the gap between batch and streaming I/Os. It also covers how to use splittable DoFn for non-I/O applications. The section ends with a detailed explanation of how a typical Apache Beam runner evaluates pipelines, and what are the typical building blocks of such a runner.

This section comprises the following chapters:

- *Chapter 7, Extending Apache Beam's I/O Connectors*
- *Chapter 8, Understanding How Runners Execute Pipelines*

7
Extending Apache Beam's I/O Connectors

In previous chapters, we focused on how to write data transformations after reading the data from *data sources*. There are two types of sources: **bounded** and **unbounded**. The difference between these is obvious – the size of the bounded type is limited (and this limitation is known in advance), while the size of the unbounded type is (possibly) infinite. A classic example of a bounded source is a file (or a set of immutable files), while an unbounded source is typically a streaming source such as **Apache Kafka**. Note that we can always convert an unbounded source to a bounded one by defining a *bounding constraint*. This could be, for example, the number of records that we want to read or the (processing or event time) duration for which we want to read the data.

In **Apache Beam**, these two types of sources historically resulted in two types of interfaces that are currently considered deprecated: the `BoundedSource` and `UnboundedSource` interfaces. While these interfaces still work and Beam runners can use them to read data from various sources, a newer approach was developed to close the gap between these two source types and unify them. This is similar to the way in which the rest of the Beam model works for both bounded and unbounded `PCollection` objects. This new approach is the last piece of the Beam model we still need to cover and it is called `splittable DoFn`.

This chapter will fully describe the concept of `splittable DoFn`, which will complete the description of Beam's core transformations. Later in this chapter, we will see how to write a custom **data sink**. While this can be done using a classical `ParDo` transform, there are some caveats we need to be aware of.

In this chapter, we will walk through the following topics:

- Defining `splittable DoFn` as a unification for bounded and unbounded sources
- Task 21 – Implementing our own `splittable DoFn` – a streaming file source
- Task 22 – A non-I/O application of `splittable DoFn` – `PiSampler`
- The legacy Source API and the `Read` transform
- Writing a custom data sink

Technical requirements

This chapter will return to the **Java Software Development Kit (SDK)**, so the tools will be the same as those in *Chapter 4, Structuring Code for Reusability*. As always, we will need a cloned version of the **GitHub** repository for this book located at `https://github.com/PacktPublishing/Building-Big-Data-Pipelines-with-Apache-Beam`.

So, let's dive directly into the (admittedly non-trivial) concept of `splittable DoFn`!

Defining splittable DoFn as a unification for bounded and unbounded sources

Beam offers a wide variety of source and sink transforms. We will not walk through them in this book because their details can be easily found online. In this book, we have used the `KafkaIO` transform heavily – other source and sink transforms are used analogously but specifically on the target storage system.

The question that arises is this: what should we do when there are either specific requirements for the way the data is read (or stored) or when we need to connect to a data source that Beam does not have a connector for? Let's first see how to implement a custom source.

A fundamental requirement for any source is that it has the ability to split itself. We need to split a bounded source in order to be able to parallelize its processing and we need to split an unbounded source to get a persistent moment in time we can return to in case of a failure. Such a moment in time is typically called a **checkpoint**. When we create a checkpoint, we have actually divided the source into two parts – one bounded (that is, the data that lies between two checkpoints) and the other unbounded (which represents the data from the latest checkpoint to the infinite future).

Therefore, we can speak about *spatial* and *temporal* splitting, as shown in the following figure:

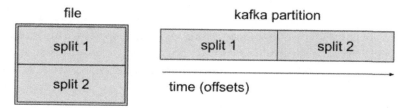

Figure 7.1 – Spatial and temporal splits

Bounded sources – such as files – are finite at the time we process them. Therefore, we can split them *spatially*. For example, we can process a file from the beginning to the middle and then from the middle to the end. We cannot do the same with unbounded sources because more and more data is arriving in them, but we can mark a specific moment in time that results in a *temporal* split. In the case of Kafka, this is represented by an offset in a partition, which unambiguously marks a specific record.

Therefore, we can see that by creating a suitable abstraction, we can handle both of these cases in a unified way. This abstraction is called a **restriction**. A restriction is a user-defined object that has the ability to split itself into two objects of the same type –Beam calls these two objects a **primary restriction** and a **residual restriction**. An important requirement is that these two restrictions must logically sum up to exactly the initial restriction before the split.

Let's explain this for the case of a file and a Kafka topic. In the case of a (text) file, we can define a restriction to be a range of offsets within the file. So, the initial restriction would be [0, size) – that is, a range from zero (inclusive) to the size of the file (exclusive). Splitting this restriction exactly in the middle would result in a primary split of [0, size/2) and a residual split of [size/2, size). These two splits together make the initial restriction – that is, the whole file – so our requirement holds.

In the case of the Kafka partition, the restriction will be initially unbounded. Kafka uses non-negative offsets for message positions within the partition, so the initial restriction would be [0, +inf). This can be obviously split in a number of ways. However, the most useful definition is that splitting the infinite restriction is done in such a way that the *primary restriction is completely processed at the processing time when we are splitting it.* So, let's assume we have processed 100 messages from a partition before we want to split our restriction. That would result in a primary split of [0, 100) and a residual split of [100, +inf). Now that we know what a restriction is, we can have a look at how these restrictions are used by the splittable DoFn process.

The first thing to note is that splittable DoFn is an extension of a DoFn object, and therefore, it needs to process an input element. This element is typically created using an Impulse transform to which a flatmap-like operation is applied. This creates from the initially empty byte-array (produced by the Impulse transform) a list of elements that can be processed independently. This could be a list of files or a list of Kafka topic-partition pairs.

The second important thing is that because restrictions can be unbounded, processing such unbounded restrictions can result in an unbounded number of output elements. This implies that we need a way to interrupt the processing to be able to create a checkpoint or process a different element-restriction pair. For this reason, Beam defined a RestrictionTracker object. Let's see what the life cycle of splittable DoFn processing looks like in the following figure:

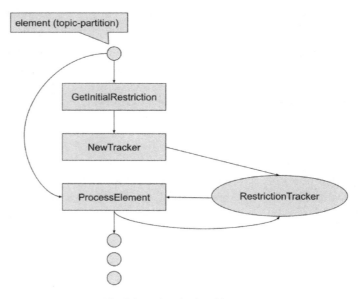

Figure 7.2 – The life cycle of splittable DoFn processing

Note that the diagram in *Figure 7.2* is simplified and highlights only the relevant parts for illustrating the difference from regular DoFn processing. It also does not include the normal methods that are used in this case – that is, the Setup, StartBundle, FinishBundle, and Teardown methods. Let's walk through the life cycle specific to splittable DoFn processing:

1. When a new element arrives at the DoFn object, it is first passed to a method annotated with @GetInitialRestriction. The purpose of this method is to return an object that will be subsequently used as a restriction. Every other place we work with restrictions we must use an object of the same type as that of the return value of this method. In the case of Kafka, we could return a [currentEndOffset, +inf) pair to start processing from the newest data.

2. When we have the initial restriction, we create a RestrictionTracker instance for it. Every RestrictionTracker instance is associated with exactly one restriction. We use the @NewTracker method for that.

3. The RestrictionTracker instance has two main duties – to split the currently processed restriction and stop processing once the current restriction is finished. It does this via two methods – trySplit and tryClaim.

4. The trySplit method splits the current restriction into a primary part – which becomes the new restriction associated with the tracker – and a residual part, which will be scheduled for later processing.

5. The tryClaim method is used from within the @ProcessElement method and notifies the RestrictionTracker instance that there is more work that needs to be processed. If that piece of work (for instance, creating a new ConsumerRecord object or a new line in a text file) fits into the range of the current restriction, it is marked as processed in the tracker and tryClaim returns true. If the piece of work is outside the restriction, tryClaim returns false and the @ProcessElement method must immediately return. This way, the runner controls the flow of the data from the (theoretically unbounded) @ProcessElement method.

6. The @ProcessElement method must return immediately after tryClaim returns false, but it can return in other cases as well. It should not block the input, so if there is currently no new data (for example, when the Kafka partition is currently empty) it should return to give a chance for a (possible) different element to be processed. It must signal the fact via the return value – this will be either ProcessContinuation.stop() to indicate that there is no more work for the current restriction or ProcessContinuation.resume() to indicate that the current restriction is not completely processed yet.

The preceding example is a simplified life cycle of processing with `splittable DoFn`. However, there are other parts that need to be done in order to make this work.

1. Although `splittable DoFn` can be used for purposes other than reading data, the I/O application is the most common. As we saw in *Chapter 1, Introducing Data Processing with Apache Beam*, every streaming (unbounded) source needs a watermark associated with the produced data. For this purpose, `splittable DoFn` has the `@NewWatermarkEstimator` method. Each `WatermarkEstimator` method can have a state, which is initialized via the `@GetInitialWatermarkEstimatorState` method. This state is then passed to the `@NewWatermarkEstimator` method via the parameter annotated with `@WatermarkEstimatorState`.

2. Users don't have to implement the `WatermarkEstimator` method themselves, as it is often convenient to use `WatermarkEstimators.Manual`, which can then be received as a parameter to the `@ProcessElement` method argument of the `WatermarkEstimator` type. The `@ProcessElement` method then manually controls the watermark by calling the `setWatermark` method.

3. Every state of a `WatermarkEstimator` method and every restriction has to have a `Coder` object associated with it. This is done via the `@GetWatermarkEstimatorStateCoder` and `@GetRestrictionCoder` methods, respectively.

We will see all of these parts in action in the following section. So, let's implement something using our own `splittable DoFn` process!

Task 21 – Implementing our own splittable DoFn – a streaming file source

In this task, we will see how to implement all aspects of a `splittable DoFn` process and we will see how to use its power and extensibility. So, let's create a streaming source from a plain filesystem! We will explain what we mean by that in the following problem definition.

The problem definition

We want to create a streaming-like source from a directory on a filesystem that will work by watching a specified directory for new files. Once a new file appears, it will grab it and output its content split into individual (text) lines for downstream processing. The source will compute a watermark as a maximal timestamp for all of the files in the specified directory. For simplicity, ignore recursive sub-directories and treat all files as immutable.

Let's illustrate that in the following discussion for clarity.

Discussing the problem decomposition

The problem effectively consists of two parts:

1. Watching a specified directory for new files
2. Processing a new file from the directory, splitting it into lines, and outputting it downstream

Note that due to the constraint that we must treat all files as immutable and therefore bounded, the only (theoretically) unbounded part is *Part 1*. *Part 2* reads an already finite-length file, which could be accomplished using a regular ParDo process. However, this would have implications for memory efficiency. A simple ParDo process would not handle large files quite as well because some implementations might buffer all of the outputs of a single input element into memory. Therefore, we will use two composed splittable DoFn processes, as illustrated in the following figure:

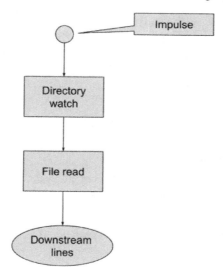

Figure 7.3 – A streaming file source

The source will begin with an Impulse transform. Note that this is a typical scenario for many splittable DoFn-based sources – the pipeline needs a starting point. Everything else then happens inside the pipeline, and therefore, a single element that kicks off the computation is usually enough.

After that, we will take our input directory, which is a static input parameter to the pipeline (we will discuss alternatives at the end of the *Implementation of the solution* section), and run a `splittable DoFn` process that will periodically scan the directory for new files. Once we find a new file, we will pass the (fully qualified) filename to another transform, which will read its contents line by line and output it for downstream processing.

> **Important note**
>
> In our implementation, we are using the local filesystem. This would obviously not work in any truly distributed environment, where we would have to use a distributed filesystem instead. In this example, we did not want to complicate the logic and deployment by using a distributed filesystem (for instance, **HDFS**), but it is important to note that a distributed filesystem would be necessary for any non-educational deployment.

Implementing the solution

The complete implementation can be found in the `com.packtpub.beam.chapter7.StreamingFileRead` class in the sources in `chapter 7`. Here, we will comment on the implementation of three independent parts – the composite transform itself, the `DirectoryWatch` transform, and the `FileRead` transform. The expansion of the `StreamingFileRead` transform itself is straightforward:

```
@Override
public PCollection<String> expand(PBegin input) {
  return input
    .apply(Impulse.create())
    .apply(MapElements.into(TypeDescriptors.strings())
        .via(e -> directoryPath))
    .apply(new DirectoryWatch())
    .apply(Reshuffle.viaRandomKey())
    .apply(new FileRead());
}
```

We can see that this exactly matches *Figure 7.3*, with one important detail. We need to insert a shuffling transform between the `DirectoryWatch` and `FileRead` transforms. The reason for this is that we need to parallelize the work produced by `DirectoryWatch`. Therefore, we need to make sure to redistribute the work to a random worker, which is exactly what the inserted transform does. The `Reshuffle` transform is currently deprecated because it has some non-portable side effects, but we can use it for the requirements of this example.

Let's now walk through the implementation of the first `splittable DoFn` process – `DirectoryWatch`.

1. The transform itself expands to a simple `ParDo` object as follows:

```
@Override
public PCollection<String> expand(
    PCollection<String> input) {


  return input.apply(
      ParDo.of(new DirectoryWatchFn(watermarkFn)));
}
```

`watermarkFn` is a `SerializableFunction` that is used to extract a timestamp from the filename and creation timestamp of each file. It is used for testing, as we will see in the next subsection.

2. For our `DirectoryWatchFn` object, we need to define a restriction and a `RestrictionTracker` object. The restriction is implemented in the `DirectoryWatchRestriction` class. The restriction has two fields:

```
@Getter private final Set<String> alreadyProcessed;
@Getter boolean finished;
```

The `@Getter` annotation is from the `lombok` library and makes the field accessible via a getter method.

The `alreadyProcessed Set` holds the filenames of files that have already been processed (that is, claimed) by processing `DoFn`.

3. The restriction needs the ability to be split into primary and residual restrictions. Note that the primary restriction must be the active restriction that is being processed after the call to `RestrictionTracker.trySplit`. In our case, once we split the restriction, we want all subsequent calls to `RestrictionTracker.tryClaim` to return `false` to split the processing. Therefore, we define the two splits as follows:

```
public DirectoryWatchRestriction asPrimary() {
  finished = true;
  return this;
}
```

```
public DirectoryWatchRestriction asResidual() {
  return new DirectoryWatchRestriction(
    alreadyProcessed, false);
}
```

4. Because our restriction has a tight coupling with its associated `RestrictionTracker` object, we can optionally implement the `HasDefaultTracker` interface and its associated `newTracker` method. This will make the implementation of the `splittable DoFn` process that uses this restriction a little easier:

```
@Override
public DirectoryWatchRestrictionTracker newTracker() {
    return new DirectoryWatchRestrictionTracker(this);
}
```

5. The last notable part is that each restriction needs a `Coder` object. We implemented ours in the `DirectoryWatchRestriction.Coder` class. The implementation is straightforward, making use of Beam's predefined coders for `Set` and `Boolean`.

6. As we already mentioned, the `RestrictionTracker` object associated with the restriction is implemented in the `DirectoryWatchRestrictionTracker` class. The tracker is defined as follows:

```
private static class DirectoryWatchRestrictionTracker
    extends RestrictionTracker<
        DirectoryWatchRestriction, String> {
```

The two parameters of the `RestrictionTracker` abstract class reporesent the type of restriction and the type of position. In our case, the restriction is our already known `DirectoryWatchRestriction` object and the type of the position (which is the type of the parameter passed to the `tryClaim` method) is `String`, representing the claimed filename.

7. The tracker has to hold a restriction, which is returned by the call to `currentRestriction`:

```
private final DirectoryWatchRestriction restriction;
@Override
public DirectoryWatchRestriction currentRestriction() {
  return restriction;
}
```

8. Next, we use our already known methods, asPrimary and asResidual, in response to the trySplit method:

```
@Override
public SplitResult<DirectoryWatchRestriction> trySplit(
    double fractionOfRemainder) {
  return SplitResult.of(
      restriction.asPrimary(), restriction.asResidual());
}
```

Note that we ignore the fractionOfRemainder parameter. This parameter is intended primarily for the optimization of the splitting of bounded restrictions, where the amount of work is known (at least) at the time we call trySplit. In our case, the amount of work is unbounded, and therefore, any non-zero fraction would be unbounded as well.

9. Once we know how to split the restriction, we need to implement the claiming of the position (filename):

```
@Override
public boolean tryClaim(String newFile) {
  if (restriction.isFinished()) {
    return false;
  }
  restriction.getAlreadyProcessed().add(newFile);
  return true;
}
```

Here, we can see that we distinguish two cases: if the current restriction is already split (and therefore, finished) or not. Once a restriction is finished, we refuse to process any new file (for example, tryClaim will return false).

If the restriction is not finished, we add the newly claimed file to the set of already processed files and return true to indicate that the file can be processed.

10. The contract of `RestrictionTracker` requires that we implement two more methods. The first one is `checkDone`:

```
@Override
public void checkDone() throws IllegalStateException {}
```

The `checkDone` method is an important part that needs to verify that the restriction is fully processed (that is, all positions have been claimed). In our case, however, we actually build the restriction while claiming it, and therefore, this constraint is trivially satisfied.

11. The last part of the contract is the `isBounded` method, which signals if the current restriction represents a finite amount of work. Note that a restriction can turn from unbounded to bounded – after the end of the work is discovered – but can never turn from bounded to unbounded:

```
@Override
public IsBounded isBounded() {
  return restriction.isFinished()
      ? IsBounded.BOUNDED
          : IsBounded.UNBOUNDED;
}
```

12. Once we have defined our restriction and its associated `RestrictionTracker` object, we can walk through the `splittable DoFn` implementation itself. The first thing to note is that the `splittable DoFn` object is defined exactly as any other `DoFn` object would be:

```
private static class DirectoryWatchFn
    extends DoFn<String, String>
```

13. However, the important differences in the way they are defined are related to the definition of the restriction and restriction tracker, as follows:

```
@GetInitialRestriction
public DirectoryWatchRestriction initialRestriction() {
  return new DirectoryWatchRestriction(
    new HashSet<>(), false);
}


@GetRestrictionCoder
```

```
public Coder<DirectoryWatchRestriction>
getRestrictionCoder() {
    return new DirectoryWatchRestriction.Coder();
}
```

> **Important note**
> We specify the @GetInitialRestriction method only and without
> the @NewTracker method that would create a RestrictionTracker
> object for a restriction. This is possible because our restriction implements
> the HasDefaultTracker interface, which is then used to create a default
> tracker for each restriction. We could override this default behavior by creating
> a @NewTracker method.

14. Next, we need to define a WatermarkEstimator object, which we will use to
    track the progress in the event time:

```
@GetInitialWatermarkEstimatorState
public Instant getInitialWatermarkEstimatorState() {
    return BoundedWindow.TIMESTAMP_MIN_VALUE;
}


@GetWatermarkEstimatorStateCoder
public Coder<Instant> getWatermarkEstimatorStateCoder() {
    return InstantCoder.of();
}


@NewWatermarkEstimator
public WatermarkEstimators.Manual newWatermarkEstimator(
    @WatermarkEstimatorState Instant initialWatermark) {

    return new WatermarkEstimators.
Manual(initialWatermark);
}
```

We will be using WatermarkEstimators.Manual to manually set the
watermark from inside the @ProcessElement method. This estimator uses
Instant – the current watermark – as its internal state.

15. The final part is the `@ProcessElement` method itself. The definition adds new arguments – `RestrictionTracker` and `ManualWatermarkEstimator` – and changes the return type. Instead of `void`, we now must return `ProcessContinuation` to be able to notify the runner if the current restriction is completely processed or not:

```
@ProcessElement
public ProcessContinuation process(
    @Element String path,
    RestrictionTracker<DirectoryWatchRestriction, String>
        tracker,
    ManualWatermarkEstimator<Instant> watermarkEstimator,
    OutputReceiver<String> outputReceiver)
```

16. The main loop inside `@ProcessElement` is quite simple:

```
while (true) {
    List<KV<String, Instant>> newFiles =
        getNewFilesIfAny(path, tracker);
    if (newFiles.isEmpty()) {
        return ProcessContinuation.resume()
            .withResumeDelay(Duration.millis(500));
    }
    if (!processNewFiles(
        tracker,
        watermarkEstimator,
        outputReceiver,
        newFiles)) {
        return ProcessContinuation.stop();
    }
}
```

The `getNewFilesIfAny` method is a plain Java method that takes the set of already processed files and scans the directory to find any possible new files that are not present in the set. Please feel free to investigate this method yourself. As its details are not directly related to Beam, we skip it here. If the set of new files is empty, we end the loop and signal to the runner that it should try it again by returning `ProcessContinuation.resume()`. We can also specify an optional delay after which the runner should resume.

17. The `processNewFiles` method tries to take all the newly discovered files and tries to claim them one by one in the `RestrictionTracker` object. If the claim fails, the method returns `false` and the `@ProcessElement` method immediately exits with `ProcessContinuation.stop()`:

```
Instant maxInstant = watermarkEstimator.
currentWatermark();
for (KV<String, Instant> newFile : newFiles) {
  if (!tracker.tryClaim(newFile.getKey())) {
    watermarkEstimator.setWatermark(maxInstant);
    return false;
  }
  outputReceiver.outputWithTimestamp(
      newFile.getKey(), newFile.getValue());
  Instant fileWatermark = watermarkFn.apply(newFile);
  if (maxInstant.isBefore(fileWatermark)) {
    maxInstant = fileWatermark;
  }
}
watermarkEstimator.setWatermark(maxInstant);
return maxInstant
    .isBefore(BoundedWindow.TIMESTAMP_MAX_VALUE);
```

In the preceding example, the most important parts are highlighted. *First*, once the tracker fails to claim a new file, we must stop the processing immediately. It is good to update the watermark (if any new file has been processed). Another important part is that we must use the `outputWithTimestamp` method of `OutputReceiver`, otherwise, all of the output files would have the same timestamp – that is, the timestamp of the input element of the `Impulse` transform, which is `BoundedWindow.TIMESTAMP_MIN_VALUE`. *Second*, we compute the maximal timestamp among all newly discovered files and use it as the watermark value by the call to `watermarkEstimator.setWatermark`.

The *final* part is the `watermarkFn` object that we use to extract the timestamp from the `KV<String, Instant>` object, representing a new file. We need this in order to make the transform testable because the processing needs to be terminated from outside – that is, from the test case – and we use a watermark for that. The `watermarkFn` object can recognize the last element from a test and set the watermark to `BoundedWindow.TIMESTAMP_MAX_VALUE`, which will cause the processing to terminate and the test to finish.

These steps complete the first parts of the `splittable DoFn` process. As we can see, the implementation is somewhat involved, which is the result of `splittable DoFn` being a low-level concept.

> **Important note**
>
> A fully distributed version of the `DirectoryWatch` transform would have to use a distributed filesystem (instead of our version, which uses the local filesystem). Here, we omitted this for simplicity, but it is worth noting that this example is not 100% correct.

The first of the two `splittable DoFn` processes that we use is inherently unbounded. The second uses a bounded amount of work per element – that is, each immutable file consists of a bounded number of rows, and this makes our second `splittable DoFn` process a little simpler.

Let's see how this is implemented in the `FileRead` transform:

1. The transform expands again to a single `ParDo` object that transforms the name of a file to a `PCollection` object consisting of the text lines in the file:

```
@Override
public PCollection<String> expand(
    PCollection<String> input) {
  return input.apply(ParDo.of(new FileReadFn()));
}
The FileReadFn in a splittable DoFn defined as:
@BoundedPerElement
private static class FileReadFn
    extends DoFn<String, String>
```

The @BoundedPerElement annotation signals that the amount of work produced is expected to be bounded. Note that @BoundedPerElement and the complementary @UnboundedPerElement annotation are both optional. When omitted, these are inferred from the return type of the @ProcessElement method. If the method returns ProcessContinuation, then @UnboundedPerElement is assumed; if it returns void, then it means @BoundedPerElement.

2. As with every splittable DoFn object, we need to define the restriction and a RestrictionTracker:

```
@GetInitialRestriction
public OffsetRange initialRestriction(
    @Element String path) throws IOException {
  return new OffsetRange(0, Files.size(Paths.get(path)));
}


@GetRestrictionCoder
public Coder<OffsetRange> getRestrictionCoder() {
  return OffsetRange.Coder.of();
}
```

We use a predefined restriction: OffsetRange. As in the previous case, this restriction implements HasDefaultTracker and therefore, we don't have to create the @NewTracker method. The default tracker for OffsetRange is OffsetRangeTracker.

3. We can see that we will not be using WatermarkEstimator because we will use watermarks that have already been computed in the upstream DirectoryWatch transform. All of the elements in a single file will have the same timestamp, so the watermark remains the same as well.

4. The last part of the FileReadFn object is the @ProcessElement method:

```
@ProcessElement
public void process(
  @Element String path,
  RestrictionTracker<OffsetRange, Long> tracker,
  OutputReceiver<String> outputReceiver)
```

5. In order to fully understand the processing logic, we must understand how the splitting of the `OffsetRange` object works. Let's illustrate a file with three lines as follows:

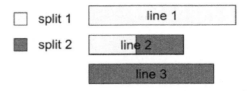

Figure 7.4 – Splitting the OffsetRange object

We see that the boundary of a split can occur inside a line (*line 2* in the previous figure). In that case, which split should *line 2* belong to? The answer is that it depends on which offsets we claim from the `OffsetRangeTracker` object. If we claim the line by the *starting offset*, then *line 2* will belong to *split 1*. If we claim by the *ending offset*, it will belong to *split 2*. In both cases, we need to adjust our reading logic appropriately. We choose to claim lines by the starting offsets, which then results in the implementation of the `@ProcessElement` method described below.

6. The `@ProcessElement` method loops inside the following `while` loop:

```
long position = tracker.currentRestriction().getFrom();
try (RandomAccessFile file =
    new RandomAccessFile(path, "r")) {
  seekFileToStartLine(file, position);
  while (tracker.tryClaim(file.getFilePointer())) {
    outputReceiver.output(file.readLine());
  }
}
```

In this case, the most important part is the `seekFileToStartLine` method, which makes sure that if the split is located in the middle of a line, the line is skipped and the processing starts at the following line.

We have now walked through the implementation of the whole `StreamingFileRead` transform. However, it is worth noting that there are some parts we omitted for simplicity and to keep the discussion focused. Besides the (already noted) fact that we used the local filesystem, which will obviously not work in distributed cases, there is also one other caveat – that is, a restriction might be split under two conditions: either when *being processed* or when *not being processed*. The former is handled by the `trySplit` method of `RestrictionTracker`, but during the latter, there is no tracker currently associated with the restriction. Therefore, Beam has a second `@SplitRestriction` method of a `splittable DoFn` object, which can split a single restriction into multiple restrictions that can be processed in parallel.

In the implementation, we mentioned several times that we had introduced something to enable testing. So, in the next subsection, let's look at this in more detail.

Testing our solution

As with the implementation, the test will be split into two independent parts: testing the `DirectoryWatch` transform and testing the `FileRead` transform. Both of these tests are located in the `com.packtpub.beam.chapter7.StreamingFileReadTest` class. We are already familiar with the Java SDK testing framework, so we will only walk through the most important parts:

1. We create a temporary directory on the local filesystem for all of the tests via `junit-jupiter-params`:

    ```
    @TempDir Path tempDir;
    ```

2. Then, we apply `DirectoryWatch` to this temporary directory:

    ```
    PCollection<String> files = p
      .apply(Create.of(tempDir.toString()))
      .apply(
            "directoryWatch",
          new DirectoryWatch()
            .withWatermarkFn(
              kv -> {
                  if (kv.getKey().endsWith("b")) {
                      return BoundedWindow.TIMESTAMP_MAX_VALUE;
                  }
                  return kv.getValue();
              }));
    ```

We must provide a custom `watermarkFn` object (as discussed in the *Implementing the solution* section) so that once we see a file that ends with b, we shift the watermark to the end of `BoundedWindow`, thereby terminating the pipeline.

3. We then assert what we expect as the outcome of our transform:

```
PAssert.that(files)
    .containsInAnyOrder(
        new File(tempDir.toFile(), "a").toString(),
        new File(tempDir.toFile(), "b").toString());
```

That is, we expect two files called a and b to be present in the output.

4. Next, we run our `Pipeline` object. Note that the call to `Pipeline.run()` might be blocking, therefore, we run it in a separate thread:

```
CompletableFuture<PipelineResult> future =
    CompletableFuture.supplyAsync(p::run);
```

5. After that, we can create our desired files in the `tempDir` directory. Note that we need to wait for some time before creating the b file to make sure that the a file is already processed. Otherwise, the test would become non-deterministic. Although waiting for a fixed amount of time is not the most secure practice in general, it should be sufficient in this case:

```
createFileInDirectory(tempDir, "a");
TimeUnit.SECONDS.sleep(1);
createFileInDirectory(tempDir, "b");
```

6. Finally, we must retrieve the result of the `Pipeline.run()` method and make sure that it terminated successfully:

```
PipelineResult pipelineResult = future.get();
assertEquals(State.DONE, pipelineResult.getState());
```

The test for `FileRead` should be straightforward, so we'll leave it up to you to walk through the details if you are interested. Now, we will focus on actually running the `StreamingFileRead` transform in the following subsection.

Deploying our solution

Note that because our implementation uses the local filesystem, we cannot use a fully distributed runner to run a pipeline with this source. This does not matter for us right now because we created the source for educational purposes only. On the other hand, it limits the way we can run it. Here, we will use `mvn exec:java` to run it on our local machine as follows:

1. First, we create a directory, `/tmp/streaming-read`:

    ```
    $ mkdir /tmp/streaming-read
    ```

2. Next, we run the reading of this directory using `DirectRunner`:

    ```
    chapter7$ ../mvnw compile exec:java
    -Dexec.mainClass=com.packtpub.beam.chapter7.
    StreamingFileRead -Dexec.args="/tmp/streaming-read"
    ```

3. This will run a pipeline and start watching the directory. The `StreamingFileRead.main()` method creates a simple word-count pipeline on top of this source:

    ```
    chapter7$ cp ../LICENSE /tmp/streaming-read/
    LICENSE.${RANDOM}
    ```

So, if we copy several files into the directory, we should see that the running pipeline starts to output counts of the words present in these files.

> **Important note**
>
> Because of how we implemented the `WatermarkEstimator` object in `DirectoryWatch`, the watermark cannot move when there is no input data. Therefore, we must copy at least two files with at least a one-second time gap in order to see any outputs. This problem could be fixed in the `@ProcessElement` method of `DirectoryWatchFn` so that it can better handle cases when there are no new files present.

4. We can try running this using the local **Apache Flink Runner** as well, which would mean adding the appropriate command-line argument as follows:

```
chapter7$ ../mvnw compile exec:java
-Dexec.mainClass=com.packtpub.beam.chapter7.
StreamingFileRead -Dexec.args="/tmp/streaming-read
--runner=flink"
```

We have now completed the walk-through of our first practical application of `splittable DoFn`. We have discussed how to implement the various aspects that distinguish `splittable DoFn` from other `DoFn` processes – that is, defining a restriction, `RestrictionTracker`, and `WatermarkEstimator`. We have also seen how to use the `RestrictionTracker` object inside the `@ProcessElement` method to achieve the splittable behavior.

The application of the `splittable DoFn` process we implemented was targeted at the primary use case of `splittable DoFn` – that is, the sources. In the following task, we will see one example of a non-I/O application of `splittable DoFn`.

Task 22 – A non-I/O application of splittable DoFn – PiSampler

Though `splittable DoFn` shows most of its strengths when providing inputs to pipelines, it has other interesting use cases as well. In this task, we will investigate one of them: a **Monte Carlo method** for estimating the value of **Pi**. Although this is not an efficient algorithm for estimating the value of Pi, it is simple enough to provide a good example of a `splittable DoFn` use case. The approach that we will investigate can be extended to other similar use cases such as **Gibbs sampling**, which might have better practical applications.

As always, let's start by defining our problem.

The problem definition

Create a Monte Carlo method (see Figure 7.5) for estimating the value of Pi. Use `splittable DoFn` *to support distributed computation, specifying the (ideal) target parallelism and the number of samples drawn in each parallel worker.*

As part of the problem definition, we will define the Monte Carlo method for estimating Pi. The method is based on creating an experiment that has a probability depending on the value of Pi and then performing a large number of such independent experiments. By comparing the observed value of the probability (that is, the number of positive samples divided by the total number of samples) to the theoretical value, we can retrieve a formula for Pi. One such possible experiment is shown in the following figure:

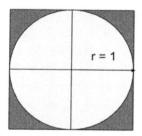

Figure 7.5 – A Monte Carlo method Pi estimation

Here, we create a circle with a radius of *1* (*r = 1*) and insert it into a rectangle with sides of length *2*. We then generate two random numbers in the *[-1, 1]* range and interpret them as *x* and *y* coordinates, with the origin (*[0, 0]*) being in the center of the circle. We count this experiment as *positive* if the resulting point lies *inside* the circle, and we count it as *negative* if it lies *outside* the circle.

Because the area of the circle is exactly equal to π and the area of the square is equal to *4*, the exact probability of a *positive* sample is equal to *π/4* (that is, roughly *78.5%*). The empirical probability can be calculated for a high number of positive and negative experiments by using *#positive/(#positive + #negative)*, which will give us the final formula for the estimation of π (let's denote the estimate with *pi*) as *pi = 4 * #positive/(#positive + #negative)*. The important thing to note is that the more samples we generate, the more precise the value of *Pi* we retrieve will be. This is a general property of Monte Carlo algorithms.

The last part to clarify is how to know if a point is inside the circle. We can determine this from the length of the vector – this is defined as the vector's distance from the origin, which is the center of the circle. The length of a vector is defined as *sqrt(x * x + y * y)*, and we need to compare this with the radius of the circle, which is *1*. Therefore, the condition for a positive experiment becomes *sqrt(x * x + y * y) <= 1*. Note that we can computationally simplify this to *x * x + y * y <= 1* due to the algebraic properties of the inequality.

> **Important note**
>
> Due to symmetry, we can generate the samples only in the *[0, 1]* interval for both *x* and *y* and retrieve exactly the same result. This is the approach we have chosen in the solution.

Discussing the problem decomposition

The first thing to note is that we do not have to count both negative and positive experiments. If we know the total number of experiments we will do, then we can use *#positive = total - #negative*. Therefore, we will count only the negative experiments and compute the rest from this total. The reason to choose the negative samples is that they have a probability of only about 21.5% and they will therefore require less work to count.

The computation **Directed Acyclic Graph (DAG)** is illustrated in the following figure:

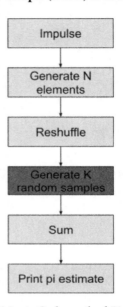

Figure 7.6 – The Monte Carlo method Pi estimation DAG

We will start with *Impulse*, then generate *N* (desired parallelism) elements, which will be then fed into the actual `splittable DoFn` process. As before, for parallelism, we will need to insert *Reshuffle* before the actual `splittable DoFn` process (that is, **Generate K random samples**). The last part is simply to sum all the negative samples and compute the final estimation.

Implementing the solution

The complete solution is in the `com.packtpub.beam.chapter7.PiSampler` class. Let's go through it:

1. The `PiSampler` object's transform expand method matches *Figure 7.6*:

```
return input
   .apply(Impulse.create())
   .apply(
       FlatMapElements.into(TypeDescriptors.strings())
           .via(
               e ->
                   LongStream.range(0, parallelism)
                       .mapToObj(i -> "")
                       .collect(Collectors.toList())))
   .apply(Reshuffle.viaRandomKey())
   .apply(ParDo.of(new SampleDoFn()))
   .apply(Sum.longsGlobally())
   .apply(
       MapElements.into(TypeDescriptors.doubles())
           .via(c ->
               4 * (1.0 - c
                   / (double) (numSamples *
parallelism))));
```

The preceding code example uses `numSamples` and `parallelism` as *K* and *N* from *Figure 7.6*, respectively. The total number of experiments is equal to `numSamples * parallelism`, and `(1.0 - c / (numSamples * parallelism))` represents the exact probability we are looking for.

2. The `SampleDoFn` object is a `splittable DoFn` object, converting a `PCollection<String>` object to a `PCollection<Long>` object of negative samples. Because we want to count the exact number of experiments (that is, samples) we create, we can use our already known `OffsetRange` object as a restriction, where each offset is a single sample:

```
@GetInitialRestriction
public OffsetRange initialRestriction() {
   return new OffsetRange(0, numSamples);
}
```

```
@GetRestrictionCoder
public OffsetRange.Coder getRestrictionCoder() {
  return OffsetRange.Coder.of();
}
```

3. The last part is the `@ProcessElement` method, which is straightforward:

```
@ProcessElement
public void process(
    RestrictionTracker<OffsetRange, Long> tracker,
    OutputReceiver<Long> output) {

  final Random random = randomFactory.apply();

  long off = tracker.currentRestriction().getFrom();
  while (tracker.tryClaim(off++)) {
    double x = random.nextDouble();
    double y = random.nextDouble();
    if (x * x + y * y > 1) {
      output.output(1L);
    }
  }
}
```

As we can see, the implementation is not that complex once we get used to the `splittable DoFn` process machinery. The interesting part is that we create a new `Random` for each restriction using a `randomFactory` object that is (optionally) provided to the `SampleDoFn` object. The reason for this – again – is to allow effective testing.

The computation is non-deterministic in nature, but non-deterministic tests tend to be flaky – sometimes passing and sometimes failing. This is generally unwanted behavior because it means we cannot be sure if a test has failed due to an error or due to a problematic implementation of the test itself.

Therefore, we stabilize the test by providing a stable random number generator for the test run, as we will see in the next subsection.

Testing our solution

The test is located in the `com.packtpub.beam.chapter7.PiSamplerTest` class. There is actually nothing particularly interesting about it, but to make it easier to reference, we have included it here. The test simply verifies that the output of the sampler is within a small margin of the actual `Math.PI` value:

```
Pipeline p = Pipeline.create();
PCollection<Double> result =
    p.apply(PiSampler.of(10000, 10)
        .withRandomFactory(() -> new Random(0)));
PAssert.that(result)
    .satisfies(
        values -> {
            Double res = Iterables.getOnlyElement(values);
            assertEquals(res, Math.PI, 0.01);
            return null;
        });
p.run();
```

We can see that the test can assert two-digit accuracy, even with a somewhat low number of samples. However, the problem with this method is that adding more digits gets exponentially more computationally expensive, which is why actual methods that compute the value of π to trillions of digits use different approaches.

So, let's see what happens when we run the code!

Deploying our solution

As with the previous tasks, we will run this example only locally. There is no reason we couldn't run this on a distributed cluster, as we implemented it this way to distribute the computation. But the environment we use (**minikube**) will not bring us any special benefit by doing so.

Therefore, we will once again use `mvnw exec:java` to execute the pipeline using local Flink by running the following:

```
chapter7$ ../mvnw compile exec:java \
    -Dexec.mainClass=com.packtpub.beam.chapter7.PiSampler \
    -Dexec.args="1000 10000000 --runner=flink"
```

We can experiment with the various settings of the two parameters, but generally, the higher their product is, the higher the precision of the Pi estimate we retrieve will be and the longer the computation will be. Note that, by default, the local Flink Runner uses parallelism equal to the number of available processors. We can change this using the `--parallelism` parameter.

With this task, we have completed our walk-through of `splittable DoFn`. We have also seen that the transform is generic enough to be useful for other non-I/O use cases. On the other hand, as it is a very low-level transform, we should always try to use simpler transforms whenever possible.

In the next section, we will describe a legacy Source API and the (currently deprecated) `Read` transform.

The legacy Source API and the Read transform

Before the creation of the `splittable DoFn` object, Beam used the **Source API** and its associated `Read` transform. Although this transform is currently deprecated and should not be used for implementing new sources, it is still supported. On some runners and under specific conditions, using the deprecated `Read` transform might still be preferred. We have already seen examples of this – for example, the `use_deprecated_read` flag passed when using the `--experiments` flag for Python's `ReadFromKafka` transform.

The `Read` transform accepts a single parameter: either an object of the `BoundedSource` type or the `UnboundedSource` type. Whether the source is bounded or unbounded then determines if the resulting `PCollection` object is bounded or unbounded.

We apply the `Read` transform as follows:

```
Pipeline p = ...;
p.apply(Read.from(new MyUnboundedSource());
```

We will not go into the details of `BoundedSource` or `UnboundedSource`, mostly because they are deprecated. However, we will highlight the main responsibilities of the source objects:

- The first step of the `Read` transform is *splitting* the source. Both `BoundedSource` and `UnboundedSource` provide a `split` method, which splits a single source into multiple parts that can be processed in parallel.

- Both sources must provide a reader – `BoundedSource` must provide a `BoundedReader` object and `UnboundedSource` an `UnboundedReader` object.

- The main difference between BoundedReader and UnboundedReader is that UnboundedReader is created for a specific CheckpointMark object. This relates to the concept of checkpointing unbounded splittable DoFn objects, which we already discussed. The BoundedReader object is supposed to read the entire split from start to finish. This is where the splittable DoFn process closed the gap between bounded and unbounded sources.

- The rest is specific to UnboundedSource. It has to provide a mechanism for creating a CheckpointMark object (thereby taking a checkpoint that can be later restored) and for computing a watermark. The BoundedSource object is simpler in this regard – it is assumed that bounded sources do not have watermarks and that the source is processed either completely or not at all. Again, this is where the splittable DoFn process enters as a unification of both bounded and unbounded cases.

With this short explanation of the legacy Source API, we have completed our discussion of sources. In order to complete the I/O connectors, we will briefly describe an implementation of a *data sink*.

Writing a custom data sink

As opposed to a data *source*, a data *sink* has much less work to do. Actually – in trivial cases – a data sink can be implemented using a plain ParDo object. In fact, we have already implemented one of these, which was PrintElements, located in the util module. The PrintElements transform can be considered a sink to stderr, as we can see from this implementation:

```
@Override
public PDone expand(PCollection<T> input) {
  input.apply(ParDo.of(new LogResultsFn<>()));
  return PDone.in(input.getPipeline());
}


private static class LogResultsFn<T> extends DoFn<T, Void> {
  @ProcessElement
  public void process(@Element T elem) {
    System.err.println(elem);
  }
}
```

This sink is very simplistic – a real-life solution would need some of the tools we already know. For example, batching RPCs using bundle life cycles via `@StartBundle` and `@FinishBundle`, or even complex, sink-specific processing such as Beam's `KafkaExactyOnceSink` for Kafka or `FileIO`, which deals with writing data to files on distributed filesystems.

Either way, there are generally no new features needed for writing sink functions. They boil down to everything we already know. However, there is one interesting exception, which we will discuss next.

The inherent non-determinism of Apache Beam pipelines

Apache Beam pipelines carry an inherent non-determinism that is related to several key aspects:

- All processing-time triggers are non-deterministic by definition.

- Event-time triggers might be non-deterministic because elements might – under some conditions – overpass their watermark (the opposite is not possible).

- User-defined processing logic might be non-deterministic.

Streaming runners normally deal with this non-determinism using their own mechanisms – for example, consistent checkpointing, external durable storage, and so on. When a failure occurs, the state of the computation is restored to the previous consistent state, and the lost computation is replayed from the data stored in the checkpoints from the sources to the sinks. This works well for all of the intermediate data inside the pipeline, but once we write to external storage, several problems arise:

- What has been written to the external storage might not be possible to *unwrite*. This problem is most prominent on commit-log types of storage such as Kafka. Once we write to a topic, the message cannot be unwritten.

- Even storage that is idempotent (that is, with multiple writes having the same result as a single write – for example, **NoSQL** databases such as **Apache Cassandra**) can suffer from the inherent non-determinism. This is because on failure, the result of the write after the pipeline is recovered might be different from the previous run, which might result in duplicate or inconsistent writes to the output database.

- Batch runners (such as **Apache Spark** or batch Flink) often rely on deterministic computation during recovery – that is, the complete data is recomputed – and inconsistencies can result in inconsistent computation.

- It is often good to plan for these non-deterministic cases and, wherever possible, deal with them inside the application logic of the pipeline (using `PaneInfo.getIndex()` to distinguish the order of the firing of panes, possibly avoiding overwriting already written data with a higher index than that being currently written).

Unfortunately, there are cases when this is not sufficient, for example, when the application logic is – for any reason – non-deterministic itself. A rerun might result in a completely different key being generated, which would prevent `PaneInfo` from being of any use in that case. For this reason, Beam has a special (and experimental) annotation for the `@ProcessElement` method in `DoFn` – `@RequiresStableInput`.

A declaration of such a method then looks like the following:

```
@ProcessElement
@RequiresStableInput
public void process(...) { ... }
```

A `DoFn` object marked with this annotation will perform a – runner dependent – effort to ensure that the input to the method will be resistant to retries. Note that the actual implementation of *how* the runner ensures this is left entirely to the runner. Some runners support this natively, some runners might introduce (possibly non-trivial) latency, and some runners might not be able to support this at all (unfortunately, this is the majority, at least at the time of writing).

A general piece of advice when it comes to I/Os is as follows: wherever possible, try to avoid non-deterministic user code. If this is not possible, use streaming runners, as these are better suited to handle these situations. Use `@RequiresStableInput` when you know your runners support it and you have tested that it meets your performance requirements.

Summary

In this chapter, we have walked through the last fundamental transform of Apache Beam – the `splittable DoFn` transform. The transform works as a unifying bridge between batch and streaming sources on one side and allows us to build reusable bounded and unbounded transforms that can be composed to deliver new functionality. As an example, we implemented a `StreamingFileRead` transform that composes two `splittable DoFn` transforms – one that watches a directory for new files and another that reads the contents of the files and produces `PCollection` objects of text lines from them. Note that we might reuse these transforms in different ways. The `FileRead` transform can be used to read filenames from Apache Kafka, thereby converting a stream in Kafka containing new filenames to a stream of text lines contained in these files. The `DirectoryWatch` transform could be used as an input to a transform that ensures the synchronizing of files between two distinct locations. It is only the *composition* of these two transforms that gives rise to the `StreamingFileRead` transform as a whole.

After exploring the typical I/O applications of `splittable DoFn`, we looked at a non-I/O application as well. We created an application that can be used to compute the approximate value of Pi in a distributed fashion. We used a Monte Carlo algorithm for this and explored how these concepts could be used to implement more practical use cases such as Gibbs sampling.

In the last part of this chapter, we looked at how *sinks* in Beam are essentially plain `ParDo` objects with custom application logic applied, which is typically defined by the capabilities and requirements of the target storage. We also emphasized that there is an inherent non-determinism in Beam pipelines that needs to be accounted for and how to do this.

In the last chapter, we will look inside a runner to see how it implements all of the machinery we have discussed in this book, and this will conclude our tour of the Beam essentials.

8
Understanding How Runners Execute Pipelines

So far in this book, we have focused on **Apache Beam** from the user's perspective. We have seen how to code pipelines in the Java **Software Development Kit (SDK)**, how to use **Domain-Specific Languages (DSLs)** such as **SQL**, and how to use portability with the **Python SDK**. In this chapter, we will focus on how the runner executes the pipeline. This will help us if we want to develop a runner for a new technology, debug our code, or improve performance issues.

We will not try to implement our own runner in this chapter. Instead, we will focus on the theoretical concepts that underpin runners. We will explore the building blocks of a typical runner, and this will help us understand how a runner executes our user code.

After describing how runners implement the Beam model, we will conclude this chapter with an in-depth description of **window semantics** and using **metrics** for observability. Improving **observability** is key when attempting to successfully spot and debug issues with our code.

We will walk through the following topics in this chapter:

- Describing the anatomy of an Apache Beam runner
- Explaining the differences between classic and portable runners
- Understanding how a runner handles state
- Exploring the Apache Beam capability matrix
- Understanding windowing semantics in depth
- Debugging pipelines and using Apache Beam metrics for observability

As already mentioned, this chapter will be mainly theoretical, so we have no technical requirements. So, let's jump directly to the description of how any runner executes a Beam pipeline.

Describing the anatomy of an Apache Beam runner

Let's first take a look at the typical life cycle of a pipeline, from the construction time to the pipeline teardown. The complete life cycle is illustrated in the following figure:

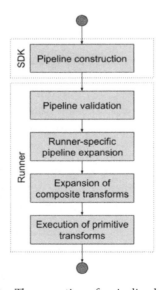

Figure 8.1 – The execution of a pipeline by a runner

The pipeline construction is already well known – we spent most of this book showing how to construct and test pipelines. The next step is submitting the pipeline to a runner. This is the point where the pipeline crosses the SDK-runner boundary, typically by a call to `Pipeline.run()`.

After the pipeline is submitted to the runner, the runner proceeds as follows:

1. Once a runner receives a pipeline, it first performs pipeline validation. This consists of various runner-independent validations – for instance, validating that an appropriate window function and/or trigger is being set and depending on the boundedness of the inputs of the pipeline. These checks apply to all runners and are typically part of the `core-construction` module (for Java runners, this is the `core-construction-java` package).

2. When a pipeline passes runner-independent checks, it is passed to the runner-specific pipeline expansion. This process walks through the pipeline DAG and searches for well-known transforms that typically have a default expansion. In this case, the runner wants to override this expansion. This might be due to performance, or it might be due to runner-specific conditions that cause the default expansion of a `PTransform` instance to be suboptimal in the context of the specific runner. The important part of this process is that the runner must ensure that the `PTransform` instance's semantics are *exactly preserved*. The Java runners again typically make use of helper classes – for example, `PTransformMatcher`, which defines which transforms to find, and `PTransformOverrideFactory`, which defines how to replace them.

3. Next, the pipeline is passed to the pipeline expansion, which expands all of the remaining composite transforms that are not meant to be directly executed by the runner.

4. The last step is to execute the remaining transforms in the pipeline DAG. This step is purely runner-specific and is typically implemented using `PipelineVisitor`, which walks through the pipeline DAG and notifies the visitor about each transform it finds.

Note that the actual procedure might vary from runner to runner. For example, the runner might use the `PipelineVisitor` instance to perform *Step 3* and *Step 4* in one pass. However, the logical view of the process is preserved.

Although the way a runner executes primitive transforms is purely runner-dependent, we can find patterns shared by runners here as well. The mapping between Beam `PCollection` instances and runner internal APIs is typically held inside a `TranslationContext` instance. For example, `FlinkRunner` currently uses different APIs for batch and streaming translation, and therefore, it has two contexts – `FlinkStreamingTranslationContext` and `FlinkBatchTranslationContext`. The first context holds mapping between a `PCollection` instance (`PValue` actually) and a `DataStream` instance (which is **Apache Flink**'s native streaming API), while the latter holds the mapping between `PCollection` and `DataSet` (which is the batch alternative to `DataStream`). Note that although Flink already supports a unified API for both batch and streaming cases, for historical reasons, the `FlinkRunner` instance still uses the legacy batch API (as of Beam version 2.34.0). It would be a great achievement if you participate in the community effort to port `FlinkRunner` to more recent APIs.

In the following subsection, we will see what the minimal building blocks of all Beam runners are.

The minimal set of `PTransform` instances of a feature-complete runner. As we have seen in the previous paragraph, a runner a runner can have two sets of transforms it implements directly:

- Primitive transforms
- Runner-specific expanded composite transforms

While transforms in the first set have to be implemented (due to there being no expansion available), the latter ones are overridden mostly for performance reasons. Therefore, a minimal runner that should be able to run any Beam pipeline will have to implement only the first set of transforms and let everything else expand to these primitives.

Let's see what the actual set of *logical* primitive transforms is:

- `ParDo`: Stateless, stateful, splittable
- `GroupByKey`
- `Window`
- `Impulse`
- `Flatten`
- `View`
- `TestStream`

We already know all of these transforms well. Note that these transforms are primitive only from the logical view – it is possible that some of these PTransform instances actually have an expansion to a *lower-level* primitive transform. For example, a Java SDK Window.into transform can actually be expanded to a Window.Assign transform. However, these are implementation details that can change over time – the more important aspect is the logical description of these transforms.

The ParDo instance relies internally on DoFnRunner – a facility that manages all of the complexities of a DoFn instance's state access, as well as managing the firing of timers and the DoFn life cycle (that is, the @Setup, @Teardown, and @StartBundle processes, and so on). It is a general rule that Beam provides pieces of code that can be reused by various runners. These runners must fulfill specific preconditions – for example, ensuring that the keyed input stream to a stateful ParDo instance is correctly grouped by key before using the DoFnRunner instance.

We haven't yet discussed the details of the Window transform; we will return to this near the end of the chapter in the *Understanding windowing semantics in depth* section. Discussing the full details of the runner API is out of the scope of this book, but if you are interested in learning more, please visit https://beam.apache.org/contribute/runner-guide/.

Identifying which transforms should be overridden

As mentioned in the previous subsection, implementing the set of primitive transforms should be enough for a runner to be able to run any pipeline. However, the ability to run a pipeline does not mean that the pipeline will run *efficiently*. Besides runner-specific concerns, there is one transform that usually needs special attention in all circumstances: Combine.

When we introduced this transform, we introduced it as a *primitive* transform. However, this is not technically correct; the transform is actually a composite with the following expansion:

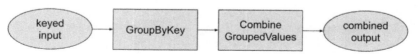

Figure 8.2 – The composite Combine expansion

As we can see, the default expansion first applies the `GroupByKey` transform, which yields `PCollection<KV<K, Iterable<V>>>`, and then it applies `CombineGroupedValues` on the resulting `KV<K, Iterable<V>>` instance. While this produces the correct result, *the performance is highly suboptimal.*

The reason for this is that the `CombineFn` instance used inside the `Combine` transform is carefully designed so that it can be applied in various contexts – and also designed so that it can be *applied partially* – and then merged to produce the final output. This way, the runner can save a huge amount of network bandwidth, and therefore, it can save computational power.

The typical development of a new runner will be split into the following two phases:

- Ensuring the runner produces the correct results (that is, ensuring its *correctness*)
- Optimizing the runner's performance

The `Combine` transform will usually be the first one to implement in any given context but deciding which transforms to make runner-specific should be based on the performance evaluation after the runner produces the correct results.

The question is – how do runners recognize which transform should be overridden and which should be left to the default expansion? We have already mentioned that this task is typically performed by a `PTransformMatcher` instance. But how is a typical matcher implemented? To answer this question, we must note an important detail – each `PTransform` instance can be assigned a `TransformPayloadTranslator` instance, which has two responsibilities:

- Assigning a unique **Uniform Resource Name** (**URN**) to the `PTransform` instance
- Converting the `PTransform` instance to a portable representation (portable representations will be explained later in the *Explaining the differences between classic and portable runners* section)

While the portable representation for a `PTransform` instance that we want to override in a runner can be omitted (for non-primitive transforms), assigning a URN is essential because the runner can then use this URN to match and replace any correct transforms. Some examples of typical URNs for well-known transforms include `beam:transform:pardo:v1` and `beam:transform:group_by_key:v1`. These URNs should be self-explanatory.

Now that we have a high-level understanding of the tasks that need to be implemented by Beam runners in general, let's see what the core differences are between *classic* and *portable* runners.

Explaining the differences between classic and portable runners

The description in the previous section – *Describing the anatomy of an Apache Beam runner* – applies to both classic and portable runners. However, there are some important differences between the two.

A *classic* runner is a runner that is implemented using the same programming language as the Beam SDK. The runner is made in a way that enables it to run the specific SDK only. An example of a classic runner is a classic `FlinkRunner` instance, which uses Apache Flink, has a native API implemented in Java, and is able to execute Beam pipelines written in the Java SDK. We used this runner throughout the first five chapters of this book.

A *portable* runner is implemented using the portability layer and as a result, it can be used to execute pipelines written in any SDK that is supported by Beam. However, this flexibility comes at a price – a portable runner implemented in Java and running a pipeline implemented using only the Java SDK (that is, without any cross-language features) will have somewhat lower performance than an otherwise identical runner. The reason for this is that the portability layer (Fn API) carries some overhead that can be eliminated in a classic runner. It is intended that some optimizations to the Fn API will be implemented that could bypass these overheads when the pipeline SDK matches, but currently, classic runners still play a significant role.

Next, let's see more differences between these two types of runners.

Classic runners

As already mentioned, classic runners share the same language (SDK) with the pipeline they are able to run. This can be illustrated in the following figure:

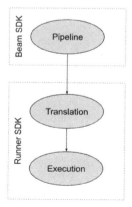

Figure 8.3 – The pipeline execution on a classic runner

The main benefit of the Beam SDK and the runner SDK sharing the same programming language is that no translation is needed between them. The runner can take the pipeline produced by the Beam SDK and act on it directly. The important implication here is that the final, translated pipeline can look somewhat similar to if it had been implemented directly in the SDK of the target runner. For example, a pipeline executed using the classic `FlinkRunner` instance will use the same API as a pipeline implementing a Flink application directly. The performance penalty between Beam SDK **User-Defined Functions (UDFs)** that need to be called from the runner SDK is generally negligible, and therefore, the translation of classic runners more closely matches the structure of the original pipeline. Again, we can illustrate this for clarity:

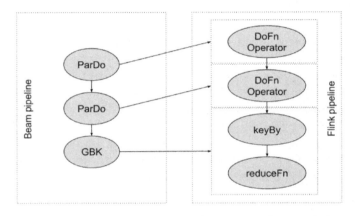

Figure 8.4 – A classic translation of a Beam pipeline on Flink

The specific details of this are out of the scope of this book – the important part to note is that *each transform is translated independently*. The `ParDo` instance is implemented using `DoFnOperator`, while the `GroupByKey` transform is implemented using `keyBy` and the reduction operation that produces the `Iterable` instance of the values. The structure of the pipeline is preserved.

Let's see how the situation changes when we switch to a portable runner.

Portable pipeline representations

When it comes to portable runners, we can no longer work directly on a pipeline produced by the Beam SDK. The target (runner) SDK can be written in an arbitrary language, and therefore, we need a *portable representation of the pipeline*. Let's look at this in detail.

The portable representation uses **protocol buffers** – that is, a language-agnostic way of serializing data into bytes that can then be read and interpreted in various languages. The details of protocol buffers are not too relevant for this discussion, but the important part to understand is that we can imagine a protocol buffer as a dictionary of (nested) key-value pairs. In this case, each dictionary is called `message`.

The complete SDK pipeline is serialized into `message Pipeline`, whose most important part is the list of pipeline components. Pipeline components are another message with the following fields:

- `transform`: This is a list of all serialized `PTransform` instances in the pipeline, including sub-transforms of composite transforms.

- `pcollections`: This is a list of names of serialized `PCollection` instances that represent connection edges between transforms.

- `windowing_strategies`: This is a list of all of the windowing functions and triggers.

- `coders`: This is a list of serialized coders.

- `environments`: This is a list of the available execution environments (for example, **Docker**).

Note that when there is any UDF needed for the specification – for example, when we implement a custom user-defined coder – this UDF needs to be serialized into the pipeline portable representation using the SDK-specific way. For example, the Java SDK typically uses Java serialization. This holds true not only for transforms but also for windowing strategies and coders. Every UDF is associated with a URN, and this URN might be defined to be well known and not carry any serialized UDF as a result. For example, the `GlobalWindows` windowing strategy carries the `beam:window_fn:global_windows:v1` URN, while `KvCoder` has the `beam:coder:kv:v1` URN. When the URN is not generally recognized, both the URN and the payload are SDK-specific. For instance, a custom Java `Coder` instance would have the `beam:coders:javasdk:0.1` URN and the associated payload would be the Java serialized class of the `Coder` instance.

Let's illustrate the execution of a pipeline using a portable runner in the following figure:

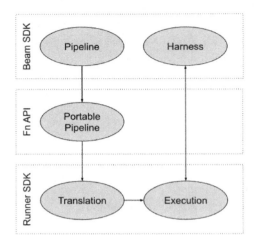

Figure 8.5 – A pipeline execution using a portable runner

The main difference we can see compared to the execution on the classic runner shown in *Figure 8.3* is that the execution (*Runner SDK*) must communicate with the Beam SDK layer via the SDK harness. This is implied by the fact that the runner cannot execute user code (for example, UDFs) itself, and therefore, it must delegate these calls to the Beam SDK.

Every request from the runner to the SDK harness has a non-zero overhead associated with the inter-process communication, and therefore, it is desirable to minimize the number of round-trips. This is where the concept of an *executable stage* and the process of *pipeline fusion* come in; we will describe these concepts in the following section.

The executable stage concept and the pipeline fusion process

Pipeline fusion is a process of optimizing the necessary runner-to-SDK round-trips. We can illustrate this concept on a pipeline with four transforms, as shown in *Figure 8.6*:

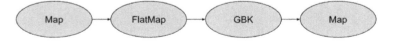

Figure 8.6 – The pipeline fusion process

The pipeline consists of four transforms: Map, followed by FlatMap, then GroupByKey, and another Map. The three mapping transforms must be associated with a UDF that will perform the actual logic. If we were to translate this pipeline natively so that every transform was a separate transform in the runner SDK, it would result in the situation illustrated in the following figure:

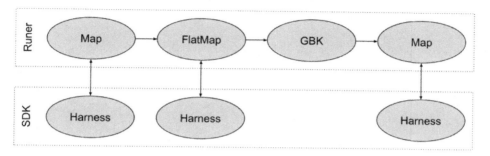

Figure 8.7 – An unfused pipeline

We can see that every data element would have to go through three runner-to-SDK communication channels. The GroupByKey instance is not associated with a UDF, as it is completely described by the input data, so there is no communication necessary. However, every other transform in the pipeline will carry a non-trivial communication overhead.

To describe how Beam optimizes this, we need to define the concept of a *shuffle*. A shuffle is an operation that requires communication between different workers in a distributed environment. This requirement comes from the fact that the operation performs the *logical grouping* of elements based on a key. This definition implies that the following transforms are shuffles:

- GroupByKey
- Combine
- Stateful ParDo

Other operations operate on isolated data elements and therefore, they can be *fused* into a single transform, as shown in the following figure:

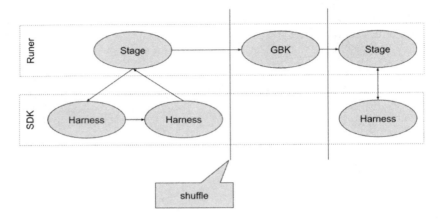

Figure 8.8 – A fused pipeline

The fused transform is called `ExecutableStage` and represents all of the operations between two shuffle boundaries. This way, data elements cross the runner-SDK boundary only as many times as there are shuffle stages. This has implications for performance. For example, imagine the following situation – a chain of two transforms within the same shuffle stage, as illustrated in *Figure 8.9*:

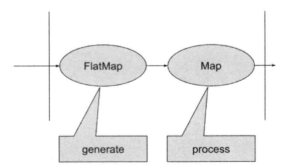

Figure 8.9 – A shuffle stage with two transforms

Let's imagine that the first transform is a `FlatMap` instance that generates a large number of elements per input and these are subsequently processed by a `Map` transform. Let's say that the `Map` transform is non-trivially expensive in terms of CPU usage. Without any additional modifications, these two transforms would be fused into a single executable stage, and therefore, all of the elements produced by a single input element to the `FlatMap` instance would be *processed sequentially, without any parallelism*. However, this might not be what we want in this situation. But how do we *prevent fusion*? The answer is that we need to insert a shuffle boundary, as seen in the following figure:

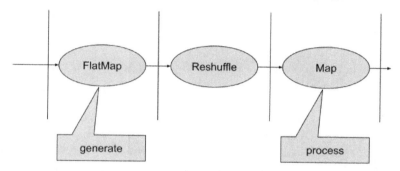

Figure 8.10 – Using the Reshuffle transform to prevent fusion

Although the `Reshuffle` transform is currently deprecated, for these purposes, it works well. However, it is important to note that fusion not only happens for chains of transforms but can also happen between *siblings*. That is, if the output of one transform is consumed by multiple downstream transforms, then these transforms might be fused as well.

Now, let's see how runners ensure fault tolerance and correctness when accessing state.

Understanding how a runner handles state

As we already know, any complex computation will need to group multiple data elements in order to do computation. Because the streaming processing cannot rely on sources being able to replay data (as opposed to pure batch processing, where this property is essential), any updates to the local state during the computation have to be fault-tolerant, and it is the responsibility of a runner to ensure this. The Beam state API is designed precisely to enable this. Any state access is handled by a runner-provided implementation of `StateInternals` (and `TimerInternals` for timers – in this discussion, we will treat timers as special cases of state, so we will not describe them independently). The `StateInternals` instances are responsible for creating the accessors for the state – for example, `ValueState`, `BagState`, `MapState`, and so on. The runner must create and manage these instances to ensure both fault tolerance and consistency during recovery after failure.

The state access is illustrated in the following figure:

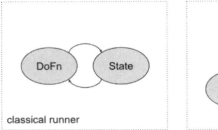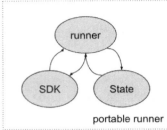

Figure 8.11 – Runner state access

We can see that the state access differs for classic and portable runners. In the classic runner, the state is accessed directly from the runner that runs the stateful `DoFn` instance, while in the portable runner, the state is accessed from the SDK harness, as the request needs to go from the harness to the runner, which then subsequently requests the value of the state from the storage. This emphasizes the need for optimizations, which are enabled by signaling to the runner if a state is going to be accessed, and therefore if it should be pre-fetched (ideally in parallel, if the `DoFn` instance accesses multiple states). This is done via the call to `readLater()` (for instance, `ValueState.readLater()`). Another useful optimization is providing a runner with hints for cases and when a state is read for every element so that the runner can further optimize the access. This is done via the `DoFn.AlwaysFetched` annotation, which can be used to annotate states in the `@ProcessElement` or `@OnTimer` methods.

Let's now see what the runner must ensure so that the state can be made fault-tolerant.

Ensuring fault tolerance

So, how does a runner ensure that the state is really fault-tolerant? The short answer – as always – is *it depends*. Different runners have different ways of ensuring this. However, there are some general requirements that must hold in all cases. These include the following:

- The state must be replicated on multiple nodes.
- The state must be able to revert itself (that is, discard changes) to a specific moment in time where it was *committed*.

Now, we will explain both of these requirements in more detail.

The first requirement is directly implied by fault tolerance. Having a state only on a single machine means that if we lose that machine, we lose the state.

The second requirement is needed to ensure consistency during recovery after failure. When a failure occurs, all stateful transforms in a pipeline are reset to the last committed state – including sources – and the processing is resumed from this state. Of course, this cannot undo changes already made to external systems – for instance, databases – so we ideally need to make writes *idempotent*. Idempotent operations are operations that can be safely applied multiple times. Any duplicate application of an idempotent operation has exactly the same effect as if it were applied only once. When idempotence cannot be achieved (for example, when writing to a commit log such as **Apache Kafka** and without transactions), the pipeline might produce duplicate writes.

Let's see two typical examples of how runners deal with these two requirements. The first will describe the implementation of a Flink runner, and the second will describe another possibility, which is similar to how **Windmill** (the streaming execution engine of **Google Cloud Dataflow**) handles state.

Local state with periodic checkpoints

Flink uses the technique of checkpointing to achieve both requirements. The state is kept in a *state backend*, which is primarily stored on the local machine and runs the computation. The pipeline performs periodic checkpoints, upon which the local state creates a snapshot that is persisted to remote (distributed) storage. On recovery, each worker fetches the snapshot and thereby rewinds itself to the *committed* position.

This is illustrated in the following figure:

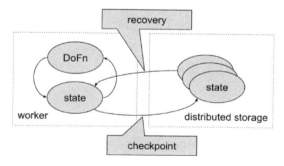

Figure 8.12 – Local state checkpointing

Note that in this scenario, the frequency of the checkpoint defines the frequency of the *bundle finalization*. As we know, a bundle is an atomic piece of work, which is either processed completely or not at all. Therefore, the bundle finalization (*commit*) can be performed for successful checkpoints only, where the state of the bundle is safely persisted. This defines how often we confirm the delivery of data to sources (for sources that need it, such as publish-subscribe types of sources), and therefore, we should not have the checkpointing frequency too low. On the other hand, too high a frequency creates unnecessary overhead, so setting the optimal value of the checkpoint frequency requires special care and testing.

An alternative to checkpointing the local state is keeping the state in remote distributed storage from the beginning.

Remote state

A state can be kept in remote distributed storage and fetched remotely from the worker for each bundle upon access (using local caching). Updates to the state are committed with each bundle as part of the *bundle commit*. Therefore, the committed remote state always contains a consistent snapshot that the worker can be reverted to during recovery. Another advantage of this approach is that workers are *effectively stateless*. This property makes it easier to dynamically scale the number of workers based on the actual load. This approach is illustrated in the following figure:

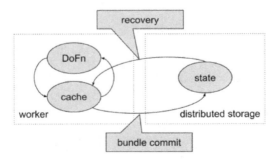

Figure 8.13 – Remote state

An important requirement is that the commit of a state update during bundle processing must be *atomic*. Otherwise, the state might not contain consistent data and a bundle might be only partially processed, resulting in some data being processed multiple times, which is prohibited by the Beam model.

Let's now explain how Beam ensures that runners adhere to the Beam model.

Exploring the Apache Beam capability matrix

Beam makes sure that runners adhere to the Beam model to ensure that pipelines are portable between different runners. There are tests specifically designed to validate the compatibility between runners – these tests are called `ValidatesRunner` suites and are annotated using the `@ValidatesRunner` annotation. Any runner author can verify the compatibility of their runner against these tests. However, because runners are developed at different rates, it is possible that a specific runner at a certain moment in time does not support all of the features of the Beam model. Therefore, the complete set of `ValidatesRunner` tests can be narrowed down by toggling specific *features* of the model. The tests in the complete suite are then annotated using features such as `UsesSetState` or `UsesSchema`. A runner is then allowed to specify features that should be excluded from the tests. These excluded features should then match what is documented in the so-called **capability matrix**. The complete matrix can be found at `https://beam.apache.org/documentation/runners/capability-matrix/`.

We will show a short excerpt of the complete matrix here:

What is being computed?

	Google Cloud Dataflow	Apache Flink	Apache Spark (RDD/DStream based)	Apache Spark Structured Streaming (Dataset based)
ParDo	✓	✓	✓	~
GroupByKey	✓	✓	~	~
Flatten	✓	✓	✓	~
Combine	✓	✓	✓	~
Composite Transforms	~	~	~	~
Side Inputs	✓	✓	✓	~
Source API	✓	✓	✓	~
Metrics	~	~	~	~
Stateful Processing	~	~	~	✕

Figure 8.14 – An excerpt from the capability matrix

The matrix has features in rows and different runners in columns. The symbols stand for fully supported, partially supported, and unsupported. If a specific feature is supported only partially (~) then a more detailed explanation of the current limitation can be found by expanding the full matrix at the URL address. It is always a good idea to consult this matrix before switching from one runner to another to avoid any surprises.

In the following section, we will explore the details of windowing semantics to understand how runners implement it.

Understanding windowing semantics in depth

In *Chapter 1, Introducing Data Processing with Apache Beam*, we introduced the basic types of window functions. To recap, we defined the following:

- Fixed windows
- Sliding windows
- Global window
- Session windows

We also defined two basic types of windows: *key-aligned* and *key-unaligned*. The first three types (*fixed*, *sliding*, and *global*) are key-aligned, and session windows are key-unaligned (as in session windows, each window can start and end at different times for different keys). However, what we skipped in *Chapter 1, Introduction to Data Processing with Apache Beam*, was the fact that we can define *completely custom* windowing logic.

The `Window.into` transform accepts a generic `WindowFn` instance, which defines the following main methods:

1. The `assignWindows` method, which assigns elements into a set of window labels.

2. The `isNonMerging` method, which tells the runner whether the `WindowFn` instance defines *merging windows* or *non-merging windows*. We will explain what this means shortly.

3. The `mergeWindows` method, which is for merging windows, if necessary.

Besides that, the `WindowFn` instance defines methods for retrieving `Coder` instances for the window label, as well as several other (mostly) helper methods. The `assignWindows` method is straightforward – it takes an input data element and returns a collection of labels that the element belongs to. A typical example of this would be returning a specific interval based on the timestamp of an element for fixed windows or returning several intervals shifted by slide duration for sliding windows.

To understand window merging, we need to define the difference between merging and non-merging windows.

Merging and non-merging windows

Non-merging windows are produced by window functions that *do not change the window label once the label is assigned*. This means the target window is fully determined by the input element itself, without the need for any additional context. The typical examples of this from our basic window functions are fixed windows, sliding windows, and the global window.

Merging windows are the opposite – that is, the window label might actually depend on multiple elements. Due to the inherently unordered nature of the elements in data streams, this context is created by assigning elements to windows separately and *merging* the resulting windows when appropriate. We can illustrate this in the following figure for session windows:

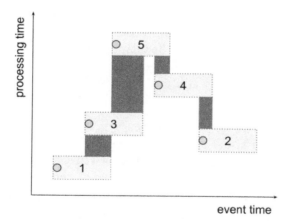

Figure 8.15 – Merging session windows

Figure 8.15 shows five data elements (for the same key) that arrive with different delays. The elements arrive in the processing time order of *1*, *2*, *3*, *4*, and *5*, however, their respective event time order is *1*, *3*, *5*, *4*, and *2*. Every data element starts being assigned to an interval window that starts at the timestamp of the element and has the duration equal to the session gap. Next, every time a new window is created, it is attempted for the new window to be merged with an already existing set of windows. The session window function defines the merge function so that *overlapping windows can be merged*. The overlapping intervals are shown in *Figure 8.18*. This will result in the following actual windows being created during the processing:

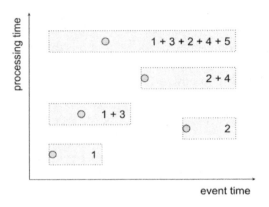

Figure 8.16 – Merged session windows

The window merge produces the first window containing element *1*, then another window containing element *2*, then window *3* will be merged with window *1* to produce window *1+3*, and this continues. At the end, all of the elements are assigned to a single window, which is what should be expected, as the distance between the elements is less than the gap duration.

Note that before the windows are merged, they are treated as independent windows, and therefore, they have an associated state (and/or timers). When the windows are merged, the corresponding state has to be merged as well. Currently, stateful DoFn does not support merging windows, as the generic merging of states is not defined. Therefore, merging window functions are applicable to GroupByKey and Combine only. In these cases, the merging is trivially defined as a union of two corresponding iterables in the case of GroupByKey and the application of an accumulator merge in the case of Combine. This way, we can easily produce the final merged output.

In the last section of this chapter – and this book – we will see how to get better insights into the performance and/or business characteristics of processed data using *metrics*.

Debugging pipelines and using Apache Beam metrics for observability

Observability is a key part of spotting potential issues with a running pipeline. It can be used to measure various performance characteristics, including the number of elements processed, the number of RPC calls to backend services, and the distribution of the event-time lags of elements flowing through the pipeline.

Although it should be possible to create a side output for each metric and handle the resulting stream like any data in the pipeline, the requirement for quick and simple feedback from running pipelines led Beam to create a simple API dedicated to metrics. Currently, Beam supports the following metrics:

- Counters
- Gauges
- Distributions

A `Counter` instance is a metric that is represented by a single long value that can only be incremented or decremented (this can be by *1*, or by another number).

A `Gauge` instance is a metric that also holds a single long value; however, this value can only be directly set. The actual value of a gauge is equal to the latest value set. Note that due to the distributed nature of the computation, the value reported by this metric might not necessarily be exactly the same as the last value reported, but it should be one of the latest.

A `Distribution` instance is a metric that is useful for the computation of more complex statistics than those possible with `Counter`. A `Distribution` instance computes the minimum, maximum, and mean of reported long values.

Each metric has a namespace and a name. The namespace is typically defined by a transform (or a class that implements a UDF, for example, `DoFn`). The name must distinguish the metric from other metrics with the same namespace.

Using metrics in the Java SDK

In the Java SDK, we can add metrics to our pipeline as follows:

```java
class MyDoFn extends DoFn<String, String> {
  private final Counter elements = Metrics.counter(
      MyDoFn.class, "elements");
  @ProcessElement
  public void processElement(@Element String elem) {
    elements.inc();
  }
}
```

All `Metric` instances (that is, `Counter`, `Gauge`, and `Distribution`) are serializable, and therefore, they can be declared anywhere in the code. When used in a UDF, they will be serialized and made available to the code on the worker. All metrics are created the same way by using the `Metrics` helper class and the `Metrics.counter`, `Metrics.gauge`, and `Metrics.distribution` methods.

Once we have a pipeline that declares and uses a metric, we can query the metrics via the `PipelineResult` class as follows:

```java
Pipeline pipeline = Pipeline.create(...);
...
PipelineResult result = pipeline.run();
// the Pipeline is running
MetricsResult metrics = result.metrics();
MetricsQueryResult allMetrics = Metrics.allMetrics();
Iterable<MetricResult<Long>> counters = allMetrics.
getCounters();
// read the current value of all counters
```

The `MetricResult` instance contains two types of results:

- Attempted metrics
- Committed metrics

Attempted metrics accumulate all attempts of tasks, including failed attempts, while *committed metrics* accumulate only values from committed work. Unfortunately, most of the runners do not support committed metrics, as detailed in the capability matrix (https://beam.apache.org/documentation/runners/capability-matrix/what-is-being-computed/).

Summary

In this chapter, we walked through how runners execute pipelines in both *classic mode* and using the *portability layer*. We have seen that classic runners are suitable only for cases where a particular underlying technology – for instance, Apache Flink – has an API in the same language as the pipeline SDK. The most practical cases for this include using the Java SDK for both the runner and the pipeline.

In cases where the language of the runner and the pipeline SDK differ, we have to use portability (Fn API), which brings some overhead. We have seen how *pipeline fusion* is used to reduce this overhead as much as possible. We have also discussed situations where we want to *prevent fusion* and how to do this by inserting a *shuffle boundary*.

Next, we discussed the responsibilities of a runner with regard to state management. We saw how the runner ensures fault tolerance and correctness upon failures. We outlined two basic types of fault-tolerant states: *local state with periodic checkpointing to distributed storage* and *fully remote distributed state*.

After that, we explained how Beam ensures the compliance of runners with the Beam model by using `@ValidatesRunner` tests. We also emphasized that all runners are not necessarily required to fully implement all of the features of the Beam model and how the supported features of the runners are documented in the *capability matrix*.

We also took a detailed look at *windowing semantics*. We have seen that we can implement our own windowing strategy using a custom `WindowFn` instance. We also learned about the differences between *merging* and *non-merging* window functions and how runners implement the merging of windows and their associated states.

In the last section, we learned how to use metrics to improve the observability of running pipelines with the `Counter`, `Gauge`, and `Distribution` metrics.

This completes our walkthrough of Apache Beam. Although we didn't cover everything Beam offers, we hope that the book has given you a good understanding of the core concepts of this great technology.

Index

A

accumulators 60
allowed lateness 21, 118
anatomy
  describing, of Apache Beam
    runner 290- 293
Apache Beam
  need for 5
Apache Beam capability matrix
  exploring 305, 306
Apache Beam metrics
  using, for observability 309
Apache Beam pipelines
  inherent non-determinism 286, 287
Apache Beam SQL
  further development 212
Apache Beam SQL shell
  reference link 212
Apache Calcite SQL dialect
  reference link 202
Apache Flink
  about 5, 99, 218
  installing 34
Apache Kafka
  about 88, 212, 303
  installing 31, 32

Apache Maven 6
Apache Spark 5, 25, 218
Apache Storm 25
associative 60
attempted metrics 310
average length of words in
    stream, calculating
  about 62
  problem decomposition 63
  problem definition 62
  solution deployment 67, 68
  solution implementation 63-66
  solution testing 66
average length of words in stream,
    calculating with fixed lookback
  about 69
  problem decomposition 69
  problem definition 69
  solution deployment 71, 72
  solution implementation 69
  solution testing 69, 70

B

batching queries, to external RPC service
  about 95
  problem decomposition 95

problem definition 95
solution implementation 96-99
batching queries, to external RPC
    service with defined batch sizes
    about 99
    problem decomposition 100
    problem definition 99
    solution implementation 100-107
batch processing
    about 6
    unifying 24-27
BigQuery 212
BigTable 212
bounded source 257
bundles 93

C

calendar windows 18
capability matrix documentation
    reference link 305
Cartesian product 166
checkpoint 259
classic runner 295, 296
CoderProvider 55
CoderRegistry 55
coders 53
CoGroupByKey
    about 161, 162
    used, for enhancing SportTracker
        by runner motivation 162
combinable operation 60
Combine PTransform object 59, 60
Combine transform 294
Committed metrics 310
commutative 60
composite transformations 59

consumer 32
Continuous Integration (CI)
    environment 42
Convert transform 194
Counter instance 309
CREATE EXTERNAL TABLE statement
    reference link 212
cross-language pipelines
    about 250
    using 250-252
custom data sink
    writing 285, 286

D

data
    assigning, to windows 18
DataFrame API
    using 247, 248
data stream
    about 10
    event time progress, measuring 15, 16
    state 16, 17
    timer 18
    triggers 17
default triggers 56
Directed Acyclic Graph (DAG) 6, 218, 280
Distribution instance 309
droppable data
    Beam 118-120
droppable data, separating from
        rest of data processing
    about 120
    problem decomposition 121-132
    problem definition 121, 130
    solution deployment 129, 130, 139
    solution implementation 122-137
    solution testing 127-138

E

early firing 58
environment
    complete environment, reinstalling 35
    setting up 31
event time 14, 26
event time progress
    measuring, inside data streams 15, 16
event time timers 103, 109
executable stage 298-301
external service
    using, for data augmentation
    about 86, 87
    problem decomposition 87, 88
    problem definition 87
    solution deployment 92
    solution implementation 88-91
    solution testing 91, 92

F

fault tolerance, ensuring 302, 303
fields 190
Filter transform 194
first streaming pipeline
    implementing, with SQL 197-200
fixed windows 18
full (outer) join 166

G

Garbage Collection (GC) 119
Gauge instance 309
Gibbs sampling 278
global window 20, 166
Google Cloud Dataflow 5, 218, 303

GroupByKey 80, 81
Group transform 196
gRPC 88, 219

H

Hadoop Distributed File
    System (HDFS) 71
hot key fanout operation 61
HTTP/2 88

I

idempotent 90
idempotent operations 303
inner join 166
input watermark 110
InteractiveRunner
    using 248-250

J

Java 102
Java Bean 192
javadoc 94
Java SDK
    about 89
    metrics, using 310
Java Virtual Machine (JVM) 9, 90
JobManager 218
Job Service 219
Join library DSL 165-167
Join transform 196
JSON 116
JUnit 5 42, 91

K

kafka-console-consumer 38
key-aligned 306
key salting 128
key-unaligned 306
K most frequent words, calculating
     in stream of lines of text
  about 35
  problem decomposition 36-39
  problem definition 35
  solution deployment 44, 45
  solution implementation 39-41
  solution testing 41-43
kubectl
  installation link 31
Kubernetes 31

L

late data 15
left (outer) join 166
life cycle of state
  defining, in terms of windows 20-23
local state
  checkpointing 303, 304
looping timers 131

M

matching windows 167
maximal length of word in
     stream, calculating
  about 45
  problem decomposition 45, 46
  solution deployment 50-53
  solution implementation 46-48
  solution testing 48, 49

MaxWordLength, implementing
     in Python SDK
  about 223
  problem decomposition 224
  problem definition 224
  solution deployment 227-229
  solution implementation 224-226
  solution testing 226, 227
merging windows 307, 308
metrics
  using, in Java SDK 310
minikube
  about 31
  code, running on 33, 34
  installation link 31
MongoDB 212
Monte Carlo method 278

N

non-merging 131
non-merging windows 307, 308

O

output watermark 110

P

pane accumulation 23, 24
parallel collection 53
ParDo transform
  implications 196
Partition 81, 82
PCollection Coder object 53

performance statistics, calculating for
    sport activity tracking application
  about 74
  problem decomposition 75, 76
  problem definition 74
  solution deployment 79
  solution implementation 76-78
  solution testing 78
pipeline
  debugging 309
  portable representation 218
  running, against streaming data 10-12
  writing 6-9
pipeline fusion 298-301
pipeline upgradability
  ensuring 72, 73
PiSampler
  about 278
  problem decomposition 280
  problem definition 279
  solution deployment 283, 284
  solution implementation 281, 282
  solution testing 283
portability layer 217, 218
portable pipeline
  components 297
portable pipeline representations 296-298
portable runner 295
primary restriction 259
primitive transform 293
primitive transformation 59
processing time 14, 142
processing time timers 103
protocol buffers 88, 218, 250, 297
PTransform 148, 149
PTransform expansion 148, 149

PTransform instance 294
PubSub 212
Python 5
Python pipeline
  implementing 220-222
Python SDK
  coders 230, 231
  MaxWordLength, implementing 223
  pipelines, implementing 220
  RPCParDo, implementing 236
  SportTracker, implementing 231
  SportTrackerMotivation,
    implementing 242
  type hints 230, 231

R

Read-Evaluate-Print-Loop (REPL) 248
Read transform 284
real-time processing 6
reduce phase 45
Reify 51
relative timer 134
Remote Procedure Call (RPC) 86
remote state 304
residual restriction 259
restriction 259, 260
retract streams 186
reusable PTransform, writing
  about 172
  problem decomposition 173-176
  problem definition 173
  solution deployment 185, 186
  solution implementation 177-182
  solution testing 183-185
RPCParDo, implementing in Python SDK

about 236
   problem definition 236
   solution deployment 241
   solution implementation 236-239
   solution testing 240
runner
   used, for handling state 301, 302

S

Savepoint 71
schema
   about 190, 191
   attaching, to PCollection 191-194
   transforms, for PCollections 194
SchemaSportTracker
   implementing 204
   problem decomposition 205
   problem definition 204
   solution implementation 205-207
SDK harness 219
Select transform 195
session window 19, 20
shuffle phase 45
side inputs 151
   used, for enhancing SportTracker
      by runner motivation 149
   using 116, 117, 139-142
side outputs 115
slide 19
sliding windows 19, 69
Source API 284, 285
spatial splitting 259
splittable DoFn

about 257
   defining, as unification for
      bounded source 258
   defining, as unification for
      unbounded source 258
splittable DoFn implementation
   about 262
   problem decomposition 263, 264
   solution deployment 277, 278
   solution implementation 264-275
   solution testing 275, 276
splittable DoFn processing
   life cycle 261, 262
SportTracker, enhancing by runner
      motivation with CoGroupByKey
   about 162
   problem decomposition 163
   problem definition 163
   solution implementation 163-165
SportTracker, enhancing by runner
      motivation with side inputs
   about 149
   problem decomposition 150, 151
   problem definition 150
   solution deployment 160
   solution implementation 152-157
   solution testing 157-159
SportTracker, implementing
      in Python SDK
   about 231
   problem definition 231
   solution deployment 235, 236
   solution implementation 231-233
   solution testing 234
SportTrackerMotivation,

implementing in Python SDK
about 242
problem definition 242
solution implementation 242-246
solution deploymnent 246
SQL
first streaming pipeline,
implementing with 197-200
SQLMaxWordLength
implementing 200
problem decomposition 200, 201
problem definition 200
solution implementation 201-204
SQLSportTrackerMotivation
implementing 208
problem decomposition 208
problem definition 208
solution implementation 209-211
state 16, 17
state bootstrapping 73
stateful ParDo 107
stateful ParDo object
theoretical properties,
describing of 108-111
stateless ParDo 92-94
streaming data processing
unifying 24-27
StreamingInnerJoin 172
streaming Python pipeline
implementing 222, 223
stream-to-stream joins 168-172

T
table-stream duality 186, 187
temporal splitting 259
TestStream 10
theoretical properties
applying, of stateful ParDo object
to API of DoFn 112-115
describing, of stateful ParDo
object 108-111
time-constrained window 11
timer 18
TimestampCombiner 52
time-varying relations 188, 212
topic 32
transforms, for PCollections with schema
Convert 194
Filter 194
Group 196
Join 196
ParDo 196
Select 195
triggering 56
triggers 17
tumbling windows 18
TypeDescriptor object 54
TypeDescriptors 54

U
unbounded data
about 10
key properties, exploring 12-14
unbounded source 257

Uniform Resource Name (URN) 251, 294
upsert 173
upsert streams 186
User Defined Aggregate
      Function (UDAF) 201
User-Defined Functions (UDFs)
      54, 201, 218, 296

W

watermark 15, 103, 109
Windmill 303
window closing behavior 57
windowed join 210
window function 26
windowing semantics 306
windows
  data, assigning to 18

Packt.com

Subscribe to our online digital library for full access to over 7,000 books and videos, as well as industry leading tools to help you plan your personal development and advance your career. For more information, please visit our website.

Why subscribe?

- Spend less time learning and more time coding with practical eBooks and Videos from over 4,000 industry professionals

- Improve your learning with Skill Plans built especially for you

- Get a free eBook or video every month

- Fully searchable for easy access to vital information

- Copy and paste, print, and bookmark content

Did you know that Packt offers eBook versions of every book published, with PDF and ePub files available? You can upgrade to the eBook version at packt.com and as a print book customer, you are entitled to a discount on the eBook copy. Get in touch with us at customercare@packtpub.com for more details.

At www.packt.com, you can also read a collection of free technical articles, sign up for a range of free newsletters, and receive exclusive discounts and offers on Packt books and eBooks.

Other Books You May Enjoy

If you enjoyed this book, you may be interested in these other books by Packt:

Data Engineering with Apache Spark, Delta Lake, and Lakehouse

Manoj Kukreja

ISBN: 978-1-80107-774-3

- Discover the challenges you may face in the data engineering world
- Add ACID transactions to Apache Spark using Delta Lake
- Understand effective design strategies to build enterprise-grade data lakes
- Explore architectural and design patterns for building efficient data ingestion pipelines
- Orchestrate a data pipeline for preprocessing data using Apache Spark and Delta Lake APIs
- Automate deployment and monitoring of data pipelines in production Get to grips with securing, monitoring, and managing data pipelines models efficiently

Data Engineering with Python

Paul Crickard

ISBN: 978-1-83921-418-9

- Understand how data engineering supports data science workflows
- Discover how to extract data from files and databases and then clean, transform, and enrich it
- Configure processors for handling different file formats as well as both relational and NoSQL databases
- Find out how to implement a data pipeline and dashboard to visualize results
- Use staging and validation to check data before landing in the warehouse
- Build real-time pipelines with staging areas that perform validation and handle failures
- Get to grips with deploying pipelines in the production environment

Packt is searching for authors like you

If you're interested in becoming an author for Packt, please visit authors. packtpub.com and apply today. We have worked with thousands of developers and tech professionals, just like you, to help them share their insight with the global tech community. You can make a general application, apply for a specific hot topic that we are recruiting an author for, or submit your own idea.

Share Your Thoughts

Now you've finished *Building Big Data Pipelines with Apache Beam*, we'd love to hear your thoughts! Scan the QR code below to go straight to the Amazon review page for this book and share your feedback or leave a review on the site that you purchased it from.

https://packt.link/r/1-800-56493-7

Your review is important to us and the tech community and will help us make sure we're delivering excellent quality content.